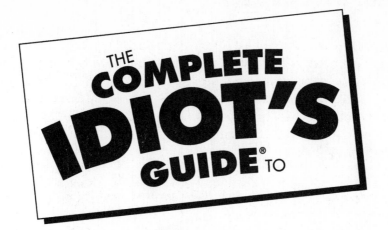

THE COMPLETE IDIOT'S GUIDE® TO

Writing
Business Books

by Bert Holtje

D1441647

ALPHA

A member of Penguin Group (USA) Inc.

ALPHA BOOKS

Published by the Penguin Group

Penguin Group (USA) Inc., 375 Hudson Street, New York, New York 10014, USA

Penguin Group (Canada), 90 Eglinton Avenue East, Suite 700, Toronto, Ontario M4P 2Y3, Canada (a division of Pearson Penguin Canada Inc.)

Penguin Books Ltd., 80 Strand, London WC2R 0RL, England

Penguin Ireland, 25 St. Stephen's Green, Dublin 2, Ireland (a division of Penguin Books Ltd.)

Penguin Group (Australia), 250 Camberwell Road, Camberwell, Victoria 3124, Australia (a division of Pearson Australia Group Pty. Ltd.)

Penguin Books India Pvt. Ltd., 11 Community Centre, Panchsheel Park, New Delhi—110 017, India

Penguin Group (NZ), 67 Apollo Drive, Rosedale, North Shore, Auckland 1311, New Zealand (a division of Pearson New Zealand Ltd.)

Penguin Books (South Africa) (Pty.) Ltd., 24 Sturdee Avenue, Rosebank, Johannesburg 2196, South Africa

Penguin Books Ltd., Registered Offices: 80 Strand, London WC2R 0RL, England

THE COMPLETE IDIOT'S GUIDE TO and Design are registered trademarks of Penguin Group (USA) Inc.

International Standard Book Number: 978-1-59257-879-5
Library of Congress Catalog Card Number: 2009923288

11   10   09   8   7   6   5   4   3   2   1

Interpretation of the printing code: The rightmost number of the first series of numbers is the year of the book's printing; the rightmost number of the second series of numbers is the number of the book's printing. For example, a printing code of 09-1 shows that the first printing occurred in 2009.

Printed in the United States of America

Note: This publication contains the opinions and ideas of its author. It is intended to provide helpful and informative material on the subject matter covered. It is sold with the understanding that the author and publisher are not engaged in rendering professional services in the book. If the reader requires personal assistance or advice, a competent professional should be consulted.

The author and publisher specifically disclaim any responsibility for any liability, loss, or risk, personal or otherwise, which is incurred as a consequence, directly or indirectly, of the use and application of any of the contents of this book. Most Alpha books are available at special quantity discounts for bulk purchases for sales promotions, premiums, fund-raising, or educational use. Special books, or book excerpts, can also be created to fit specific needs.

For details, write: Special Markets, Alpha Books, 375 Hudson Street, New York, NY 10014.

Publisher: *Marie Butler-Knight*
Editorial Director: *Mike Sanders*
Senior Managing Editor: *Billy Fields*
Executive Editor: *Randy Ladenheim-Gil*
Development Editor: *Ginny Bess Munroe*
Senior Production Editor: *Megan Douglass*
Copy Editor: *Teresa Elsey*

Cartoonist: *Steve Barr*
Cover Designer: *Bill Thomas*
Book Designer: *Trina Wurst*
Indexer: *Brad Herriman*
Layout: *Chad Dressler*
Proofreader: *John Etchison*

Contents at a Glance

Contents

Foreword

True or false: The skills it takes to write a successful business book are exactly the same skills that come into play in writing any nonfiction book.

The accurate answer is both "yes" and "no." Yes, because you'll certainly want to employ clear writing and a good narrative style, as you would in any nonfiction. No, because business books are typically read for specific reasons. They must employ clear writing and readable style, but they must also do much more.

Whether the topic is a biography of a major business figure or a corporate history, how to invest wisely or how to start and run a small business, readers of business books are looking for insight, guidance, and practical help every step of the way. If you need a book about writing general nonfiction, this is not the book for you.

This book is about focusing your attention on the specific interests and precise needs of a special audience—business readers. It describes at least a dozen different types of business books, including those on leadership, entrepreneurship, marketing, corporate history, career planning, investment, and more. And it provides detailed information on the entire process, including refining your idea, identifying the market, finding the right publisher, negotiating the contract, working with agents and co-authors, and so on.

In the pages of this book, you will meet editors, literary agents, and other authors of business books. In addition to the practical advice dispensed throughout the book, you will find anecdotes, tips, and quotes bringing the advice to life.

Bert Holtje is extraordinarily well qualified to write this book. In 30 years as a writer, editor, and agent, he developed expertise in every facet of publishing. He is the founder of James Peter Associates, Inc., where he served as an independent book producer and literary agent for three decades, representing 87 authors of nonfiction books and placing more than 600 books with major publishers. Bert has consulted with publishers on the marketing of books. And he is himself the author of some three dozen books.

I think you will enjoy reading this book and I'm sure that you will benefit from the solid and practical help you will find in its pages.

—**Grace W. Weinstein** was a two-term president of the American Society of Journalists & Authors and has served on the Board of Governors of the New York Financial Writers Association. She is the author of 13 books, most of them on personal finance, and has written business and financial articles for a wide range of magazines, from *BusinessWeek* to *Wealth Manager*. She currently contributes columns, primarily on tax and estate planning, to the *Financial Times*.

Ms. Weinstein was the editor of the monthly newsletter *Money Matters: A Woman's Guide to Financial Well-Being*. She has been a syndicated columnist, a speaker on personal finance and tax issues, and a regular financial columnist for *Good Housekeeping* and *Investor's Business Daily*. She served for three years on the Consumer Advisory Council of the Federal Reserve Board and has been on the board of the Copyright Clearance Center. As a corporate consultant, she writes white papers, brochures, annual reports, and educational publications.

Introduction

Writing a book about writing a book is an interesting experience. I know that you will probably spot some split infinitives and clunky constructions and maybe even some signs of fuzzy thinking. I'd say it's like walking a tightrope except that you'd probably nail me for the cliché. So, before we get going, I'm not going to apologize for anything. If you spot a mixed metaphor, good for you! However, if this book helps you write your book and get it published, you will have had a good experience in the pages that follow. Even if you don't get published, you will probably know why after reading my book. If nothing else, everything we do should always teach us something.

There, that's out of the way. It's not a disclaimer. It's just my way of saying that if you really want to write a business book, you can and I can help you. In my nearly 40 years of work in book publishing, I have written many books, edited many more, written advertising copy for other people's books, written many magazine articles, and even provided the total editorial content of a monthly business magazine for over 15 years. On top of all that, I started and ran a literary agency for 30 of those 40 years, managing the careers of more than 80 successful authors.

I'm not bragging; I'm sure I'd be impressed by what you do and have done. And it's what you have done and are doing that you probably want to write about. So here we are, two experienced people in very different fields, working together to achieve a common goal: getting your ideas on paper in a form that a publisher will love to publish.

There's a lot more in this book about getting you published than there is about writing. The chapters on writing, however, can set you on the right track, but they won't bore you with the details that would only interest an editor. With what you already know about the craft, you can more than likely create an acceptable manuscript or one that, with a little help, can be turned into one. But you want to write a business book, and business books are different from other books.

What makes business books different from other books is what their readers expect to get from them. I'm sure you have read your share of business books, whether they were how-to books or biographies of famous and successful businesspeople. Why did you read them when you could have been reading good novels or biographies of people who have led far more exciting lives than most businesspeople? You read them because you wanted to learn something. There's no other reason to read a how-to business book. And by reading the biography of some terminally boring business executive, you hoped to learn his or her secrets of success.

Does this really mean that business books are different from other self-help books or biographies? The answer is yes. Just as a biography of a sports star will differ from a biography of a businessperson, a book about how to sell will differ from a book about how to coach a soccer team. It's the audience that dictates the difference. Readers have specific expectations for the books they read. They not only expect information, they expect to read about it in ways that are comfortable for them. If you don't address your readers in ways they have come to expect, you will lose them quickly. This is one of the major topics of this book.

Getting your business book published well is another key feature of the book. While self-publishing does offer opportunities to publish, there can be no discounting the value of a book published by a major publisher. The publisher's imprint says something that even the best-designed self-published books cannot say. Yet not all self-published books have been rejected by larger publishers because they fall short qualitatively. Many are turned down no matter how well they are written simply because the publisher can't see a large enough market to make publishing the book worthwhile. But there are alternatives, and you will read about them in this book.

You can't spend as much time in book publishing as I have without having learned most of the tricks of the trade. I have tried to include everything that will be of help to you in this book. These aren't the "hidden secrets" so often touted to sell books on just about any subject. Rather, they are the easier ways over the bumps, the shortcuts, and the ways to determine what's real and what isn't, plus a lot more. Authors with more lofty views of themselves might call it their wisdom. I prefer to think of it as what's needed—not just to get things done, but to get them done faster, better, and with some style. I hope they work for you as well as they have worked for me.

How This Book Is Organized

The Complete Idiot's Guide to Writing Business Books is divided into six parts that cover everything you need to know to write business books, find interested agents and publishers, and see that your published book sells well, gets good reviews, and helps you achieve your personal goals.

In **Part 1, "Testing Your Business Book Idea,"** I show you why it's necessary to have solid competitive information to make your case to publishers, and how to present the material in the most meaningful way in a proposal. I also describe the kind of personal commitment that is needed and how to blend your writing with your "day job."

In **Part 2, "Writing Your Proposal and Sample Chapter,"** I introduce the three key people who must all agree on your proposal if you are to be offered a contract. I tell you what each looks for and how to pitch each for best advantage.

Part 3, "Finding an Agent and Other Helpers." There's plenty of help available if you need it. Here you will learn what collaborators, ghostwriters, book doctors, and consulting editors all can do to make the job a lot easier for you. You will also learn how to evaluate the credentials of each of these professionals.

Part 4, "Finding a Publisher and Negotiating a Contract.," is a mini course in negotiation as well as the terms and conditions you will have to understand in order to have a fair and just contract. You will see what publishers want, what you should expect, and how to make sure that both of you are satisfied.

Part 5, "Writing and Publicizing Your Book." Here you will meet the various publishing editors you will encounter while writing your book and learn how to work with each for maximum productivity. You will also meet the sales, marketing, publicity, and other pros who will have an active hand in creating and launching your book.

Part 6, "Using Your Published Book to Enhance Your Career." This part is a guide to making the best use of your book, from getting career-building publicity to helping you launch a successful business.

Publishing Tip
These boxes are full of advice or practical tips about writing business books and the publishing process.

Backspace
These warnings provide you advice about how to deal with specific things you should watch out for when writing your business book.

Quote/Unquote
These notable quotes will teach you something or inspire you to write.

Trademarks

All terms mentioned in this book that are known to be or are suspected of being trademarks or service marks have been appropriately capitalized. Alpha Books and Penguin Group (USA) Inc. cannot attest to the accuracy of this information. Use of a term in this book should not be regarded as affecting the validity of any trademark or service mark.

Part 1

Testing Your Business Book Idea

If you're thinking about writing a business book, you probably know that market research not only prevents you from making big mistakes, it also points the way to making better products. I know that my editor will never forgive me for saying this, but a book is a product. Editors have to answer to publishers, and publishers are not happy when their books don't sell well. So the whole process of pitching a book to a publisher is really a mini research program for all who are involved with it.

Getting published begins with testing your idea and goes from there to testing whether your idea, as good as it may be, is salable. And then it proceeds to an evaluation of whether you are capable of writing the book you propose to write, whether you will have the time to devote to it, and whether the wind is blowing in the right direction for your subject to catch the momentum it needs to sail through all the rocks and shoals it will encounter on the way.

Test Your Idea First

In This Chapter

- Discover the hidden author within
- Test your book idea—and even get paid for doing it
- Uncover markets you never thought existed
- Get endorsements for your book before it's even written
- Get started by writing short magazine articles

Those who read business books seldom read them just for pleasure. Sure, they may get pleasure from some, but the reader's real goal is to learn something. The most obviously educational business book titles begin with "How to." Less obviously educational, however, are business biographies. But even biographies are usually read in the hope of learning someone's secret of success. The recent rash of autobiographical books by celebrity CEOs plays well to this notion.

As someone interested in writing a business book, you have the same goal as the company you hope will publish your book. You both want to sell a lot of copies of your book. And one of the best ways to do this is to write a book that people will read because they want to learn something. So before you write a word, you must know exactly what your readers want to learn, you must have an idea that will help them, and you must know whether there is a large enough audience for your book to make the project attractive to a publisher.

Once you have your idea, your first step—before you even write a word—is to test your idea and your market. This is not as daunting or expensive as you might imagine. In fact, you may even be able to make money while discovering whether you have a salable idea and a good market.

Sell It, Then Write It

Before we get into the details of testing, you should know that you never first write a business book and then try to sell it to a publisher. A finished manuscript offered to a publisher or an agent is a big mistake. I go into this in detail in Chapter 4, but for now please take my word for it. Business books and most other nonfiction books are sold as a detailed proposal and a few sample chapters. Then they are written. Business books, like all other books, are trendy. A few years back, the celebrity CEO du jour could count on a six-figure advance, reviews by general print media as well as the business press, and even talk show spots on radio and TV. That's pretty much over. So are the excruciatingly long business books that hit the charts until fairly recently. In fact, some of the major business book publishers have begun to introduce series in which the titles have about a hundred pages each. And we are seeing some business book material appearing in digital form for use on portable electronic readers.

Now to the issue at hand, testing your idea.

What Is the Purpose of Your Book?

When you test your idea, you need to be able to state the purpose of your book, and you need to do so in a succinct way. When I ask clients what the purposes of their books are, most of them give me what I call the "Miss America" answer. If you have ever watched this annual contest, you might have noticed that the beautiful and talented women are asked questions that could be answered in a few succinct sentences. However, the contestants occasionally go on forever, seldom answering the question satisfactorily.

In my proposal to the publisher of this book, I stated that the purpose of this book would be to enable readers to write and publish successful business books. There are many steps in writing a business book, and those steps are written about in this book. However, whether I write about the use of active voice versus passive voice or about how to work with a literary agent, my purpose remains the same: to help you write and publish a business book. Period!

Generalities are the kiss of death. I can't tell you how many proposals I've read and rejected in which the author said something like, "This book will give you everything you need to start and run a successful business and retire with untold riches." This is a bit of an exaggeration, but you see my point.

Backspace

Most business book ideas fail to ignite an editor's interest because they try to cover too much territory. Make your book's purpose a tight one and stick with it. If you lose your narrow focus, you lose your editor's.

Do You Have Something Original to Say?

Another test of your book's purpose is whether it's original. This may surprise you, but most of the many business books published every year actually do have something original to say. How can there be so much new in a field that is already choked with books? The answer is that ideas already tested in one area can often be used in new ways in totally different areas. This is especially true in some areas of management: hence all the management books.

During World War II, a bunch of engineers at the Lockheed Corporation (now known as Lockheed Martin) began working outside the company's usual management structure on a design that ultimately became the famous P-38 fighter plane. The group, called the Skunk Works, was neither sanctioned nor disbanded, and it operated almost autonomously within the company. Because of its success, the idea of creating an autonomous group within an organization to avoid bureaucracy was adopted by many other companies and hailed as the management method of the future. Literally hundreds of books and articles were published on the subject. Each drew on the concept and each applied it in a different way in various industries. To this day, the notion is being used in new ways, and people are still writing about it, although mention of the Skunk Works has all but disappeared from the vernacular of contemporary management theory and business book writing.

I'm not suggesting that you rehash old ideas. I'm merely saying that ideas morph to suit changing times and needs, and a fresh approach is often worth writing about. When you think about it, almost everything is based on work that was done earlier by someone else. Nuclear submarines, for example, are still powered by steam engines. Atomic reactors create the heat that produces the steam, which runs very sophisticated engines, which are still, technically, steam engines. So what can you do with the old, but still very practical, management system called Management by Objectives? If you publish an article or a book on it, give me a footnote!

Publishing Tip

Don't shy away from controversy. If you have an idea that is at odds with what someone else has said, and you can defend your idea, go for it. There's no faster way to get attention than to slay a dragon on the public square. But make sure you know what you are doing and that you are capable of winning the fight. Pick your battles carefully.

If you plan to write about something that will stir up some controversy, the best way to make sure you have solid footing is to find support you can quote. If you don't do original research, contact those whose authority would add weight to your argument and discuss the idea with them. Be sure to get permission to quote those authorities and get their endorsement of your idea in writing.

Is Your Audience Large Enough?

Another test of your book is whether it has an audience. Beginning business book authors learn that the larger the audience, the more interested a publisher will be. So it's not uncommon to see an over-the-transom book proposal in which the writer states that every businessperson will want to read the book. In all my years in this business, I have yet to see the book that fulfills that promise. What a publisher wants is a large *and* well-targeted audience, though it will settle for a small audience with proven book-buying habits.

Check the business book shelves in libraries and bookstores, and you will get an idea of just how publishers segment their titles. Sure, there are plenty of books that will appeal to different audiences, but your book must have a large enough market to reach a key audience, or your chances of getting a contract are pretty slim.

Although you must be able to demonstrate that your key audience is large enough to get a publisher interested, you can enhance your case by discovering and describing as many secondary audiences as possible for your book. For example, you probably found this book either in the business section, the writing section, or possibly the career section of the bookstore. But if I had been unable to prove that there was a large enough key audience for the book, you would have been deprived of all this wisdom.

Publishing Tip _____

The larger the audience, the more leverage you have when negotiating contract terms with a publisher. A book publisher's advance offer is based mainly on what it believes it can recover from the first-year sales. In Chapter 17 I discuss this in detail.

When you estimate the size of your potential market, don't overlook foreign sales. Today, the foreign rights to many business books published in America are sold to book publishers all over the world. A book I wrote on marketing more than 20 years ago has been translated into Spanish, Italian, Portuguese, and a few other languages. It was even adopted as part of the graduate school program of a major Italian university. Although you can't really nail down these things when making your case to a publisher, a rough guess of where your book might find legs offshore should be included in your estimate of the potential market.

Your estimate of the market must be based on facts. The facts will be historical—how many books on the same subject or similar subjects have been sold in the past—but publishers are pretty good at using them to run their own numbers when it comes time to talk about advances and royalty percentages. Your agent should be able to help you with some of the market data. If you are going it alone, the magazine *Publishers Weekly* can be very helpful. It's expensive to subscribe, but most public libraries subscribe to it.

Your book may also have subsidiary rights potential. Sub rights, as they are commonly referred to, are essentially licensing agreements your publisher might make with other users, including foreign publishers. Paperback books sold after initial publication in hardcover are the most common sub rights deals. I talk a lot more about sub rights in other chapters, but for now try to envision whether your book might warrant a paperback edition. Also think about whether any of the material might be sold to other users, such as online course producers. However, I think you can safely rule out movie deals!

Testing Yourself

Are you capable of writing the book you have in mind? This represents two questions. The first raises the issue of your skills and commitment to the project. The other raises the issue of whether you will be able to get all the information you need to fill out a few hundred pages of a book. Many of the proposals I have seen over the years raised interesting and important questions. However, more often than not, either the author was unable to get the material needed or the material available wasn't sufficient or reliable enough to make the case to publish a book.

Writing a book is easy. You just write chapters until you have enough to make a book. This is said in jest by most professional writers, yet it is pretty much the way we look at our work. As I write this book, I am writing another. Both are due at about the same time. If I write 1,000 words a day for each, I will meet the deadlines. If I miss a day, I have to write 2,000 words for each book the next day. I'm not trying to intimidate you or to brag. But you must have a realistic attitude about what writing a book requires of you. Chapter 3 will help make it easier—though not easy—for you.

Publishing Tip _____

Years ago, I had the pleasure of meeting Isaac Asimov, one of the most productive and creative writers of his time. He claimed that he had eight IBM Selectric typewriters—this was pre–word processing—and was writing a different book on each machine. He claimed, further, that he would start at the head of the line and write for an hour on the first machine. Then he would move to each of the others in hourly succession until he had spent eight hours a day writing. He was actually writing eight books simultaneously. Don't try this!

Most people who set out to write a business book have the basic skills. However, writing a compelling memo or press release is a 50-yard dash compared with the 26.2-mile marathon of writing a book. If your contract gives you enough time, you can probably hit your stride by the second or third chapter. If you do find it a slog, there are editors, book doctors, collaborators, and even ghostwriters who can help you out. In the spirit of full disclosure, you should know that although I call myself a consulting editor, I am actually a ghostwriter and a collaborator. Those for whom I work usually prefer to introduce me as an editor rather than admit that I am actually writing their books. We of this dark corner of book publishing have no problem with anonymity, as long as our names are spelled correctly on the checks.

An editor with whom I have published a few books told me of a simple test she uses when considering a proposal from an unknown author: she asks the author what he or she reads. A person who reads *The New York Times* or one of the other better papers is a good bet. One who reads *USA Today* could be problematic. One who prefers literary fiction to mysteries gets positive points. There's nothing wrong with *USA Today* or good mystery stories. However, most of us who make our livings with words will tell you that we probably learned more from reading good writers than from any courses or books on the subject. Why not? Part of an artist's training is learning to appreciate the work of great artists. If you aren't reading works by good authors already, take some time to do so.

Even if you've never written more than a few hundred words at a time, don't let the thought of writing 100,000 words throw you. If you do it in small, regular steps, you can accomplish it.

Testing the Market Potential for Your Book

I hate to put it this way, but books are products. They are the product of your labor and your publisher's investment and labor. As such, it makes sense to test the market for a book idea before any time and money are spent on the project. Remember, we are talking about business books, not great works of art.

Publishers often do their own research on what's hot and what should be written and published. When publishers think that they have an idea that will sell, they approach agents and authors about doing the book they want. But as a first-time author, you won't get these calls. So you have to do your research and then convince a publisher that your idea and your ability will result in a book that will sell enough copies for the publisher to make a commitment to you. That is the reality of commercial book publishing.

As I said earlier, you never write a book first and then try to find a publisher for it. You do your research on the subject and the market, you write a proposal, and then you or your agent seeks the best publisher for your book. Follow these steps and you will know soon enough whether you have a salable idea.

Informal Research

One of my clients calls this the "You've gotta be kidding" step. She says that most of her ideas are pretty wild, and when she gets a "You've gotta be kidding" response from people she discusses an idea with, she knows she is either on to something really big or something really weird. If she gets this response from enough people, she goes further with it. It's a noncommittal "that might work" response that tells her that she better drop the idea.

The informal research step is a bit more formal than asking your mother whether your idea for a book on nonparametric statistics for human resources executives might fly. Of course, if your mother can compute a Kolmogorov-Smirnov equation in her head, you should really listen to her. Otherwise, pitch your ideas to people you know are capable of giving you a well-reasoned response.

Because you are considering writing a business book, the best place to begin is with your work colleagues. Be upfront: tell them that you are thinking about writing a book. Sure, there are people who steal ideas, but few people steal book ideas. After all, an idea is worth something only when it's put to use. And anyone who might steal your idea has to realize that, to put it to use, he or she is going to have to knock out a book manuscript. That could mean no TV for a long time—and maybe even working Saturdays and Sundays. So fear not. In my 30 years in this business, I have never had anyone hijack an idea, and I have discussed my ideas with plenty of people who could have taken them and run.

Quote/Unquote

"Don't worry about people stealing your ideas. If your ideas are any good, you'll have to ram them down people's throats."

—Howard Aiken, American mathematician

Many writers I have worked with claim that they get some of the best comments on their ideas from their closest work or professional colleagues. The possibility of being quoted in a book you are writing is often enough to elicit honest and thoughtful responses from colleagues. Those of you thinking of writing for a professional or academic publisher know about the value of a footnote mention in a successful book.

Formal Research

Once you feel you are on solid ground with your idea, it's time to see if anyone has beaten you to the punch with a book. This used to be a boring and time-consuming task. However, the Internet has made it possible to compress weeks of tedium into a couple of days of facing the flickering screen.

This is not the place to teach you how to use the Internet. There are plenty of books on the subject, including several excellent volumes in the *Complete Idiot's Guide* series. So let's jump to a strategic plan that will make your search easy, fast, and rewarding.

Go right to the Library of Congress website (www.loc.gov) and do a keyword search. The Library of Congress is the best source of information on just about any subject, but it takes a little getting used to in order to make the best use of it. Take your time. After all, your tax dollars go to support this wonderful resource, and you want to get your money's worth.

You probably know which publishers do the best books in your field. Go to their individual websites and see whether they already have a book or two in print that complements your idea or competes with it. Many publishers' websites allow you to see the table of contents and introductory pages of their books. You can get a quick idea of where your idea stands by scanning this material.

Then, of course, you can go to websites like Amazon.com that seem to have every book ever published. You can even get relative sales information on most of the titles. And even if a book is out-of-print, Amazon works with independent dealers that specialize in hard-to-find books.

Check the magazines that cover the market you plan to write for. Again, the Internet is the hands-down winner for this information. Most periodical publishers have online archives listing the titles of the articles they have published over quite a few years. Some even give you free and immediate access to the actual articles. Others allow you to download articles for a fee or to request hard copies to be sent by snail mail, again for a fee.

If you work for a company that maintains a comprehensive library of books and periodicals that cover your field, you are home free. Check with the office librarian and see what he or she can turn up.

Do Your Own Content Study

After you have determined that your idea might be salable, the next step is to discover what your potential readers might think of the idea and to discover if there is anything you might have overlooked. You can, of course, round up the usual suspects, but there is a better way. And that is to write an article on your subject and try to have it published by a periodical whose readers would also be prospects for the book you plan to write.

Needless to say, you don't want to give away the key idea of your book. But you do want to cover enough material so that responses from readers will tell you if you are on the right track.

Some periodicals want potential contributors to submit proposals for their articles, and others prefer that you submit the article itself. Whether you choose an Internet-based periodical or a paper-and-ink publication, check first to see what is wanted and how the editors want it presented. You will usually find this somewhere in the first few pages of a print magazine, on or near the masthead. Electronically delivered periodicals usually provide this information under a heading something like "How to contact us." Follow the instructions to the letter. Most periodicals get an awful lot of submissions, and unless your material is presented in the asked-for format, it just might go unread. Remember, every periodical has its own individual requirements.

Backspace _____

Every periodical, whether it's delivered electronically or by snail mail, has its own special submission requirements. Don't make the mistake of thinking that one style will work for all. It won't!

Selecting the Best Periodical for Your Test

It's a mistake to scatter your proposal or article to every publication you can find and hope that one will accept it. The best approach is to make a list of publications that might publish your article and rank them in their order of importance to you. These are the factors to consider when evaluating a periodical:

◆ Does the publication reach the largest possible segment of the audience you imagine for your book? Circulation figures are often available directly from electronic periodicals and in print for others. Check out a publication's advertising rate card and you will probably find the circulation numbers you need.

◆ Are the publication's readers ones you believe would also want to read your book? Most periodicals, at least those that depend heavily on paid advertising, can provide you with all sorts of demographic data to help you make this decision.

◆ Is the editorial content of the publication compatible with the article you want to submit? Again, those with paid advertising will usually have extensive data to help you with this issue. Further, most periodicals offer lists of the articles they have published in the past. Some provide free reprints, but most charge for copies of articles. However, the titles and the abstracts, if the journal includes them, will tell you a lot about what the journal's readers might want to read.

◆ Does the periodical publish frequently enough to give you an opportunity to test your material? Suppose a quarterly periodical accepts your material and then tells you that your article will appear a year later. This, incidentally, is not unusual. Under most circumstances, this is seldom a problem. But if you are looking for information quickly, this is probably not the periodical for you.

As you have probably guessed already, ranking the magazines to which you might send your article or proposal will be based on some compromises. You may discover that the periodical that targets your potential audience most closely only publishes quarterly, when you want feedback quickly. So you would probably want to choose a magazine with a more frequent publication schedule and hope that it, too, covered the audience reached by the quarterly.

Pitching Your Story to the Editor

Most periodicals provide potential authors with detailed writers' guidelines. Make sure you understand exactly what the editors want and provide all the information needed, exactly as specified. If the publication requests that you include a self-addressed stamped envelope for a reply, send it.

When the Editor Calls

When you get a nibble, an editor will probably phone or write with a few questions about what you propose. Be ready to provide immediate and helpful answers. If there seems to be genuine interest, don't hesitate to ask if the editor has a publication date in mind. You can always say that you would like to use reprints at an upcoming meeting or conference.

Writing Your Article

If your proposal is accepted, or even if you submitted a finished article, the editor will probably have some suggestions and requests for you. Take them seriously and do whatever is asked. More than likely, the publication will either have a style sheet to guide your writing or tell you which published style manual it prefers contributors to use. Don't be overwhelmed by these manuals. Some of them are big and intimidating. Write as well as you can, and use the style manual to answer questions as they arise. Just reading a few issues of the magazine should give you a feel for style and tone.

Somewhere in the text of your article you should raise issues that will encourage readers to contact you. This is where your feedback is going to come from. Reader comments, whether in the letters to the editor column of the magazine or sent directly to you, will tell you a lot.

Analyzing the Feedback

You're not going to get a lot of feedback, but what you get will probably be extremely helpful. When people take the time to contact the author of an article, they usually have something significant to say. Apart from using the comments to further shape your ideas, you can also use them when you pitch your book idea to a publisher. One of my clients got an e-mail from a reader of an article he had written for a business magazine. The reader was the CEO of a major corporation and had several suggestions that my client used. Further, with the CEO's permission, he used the correspondence as part of his book proposal. Even better, the CEO agreed to blurb (publishing lingo for endorse) the book when it was published.

Publishing Tip _____

Oh, I almost forgot! Some magazines will pay you to write for them, but many don't. You won't get rich with the fees magazines pay—if they do pay—but at least you will not have had to spend a lot of money on researching the potential for your book.

The Least You Need to Know

- You can write a business book if you plan and test the idea first.

- The market for your book doesn't have to be big, but it has to have a proven record of book-buying activity that will be attractive to a publisher.

- Your idea doesn't have to be a breakthrough. All it has to do is help someone do something better or do it for less money.

- A simple magazine article with your byline is often all that's needed to get you started. And you may even be paid for writing it!

Chapter 2

Is There a Market for Your Book?

In This Chapter

◆ Uncover all the books in print that may compete with yours

◆ Discover how publishers use market estimates to make the accept/reject decision

◆ See why bookstore sales are often the smallest portion of a competitive estimate

◆ Learn how to make marginal numbers work—without cheating

Whether or not a publisher makes an offer for your book depends on several things: Is there a market for your book? Is the subject of sufficient interest to those who make up the potential market? And can you write well enough to pull it off? Basically, can the publisher expect to make money by publishing your book? You or the publisher can always find someone to help you write your book if this is not your strong suit. But if the publisher can't see a buck in the bargain, no matter how well reasoned the book, and no matter how well you write, you won't be invited to the party.

Most publishers, even the largest and most well respected, seldom do a lot of research to determine the salability of a proposed book. They may do it for a well-known author they want to attract or for a "house" author who has done other successful books on their list. But for you and most others whose proposals they consider, it's up to you to convince them of a market potential. The information you give a publisher will be carefully scrutinized by an editor, a sales manager, a marketing manager, and probably even someone from the management and production side. Only the editor has responsibility for deciding whether you can or cannot write.

So read this chapter carefully and see just why I focus on writing in only 4 of my 26 chapters. I assume you have some writing experience, even if it's only letters, memos, and e-mail. And I also assume that you don't know why writing a business book is different from writing any other kind of book. You learn why in Chapters 8, 9, 18, and 19. Now, let's see what it takes to motivate a book publisher to put some money on the table—your table!

Selling Your Business Book

Business books appeal to businesspeople, and these businesspeople can be divided into many specialized categories. This means that if you are planning a book on marketing, your potential audience will have to be estimated in specific terms. Not many human resources people will spring for your $50 tome on marketing gimmicks over the Internet. Keep this in mind as I discuss the most productive sources of information on business book sales.

> **Backspace**
>
> Business books are sold in many ways, and sales to bookstores may represent only a small part of a publisher's effort. As you research the potential for your book, don't be discouraged if you see low bookstore sales figures for some titles.

Think about it. Every book a publisher acquires becomes a new product. While it's true that these new products are often largely based on a pleasant experience the publisher might have had with a similar book, each book is still essentially a new product. Just about any other company can crank out its only product for years. But as each book is based on ideas and intellectual effort, publishers must think of each book as a new product. And this puts an interesting spin on the author/publisher relationship. It's a codependent relationship, without all the trappings of hostility that term often churns up.

Where and how your book will be sold by a publisher is a key to discovering if there is a market for your book and to estimating sales to that market. Note, however, that some business books, no matter how important the subject may be and how well the book is written, may never be published by a commercial publisher. If the market is too small, a commercial publisher just won't be interested. Some commercial publishers will, however, take on books with limited sales potential if the author agrees to buy enough copies to cover expenses and meet profit requirements. And there is, of course, the possibility of self-publishing or working with a custom book publisher.

Sources of Competitive Information

There are plenty of places to look for the information you need for your proposal. However, you will probably discover that different sources reporting on the same book may show widely different numbers. Sample timing is usually the reason for this. If one source samples weekly and reports the cumulative sale of a competitive book at 1500 copies, while another source shows 500 copies, check to see how often each reports its data and check the dates of the reported data you have. The source reporting the larger number is probably sampling more frequently than the one reporting the smaller number.

The Book Itself

Suppose you have discovered that your book competes with or augments a book that has been in print for a while. This is information that should be included in the competitive data section of a proposal you will write to interest a publisher. Check the book out of a library or locate it in a bookstore. Then open to the copyright page and look for a line of numbers that appear to be counting backward (5 4 3 2 1). This is the book's printing history. The smallest number in the line indicates how many times the book has been printed; in this example, the book has had only one printing. With each successive printing, the smaller numbers are eliminated sequentially. The more often the book has been printed, the better the book has been selling. However, be aware that recent developments in book printing technology make it easy and relatively inexpensive to produce a small number of copies on demand compared with the costs of only a few years ago. This means that many book runs are a lot smaller than they used to be. But in general, the more printings a book has gone through, the more interest there has been in the book.

If you are looking at a library copy, see if you can get a feel for whether the book has been handled a lot. A book that has never been opened feels different from a book that has been read many times.

If your library still uses the old stamping system, see how many times the book has been checked out. The new digital systems don't leave this kind of trail in a book, but most librarians can check their data files and can usually let you know the number. Just don't bother a librarian when there is a long line at the checkout desk.

Local libraries seldom carry much more than the top tier of business books, so you may have difficulty getting your hands on books that might compete with yours. If you are near a college or university with a business school, see if you can gain access to its stacks. Most universities, as part of their Town-and-Gown activities, will give library privileges to local writers. And if you kept up your membership in your college alumni association, you may have access automatically.

Do more than just peruse the stacks. Books come and go, and unless you check every day you will probably miss some titles. So, of course, the best way to do your initial survey is either with the library's card catalog, if they still have one of those quaint antiques, or by using their computer search database. You can also search on Amazon. com.

Best-Seller Lists

I'm sure there is a best-seller list for every class of book. However, you are on safe ground when you go to the well-recognized lists and those published by well-known sources. All of the major business periodicals have book columns and most rank the books they review according to one standard or another.

You can even access some of these lists online without subscribing to the magazine. The *BusinessWeek* best-seller list is one of your best sources. This thorough list not only includes the top 15 hardcover books, but also the top 15 books in trade paperback format. The magazine also includes a very helpful feature of long-running best-sellers.

The New York Times publishes an excellent book review section each Sunday. It includes hardcovers as well as trade paperbacks. This is a review of general books, not specifically business books. However, the *Times* often publishes reviews of biographies of well-known businesspeople.

Magazines that cover the book publishing field, such as *Publisher's Weekly*, have all sorts of excellent information, including sales rankings of books by major categories. The annual subscription fee, however, is high.

Backspace _____

The term *best-seller* is one of the most used and abused in the publishing business. Professional and trade groups publish lists of "best-sellers," as do popular and general circulation magazines. Many of these lists are pure hype and the book's' authors can only hope that their vaunted status results in royalties that live up to the rankings. You're on safe ground with lists by the major media. Take the others with a grain of salt.

And remember that the major best-seller lists are based on the number of books sold to distributors and bookstores—not to readers. Many of these "sold" books are later returned to the publisher for a full refund. Returns often exceed 50 percent of the sales of overly hyped books. Bookselling is one of the few fields of business that allows retailers to return what they don't sell to their publishers for full refund.

A few years ago, the major media broke a story about an author who understood and profited from the criteria by which best-seller lists were created. I won't bore you with the details, but, in short, he knew that he could buy large quantities of books and later return them for a full refund. Books are sold to booksellers on this basis. The jump in sales was duly noted and reported by some of the media that cover the field. The result was that an apparent best seller became a best seller in fact because of this fraud. It won't work a second time, so forget about it!

Online Sales Information

There is a treasure trove of information online that will help you determine how many books are being sold. Because sales of books that compete with or complement your book will be a significant factor in a publisher's decision to acquire your book, you should look carefully at all the sources.

The most obvious, and often the most helpful, source is Amazon. The sales ranking information alone can tell you a lot, but only when you compare apples with apples and check the trends regularly. Amazon and many other online booksellers give you a limited peek inside the books they sell. Check the copyright page and you will have the number of printings if the edition they list is the latest edition. Check the intros and the tables of contents and you will have a pretty good idea of where you stand relative to the books that have already been published.

A key phrase search will turn up the websites that cover your topic. Just the number of sites alone will give you a clue to the interest in your proposed subject and book. Check into some of the groups on Yahoo! and Google that are devoted directly—and even indirectly—to your topic, and see the level of interest in the project you plan to write about. Most of these interest groups are free, and if you can prove a serious interest in their subjects, you can become a member.

If you can get a discussion going on your topic—without announcing that you are planning to write a book—you will get some interesting feedback. However, remember that all the feedback you get will be unfiltered. That is, the group members are self-selected. They could be just plain cranky people with nothing better to do or people with a serious interest in the subject. You may even turn up people with the credentials and interest you need as resources when you actually go to write your book. Don't go for numbers at these sites; go for comments by people who seem to have the credentials and reliability you need to discover whether there is a significant market for your book.

Book Distributors, Wholesalers, and Friends in the Business

Most books sold to retail outlets are sold through wholesalers or distributors. There are similar organizations for the sale of textbooks and professional books. Some of these companies can provide a lot of very helpful information. You'll find them by simply typing "book distribution" in your search window. Ingram, the largest book distributor in the country, has a wealth of information online. If you have a book's ISBN (International Standard Book Number), you can get its stocking and sales data online. Navigating Ingram's website is complicated, but it's really worth the effort.

Chances are, you either know someone in book publishing or know someone who knows someone in book publishing. If that person works for one of the larger international houses, chances are that his or her company subscribes to one or more research services, such as BookScan by Nielsen. If you don't ask for the moon, that person can probably get you some of the critical numbers.

No Competition

You have a book idea. You have checked every possible source and have discovered that no one has written on the subject. You're sure to be a shoo-in with even the best of publishers, right? Not necessarily!

Yes, you may have found the sweet spot and have everything you need to do the book, but why hasn't anyone else ever done it? Nine times out of ten, it has been done—and failed often enough for editors and publishers to know that your idea just won't work with them either. It may be a question of too small a market, in which case there is a good argument for custom publishing or even self-publishing. Or it could just be that you did discover the hiding place of the pot of gold. In any case, do your research and be sure to look into the books that bit the dust in the past.

What Your Editor Should Already Know

The person who goes to bat for your book proposal is known as an acquisitions editor. On more general business topics, chances are that your editor will have solid competitive information at his or her fingertips. However, the narrower your focus, the greater the attention you must pay to your research. For a book titled *Ten Winning Sales Tips for Every Sales Situation*, your editor will probably be able to quote numbers immediately. But propose a book that tells how to sell to purchasing agents in the gourmet pet food industry, and you had better include the numbers in your proposal.

New writers often bring too much to the table. Editors and agents are constantly bombarded with proposals, so the easier you make it for them to see the potential for your book in real terms, the better your chances of winning a contract. Acquisitions editors are very interested in knowing whether there are any books that directly compete with your proposed book and whether a large number of books have been published on the subject you propose.

Don't try to hide this information. The larger the number of books in print on a given subject, the more likely an editor is to become interested in your proposal. A large number of competitive titles is a sign that there is a healthy market for books on your subject.

How to Get Marginal Estimates to Work

If you have a good idea, but you just can't get the numbers to work for a publisher, there are several other possibilities. One is to self-publish, and another is to work with a custom publisher. There are good reasons to go either way, and I discuss them in Chapter 14. Before you go that route, however, it's still often possible to sweeten the pot enough to entice a publisher who thinks the book should be published but just can't get the numbers to work.

A publisher's name is important. I don't think it comes as a surprise to you to know that "Viking" on the spine of your book carries a bit more weight than the name of a lesser-known publisher. And that imprint often makes the difference between your book being reviewed and not being reviewed.

If the publisher's name is that important to you and your numbers are close enough to what a publisher might need to take on the project, you might be able to tip the balance with a pre-publication sale. A pre-pub sale is one you, the author, bring to the publisher; it guarantees that either you or someone else will buy a specified number of books. This is a deal that must be done before a contract is signed. And when it is done, the numbers just might be enough to put the publisher's initial sales estimate into a profitable range.

If the amount needed to make the deal work is close enough to the publisher's estimated sales need, you might even consider doing this yourself if you have a way of selling or using the books. More than a few consultants who do the lecture circuit work deals like this, then either include free books with registration fees or offer them to registrants at a significant discount.

> **Publishing Tip** _____
>
> Publishers usually start their negotiation for pre-pub deals with a discounted price based on the retail price of the book. A 20 or 30 percent discount off retail sounds great until you look at the actual numbers. Publishers sell their books to bookstores and wholesalers at discounts that are around 40 percent off retail. Even at deeper discounts, the publishers are still in a profitable range. They have to be! So see if you can negotiate a pre-pub price based on the publisher's actual cost per book plus an acceptable markup. It's not easy to do these deals, but it's worth a try.

Pre-publication deals most often involve an organization, company, or other group with which you are involved and which could benefit from the exposure a published boom might offer. Most of the deals I have seen over the years involved people who were employed by very large companies. The company sees the benefit to it as well as to the author. A pitch to your employer's public relations or corporate communications department is a good place to start the ball rolling.

Foreign Market Potential

Not many business books travel all that well when it comes to the sale of foreign rights. Your publisher or your agent usually handles these rights sales, and I discuss them in detail in Chapter 17. For now, when thinking in terms of building your case for a significant market for your book, try to determine whether the rights to publish it abroad would bump up the market estimate needed to get a contract.

The best way to do this is by trying to discover how well similar books have done when sold to offshore publishers. There is no easy way to do this, but the best way to get started is with the titles you know have sold well to the United States market. If you have an agent, he or she might be able to help get you the information you need, but in most cases the burden is on you to prove that there might be a market in Greenland for your book on selling summer cruise wear.

You can often get the information you need directly from the publishers of the books you have selected. The publishers will probably not share their foreign sales figures with you, but most will tell you if they have sold any foreign rights to the books and to whom they have been sold. Then check with the foreign publisher and see just how far you can go.

Except where foreign rights appear to be a possibly significant source of sales for a publisher, I don't suggest that you spend lot of time chasing these numbers. It's hard work, and even with good numbers, it's a crapshoot whether the foreign publisher would be interested in a second act.

Money from Periodical Publishers

If your entire book is interesting enough to a periodical publisher that the publisher wants to serialize it all, there could be enough money on the table to turn a weak sales estimate into a workable one. But a single chapter sale here and there probably will not tilt even a close estimate in your favor. Keep in mind that these rights (and other rights), depending on your contract, may be controlled by you or may be controlled by your publisher.

Online Booksellers

Amazon and its imitators move a lot of books, and their estimated purchase of your book can represent a major factor in the success or failure of your proposal. However, you are better off letting your publisher's marketing people get estimates from them rather than trying to do it yourself. The truth is that many business books sell far better through online booksellers than they do through the more traditional brick-and-mortar network.

You probably won't be able to get the kind of information you want directly from Amazon, but you can get more than enough help by looking at Amazon's book sales rankings and relative positions on the website. It is important that you include these figures with your proposal. Many larger publishers actually have salespeople dedicated to selling only to Amazon and some of the other online booksellers. If your editor is intrigued enough by what he or she sees in your proposal, it's a sure bet that one of the first steps on the path to pitching your book at an editorial meeting will be a request that marketing get an estimate from Amazon. A low estimate from Amazon can be the kiss of death, even when some of the other numbers fall in line.

Can the Publisher Make Money?

The final factor hinges on the price the market will support. If you are planning a book that will end up with many pages and many complicated illustrations, the cost to produce that book may be more than a publisher is willing to bear. If this is the case with your book, you should research the prices of similar books that have been published and sold to similar markets. Most bookseller listings will give you a retail price and a page count. Make sure your book falls in the same range as competing titles. If you can't, you better have a good reason why your book will be more expensive to produce and why the publisher can expect that a higher cover price will fly.

Writing and publishing is a collaborative enterprise. Publishers depend on authors to provide them with their best creative efforts and authors depend on publishers to provide their best production, marketing, and sales efforts. If you think in terms of other areas of business, there are many parallels. The movie business works pretty much the same way.

Some publishers do fairly extensive research on books they believe could and should be published. When they do this, they often commission writers to create the books for them. These projects are often contracted on a work-for-hire basis. Others do things more informally, simply suggesting to authors they know that a book proposal on a subject they would like to publish would be welcomed. This all boils down to the fact that you must have the numbers, and the numbers you have must be accurate and sufficiently large to warrant the offer of a contract.

The Least You Need to Know

 ◆ A publisher's interest can turn into a contract only when the numbers work.

 ◆ Most of the competitive marketing information you need is available from easy-to-access sources.

 ◆ Best-seller lists may not always be the best source to use to convince a publisher of the market.

 ◆ A field in which there are a lot of competing books is a good sign.

Chapter 3

Making the Commitment and Keeping It

In This Chapter

◆ The one mistake that most writers make and what you can do about it

◆ Learn why you should focus on the dark side

◆ Miss a delivery date and you'll never write in this town again!

◆ Writer's block is not a disease, but it sure feels like one

◆ Never write on an empty stomach

Back in the days when I was a literary agent, an editor phoned me to complain that one of my authors had missed two deadlines and was in danger of having her contract cancelled. After offering a feeble apology on her behalf, I got on the phone with the author and asked what was happening. She replied quite calmly that the dog had eaten the manuscript. After I told her that, as a writer, she should be able to come up with a better excuse than that, she said, "Well, if you don't want to do something, any excuse will do." I reminded her that she could do better than to quote an old proverb, and she finally blurted, "Look, I really don't want to write this **** book!"

Don't get yourself in this kind of a pickle. Writing anything takes commitment. Writing a book takes serious commitment. Typical business books run between 50,000 and 120,000 words. To anyone who writes for a living, this is pretty close to a walk in the park. But to a first-time author this can be seriously intimidating. I have written an entire chapter on this subject because it is so important. And while what I am about to tell you may be all you really need, please read the rest of the chapter. I made a serious commitment to it.

Keeping Things in Perspective

The biggest mistake most people make when facing a complex project like writing a book is keeping the entire job in full view all the time. Make a commitment to clean the cellar and all you can see is a crummy, damp, and dark place, spiders and all, staring you in the face. But if you were to break the cellar-cleaning project down into four separate projects—for instance, cleaning one corner a week—you probably would be able to clean the entire cellar with ease. Writing a book is no different. If you have a contract to deliver a 12-chapter book in one year, all you have to do is write a chapter a month. When you have 12 chapters, you have a book.

Yes, I know, you have heard all this before. And you know how easy it might be to skip a month and write two chapters the next month. That's why I have not stopped with this simple advice.

Any project, including the writing of a book, requires serious commitment. Unless you want to spend just as much time doing the rewrites an editor may demand, and if you don't want to return that enormous advance, make the commitment and stick to it. Before we get going here, humor me and take this other proverb seriously: Bad habits are easier to break today than tomorrow. That's it for the clichés!

Making the Commitment—the Basics

Let's begin with a simple plan that seems to work well, whether you are cleaning a cellar or writing a book. Then, I'll take you through the book-writing process and show you where you are likely to hit snags and dry spots and what you can do about them. It works for me and it works for many of the authors I have worked with.

- ◆ Take an oath.

    Allow me to share the system of a well-published author I know. He takes a simple oath in front of a mirror on the day the contract for his next book arrives. As he explained to me, "I do it in front of my shaving mirror, the same mirror I use every morning." He claims that's all it takes to keep him focused. He also added with a wry smile, "It helps to think about paying the mortgage and the kid's college tuition while you take that oath."

◆ Impose your own personal Management by Objectives system

Management by Objectives is a very practical system based on a worker and an employee agreeing collaboratively on work that has to be done and how it is to be done. It's not top-down management. Because you are both boss and worker, the job of managing yourself can get sticky. As one of my clients put it, "I work for a really lousy boss … me! But by wearing both hats and putting everything in writing it's easier to stay on track."

◆ Set specific and attainable deadlines

It's tempting to plan to write a chapter a month for a year if you have one year to complete a book. But this seldom works, simply because some chapters write themselves and others can be a real slog. When you set your dates, keep this in mind. If one chapter requires more research than another, give yourself a flexible deadline. Interestingly enough, most writers discover that setting varied deadlines like this makes the work go much more easily than going by calendar dates. The psychology behind this notion is well documented.

◆ Focus on the negative

What happens if you miss the date set for delivery of half of your manuscript? Depending on the publisher and the specific contract, it could mean cancellation of the contract. Cancellation of the contract usually requires an author to repay any money advanced on the project. Repaying an advance might mean beans rather than steak for dinner or missing a car payment. When you focus on what will happen rather than just on missing the deadline, the picture gets a lot clearer.

◆ Reward your effort

A little positive reinforcement goes a long way. Finish a chapter and enjoy one of your favorite pleasures. An author I met years ago told me that she scheduled dinners at successively better restaurants as she completed each chapter of a book. "At the end of chapter one," she explained, "it's usually a burger and fries at a local fast food joint. By the time I complete the final chapter, I'm ready for my celebratory dinner at Chez Andre." In psychological terms, she has set an ascending goal gradient that works for her.

Make It Easy on Yourself

Most project planning and self-discipline systems read like manuals for running a prison. There are times when writing may seem like being in prison, but it's no different for those who work at regular jobs—no matter how much they usually enjoy their work. I asked several colleagues how they smooth the path.

"I have music playing in the background all the time," an author told me. "I check out a bunch of discs of music that is unfamiliar to me at my local library and keep it playing at a low level, whatever I am doing. I discovered that if I listen to familiar music I would immediately find myself comparing the rendition I'm listening to with the way another musician might have played it. That is very distracting. But listening to unfamiliar music is comforting." Interestingly enough, this works for me, too.

The author of well over 50 books said, "I look for the sweet spot in the work at hand. If I'm writing about a particular period of history that intrigues me, that excites me, all the other writing goes a lot easier then."

An equally prolific author explained that she steadfastly avoids looking at the "big picture" as she works. "If I have my material organized in my head and focus on the small steps, the big steps pretty much take care of themselves."

Read any of the periodicals for writers and you will see this kind of advice laced throughout every issue. The best advice really is to do whatever you want that makes your work go smoothly. Don't resist anything because it might seem odd to others.

Write naked? Why not! Just be sure you have clothes handy for when the postal service arrives with a registered letter containing your latest royalty check.

Writer's Block

Last night, Ed Claflin, my agent, called and suggested that we take advantage of the weather and spend a few hours sailing today. The thought of launching a spinnaker in a good wind was more than a little intriguing, but I am a bit behind with two books I'm writing for Ed, so I turned him down. Now, as I sit here trying to write, all I can think of is sailing. In fact, it took me about 10 minutes just to write this paragraph. I should have written at least a page in that time.

Writer's block? You could call it that, but why call it anything? As soon as you give something negative a name, you have given yourself an excuse. How easy it is to say, "I have writer's block," and quit for the day. I'm not saying that there aren't times when all you can do is put one word in front of another, but I am saying don't dignify the situation by saying you have writer's block.

Publishing Tip

We all have bad days. Don't beat up on yourself. It happens to everyone in every field. We writers have just given the problem a name: writer's block. Think of how lucky you really are. You can get up and walk away from a bad day and have a good one tomorrow. The pilot landing a 747 in a 50-knot crosswind doesn't have that option. There, feel better now?

I usually get over the problem by reminding myself that writing is, for me, just work. I don't think of what I do as art. When I'm stonewalled, I turn to artifice, a deceptive maneuver to get me going. Inside, however, I know that someday a great novel will find its way onto my hard drive. But enough about me!

Before I get into some of the techniques you can use to keep the words flowing, I should say that writer's block, or whatever you choose to call the problem, is not something to joke about. The history of literature is littered with examples of great writers being stalled for years. There are those who wrote blockbusters the first time out and never wrote another word. Psychologists have studied the problem and some have linked it with a few of the major mood disorders. Sociologists have linked it to issues of class difference and even to a possible natural ebb and flow of creativity. They've written about it, usually with prose that gives me what might be called reader's block.

Now that I have set you up to avoid thinking that writer's block is a disease, condition, or syndrome, but rather is simply a problem you can deal with, let me tell you how three of my favorite authors deal with the problem. When I was an agent, these writers were clients of mine. Each of them makes all or a good part of his or her living by writing and each of them gets stuck from time to time. Today is your lucky day, because all of them have agreed to share their secrets.

◆ **Alan Axelrod** has more than 90 books in print. His books have been reviewed well in *The New York Times*, *Publishers Weekly*, and many other periodicals. Alan is prolific. He told me, "I get stalled from time to time, but never long enough to worry about it. I usually have three or four books under contract at any given time and shifting from one book to another is all I need to keep the work going. But for anyone just getting started, I suggest that they just keep at it." Alan makes a good point when he suggests just sticking with it. Putting writing aside when you get stuck can turn into a bad habit. You can quit after you get moving and achieve your goal; it's your reward for sticking with it.

Another author says she finds it difficult to shift from book to book, but when she gets stalled on a book, she does a quick magazine piece and finds that to be most helpful. The bottom line is really just putting the offending work aside and doing something else, whether it's writing something else or hoisting a sail.

◆ **Susan Shelly** also has an impressive number of well-reviewed books in print. Along with her book writing, she does journalism, corporate histories, and collaborations. As impressive as her writing is, she insists on looking at her writing as just a job. She's modest almost to a fault, but it's easy to put up with when you know that she seldom misses a deadline and always turns in work that requires virtually no editing. "When you think about it," she told me, "we just use words like a bricklayer uses bricks. Put the words or bricks in the right place and you have something to be proud of. Besides, it beats any other way of making a good living."

◆ **Carol Turkington** was a client of mine for more than 30 years before her recent death. Early in our happy and very productive relationship we had long conversations about craft. She was a staff writer at the American Psychological Association when we met and was just beginning to write books on her own. She was concerned that her day job writing might make it difficult for her to write a book in her spare time. She discovered that reading about her concerns from a psychological perspective put her in touch with the work that was being done in the field. She discovered early on that many of the famous writers she had read about who had blocking problems solved them intuitively and pretty much the way theory might predict. In short, she discovered for herself that she was not alone and that all artists, writers, and even scientists face the same problems. Her way of coping was to take short breathers, even when the work was going very well. "It charges my battery when the work goes well and takes the heat off when I'm stalled," she explained.

Okay, these writers are all pros, and you just want to write one business book and sit back and bask in the glory and collect the royalties. How should you deal with the blank page that refuses to fill itself with words? What the pros do should work for you. But if you find that these three approaches fail to do the trick, here are some other suggestions. Each addresses a different blank page problem.

When Apprehension Sets In

You're halfway through your manuscript and things seem to be going well. So you look back at a few earlier chapters and the only word that comes to mind is *drivel*. All your planning is on target and you are comfortable with your research, yet now, after all those words, it just doesn't seem to work.

First of all, this is as common to professional writers as it is to those doing their first book. Chances are that it is not drivel. It may need some polishing; all manuscripts can benefit from the ministrations of a good editor. What has happened is that, as you wrote, your overall idea of the book has probably shifted a little. And what you are currently writing doesn't jibe too well with your earlier material. In short, you haven't written drivel, you have drifted off course.

If the idea has matured as you wrote, you may be on a better track than when you started out. It's usually pretty easy to make adjustments in the earlier writing if the drift is minor. And who knows, maybe you will be the only person to notice it. But if you are way off course, you better stop and decide whether your current writing is going the wrong way or your initial stuff has to be revised. This, incidentally, is a good argument for rereading your stuff as you go along.

Here are some problems other than writer's block you might face.

- You are anxious about your ability to write the book.

   In most cases you will find yourself having conversations with yourself (in your head, of course). "I'll never pull this off," is the most common. It may seem corny, but just tell yourself that you will pull it off and write a couple of paragraphs as quickly as possible. Don't stop to read what you have written; just get the words on paper. Don't do more than one page of double-spaced text; then stop. Put your writing aside without reading it. Shut off the computer and do something entirely different for a couple of hours without thinking about your writing at all.

   Then go back and read what you have written. It won't be perfect, but unless you are a lot different than most people, you will see that, with some editing and revisions, you aren't all that bad as a writer. Believe me, most writing is editing. Get the words on paper, polish them, and move on. Some people write entire chapters before they go back to edit themselves. Others do it a page at a time, and others pick at each finished paragraph. I tend to polish each paragraph, but that's just my way.

- You just can't seem to get started.

   Trouble getting started can usually be traced to two conditions. The first is that you know you don't have enough research done to make the book work. The other is that you know you have much more material than you really need. In the first case, you are fearful that your lack of material will result in your having a short book or one with a lot of irrelevant fluff. Too much information is just as scary, because you know that you're going to have trouble sorting and using all the stuff, and you may leave out something important.

The solution is to sort your material first, until you know what is going to be needed, and then begin to write. I wouldn't chuck the other stuff right away. Just get it out of the way and dig into what you know will work for you. If it looks as though you might be coming up short, you can always go to pile.

If your research shows that there isn't enough material, maybe the topic is not worth writing about. If it is, consider blending it with material that relates to it.

◆ You can't seem to stick to your schedule.

Once broken, a commitment is diminished greatly in your roster of good intentions. Even if you can't write the 10 pages you scheduled for the day, sit down and write 5. But keep the schedule. Chances are that you will be able to do 15 in the next session. Keep the commitment, even if you turn out fewer pages or turn out work that your high school English teacher would mark with an F. Once you let yourself off the commitment hook, you are in trouble.

◆ You can't seem to end the book.

More often than not, this is the result of poor initial planning. If you have done all your research and prepared a comprehensive outline, your book should pretty much end itself. But when you reach the last word of the publisher's suggested page count and you are uncomfortable about ending the book, something is probably wrong.

Rather than just writing more and hoping that you will find the end somehow, go back to your outline and read key material in what you have written so far. You will probably see weak spots in your argument, the material you present, or the conclusions you have drawn. In other words, the problem with your ending just may be somewhere in the earlier chapters.

Publishing Tip

As a writer, you are working with words. But visual images can be powerful tools to help you keep your commitment. Early on, try to envision what the cover of your book will look like and how your name as the author will be presented. Keep this vision in mind. Along with this vision, just tell yourself that unless you keep moving, there will be no book, no fame, and no fortune.

It often helps to have someone who is familiar with your subject read your material. Ask the reader to focus on content. All too often, people who are not writers and who are asked to comment on writing become instant editors. You don't need that at this point. You may need editorial help later, or elsewhere in the manuscript, but an ending that doesn't satisfy you is seldom an editorial problem.

Distractions and How to Deal with Them

Early on, daydreaming can be very productive when writing a book. Chances are that you will write and rewrite early material several times. As you settle in to a regular pace, however, the real distractions will be real distractions—ringing telephones, pressure from other work, unanswered e-mail. It's a long list. But as you have probably already discovered, if you stop mid-sentence to answer the phone, it may take you a long time to pick up the thread, even if it was a wrong number and the caller never apologized. Don't you hate that?

It's tempting to say that total isolation is the best way to deal with the distractions of the real world, but silence and isolation can be as distracting to some as the clatter of noisy kids is to another. What distracts you might spur me on to write more. Until you actually get into your writing routine, you may not realize what really bugs you as you try to write. Answering a ringing phone doesn't bother me, nor does street noise. But I am easily distracted by the calls of birds. I'm not a devoted bird-watcher, but I enjoy watching what any birds do, whether they are chattering sparrows or the occasional red-tailed hawk that perches in a tree about 50 feet from my window. Things don't have to be annoying to be distracting. I'm distracted by music I know and like. Unfamiliar music is not a distraction.

I asked a few friends and colleagues what bothers them when they need time and space to concentrate. All share the same concern: a distraction doesn't just interrupt their thinking and output, it means running faster and harder to get back on track.

"I go to the library to work," a management consultant who also writes books told me. "I take my laptop and work in one of the rooms the library has set aside for the key-clacking that accompanies even the quietest of keyboards." His laptop is Wi-Fi equipped, so his wife can send him a silent e-mail message immediately if there is anything that needs his attention. And being in a library also means that he has access to material he might need that he doesn't have at home.

"I tend to work at random times so that regular distractions are not so much of a problem," an editor told me. When she knows that a church bell is going to ring nearby every hour, she tends to start thinking about it five or ten minutes before ring time. Psychologists refer to this as habituation, and it can be a big problem for anyone whose work requires long periods of concentration. Random events become far less intrusive when you don't follow a rigid schedule in which you can anticipate every annoyance.

"Never read the mail until you have written at least a thousand words," another writer told me. He claims that whether it's his monthly credit card bill or a surprisingly high royalty check, the mail is far too intrusive in his creative life.

"I am easily distracted by any sound," another writer told me. He solved this problem by wearing a pair of sound-canceling headphones as he works. I asked him about phone calls, and he said that phone calls don't bother him and that he can hear the ringer even when he wears his headphones.

I suppose the list of things that keep people from writing is endless. So when you know what it is that prevents you from keeping your commitment to writing, do something about it. Don't sit and stew over it, as far too many people do.

The Least You Need to Know

- Without firm commitments, your chances of finishing a book on time are pretty slim; with them, you will probably be done ahead of schedule.

- Writer's block is not a disease.

- Getting started is often easier than writing the ending.

- What distracts others just may energize you.

4

Before You Write a Word

In This Chapter

- ◆ What to read first to get you off to a fast start
- ◆ Discover how to get the help you need quickly
- ◆ Learn why you should keep your writing a secret
- ◆ You may already have the credentials to attract a top publisher
- ◆ You can write your book with two fingers, but you must be able to file accurately

Any marathon runner will tell you that you don't prepare for long-distance running by doing sprints. The same advice applies to writing a book. You are planning to do some long-distance writing, so I strongly suggest that you prepare very carefully before you write a word of your book. The guidelines and suggestions that follow should get you in shape. You're not entering the 50-word dash, you're planning to go the distance with a book.

Read the Good Writers First

Read all the books you can get your hands on that cover the topic on which you plan to write. Read not just for content but also for style. You're not cheating if you adopt the style of an author you admire any more than a painter cheats who is inspired by the brushstrokes of a famous painter.

When you find a business book writer whose style is comfortable for you, read his or her books several times and try to put your finger on what it is that has drawn you to the writer. Your readings will probably be quite revealing. Content won't be sacrificed to style, and the style will keep your attention.

It's best to read several books, skipping what you ordinarily would read for pleasure for the time being. And do this reading armed with a pile of Post-it notes and yellow markers. In your own words, note what impresses you about the passages you highlight.

Publishing Tip

Good writing is more than accurate spelling and grammatically and syntactically correct prose. Good writing makes a point clearly. It is tightly structured, it is substantively satisfying, and it should be a pleasure to read. You'll know it when you see it; you won't be able to put it down.

Pay particular attention to pacing. The positioning of long and short sentences and even long and short words can make the difference between dull and interesting writing. Book writers are seldom paid by the word. But those with less experience tend to overwrite as if they were. They usually do this by repeating what they have already said in different words. Brevity is not only the soul of wit, it's the soul of good business book writing.

For now, just try to get a feel for what you think is good writing. If the author holds your attention and you are not easily distracted as you read, you can bet that the author you are reading knows what he or she is doing.

Read Reviews of Other Books on Your Subject

Most ideas that are the subjects of business books are extensions and enhancements of other ideas that have worked in the past. Improvements in any field are usually incremental and are based on new ways of looking at older concepts. Most of these improvements can be seen as a continuum when you read what others have written earlier. You should read some of the critical books in the progression, but you can get a very real sense of your idea in this context just by reading the reviews of the earlier books. Reviewers' comments can often summarize the trends quite clearly for you. Not only can this help you focus your idea, but it can also give you critical marketing information to pass along to your publisher. It also shows you which publishers are doing books in your field and what kinds of books review publications choose for review.

Identify the Organizations That Publish on Your Subject

I say identify "organizations" because there are opportunities to publish book-length manuscripts with groups other than those who call themselves book publishers. Just about every general trade publisher does some business books. And there are many houses that do nothing but business books. Don't forget the professional associations in your field that might publish the work of their members.

> **Backspace**
>
> While you're gathering information from the publishers you know, also check out those you don't know, as well as some of those that offer private publishing services. More than a few books are rejected by commercial publishers just because the proposed market won't support the investment. Private publishing can often put you in print and help you reach a narrow, but influential, audience. One of the better private publishers is The Jenkins Group. Contact Jerry Jenkins at jrj@bookpublishing.com.

At this point, you should begin to collect catalogs from all the organizations that could be your publisher. Most will respond to e-mail requests and send you their material. Many, however, have the same information already online. Your goal here is to see not only who might publish competitive material, but also who is publishing complementary material that might help you when you go to write your book.

Scope Your Competition

You should begin to see the trends in your field more clearly than ever. Your research can also point to the need for a follow-up book on the same subject. This is important information to be able to pass along to the editors you pitch for your first book. Every editor likes to think that the author he or she has just discovered is capable of more than just one book. It's the economies of scale idea in action in the book trade. Make it work for you.

Do All Your Heavy Research First

I have written many books and I can tell you that three quarters of the work is doing the research. Writing while you do research is no way to go. With most of the material in hand, and a solid outline in front of you, you can concentrate on writing.

I wrote my first few books on the fly, researching as I went along. But my wise agent back then, Walter Pitkin, told me that I could cut the time in half by getting all the research done first, and that I would be a lot less frustrated during the process. Thanks, Walter, wherever you are!

Line Up Those Who Can Help You

If you are planning a book in which you include a lot of interviews, contact the people you hope to interview now. Most authors prefer to send questions or topics to those they plan to interview to give their interviewees plenty of time to think about what they will say. You will get better and more carefully considered answers when you get to the interview than you will get if you call cold. And the people you interview are usually much more willing to participate when given time to think about their answers.

> **Publishing Tip**
>
> Writing with a professional collaborator often opens the door to interview sources not normally available to new writers. Ghostwriters and collaborators frequently maintain contact with professionals, who can either be interviewed or provide access to those who might be willing to be interviewed, in the fields in which they specialize.

If you are thinking about working with a professional collaborator or consulting editor, now is the time to interview a few. Most independent book people have work scheduled out many months ahead. Waiting to call for help until your publisher more-than-hints that you might need help is not the best way to engage a back-up professional.

Do the Numbers

Do a rough cost-benefit analysis of the time you spend doing your regular work and what you might lose by devoting more time to writing a book. It is, of course, difficult to project the actual economic gain from having a book in print, but it's relatively easy to allocate time and resources in terms of your present situation.

> **Quote/Unquote**
>
> "Some day I'm going to write a book where the royalties will pay for the copies I give away."
> —Clarence Darrow
> Mr. Darrow would be surprised to know that's just what happens—intentionally—when you write and publish a business book. More on this later.

It's not too soon to introduce you to some of the economic realities of book publishing. First, your chances of getting an advance like that paid to Jack Welch and the other heavies who feel compelled to tell their stories are zero. It gets better, but not that much better. An advance of more than $15,000 for a first-time author of a book on any of the typical business subjects is rare. Most advances are less; some are far less. But remember, you are not considering a career as a business book writer. You are writing your book for other reasons, reasons that should in the long run greatly enhance your career and make you more valuable to employers or clients.

A Publisher Is Your Partner

Contrary to publishing folklore, most book publishers are pretty fair in their dealings with authors. They use a market model for their business just as most other companies do. When I discuss publishers in Part 4, I give you real numbers to look at.

You will probably be paid an advance, and you might earn royalties on sales and the sale of subsidiary rights to your material. But consider this: if you were to hire an advertising or public relations agency to promote you or your business, it would be pure out-of-pocket cost to you. When you factor this notion into your equation, it makes it easier to take an advance that might be less than the cost of a mid-level home entertainment system. In short, there is more to the value factor of the equation than just an advance and some hoped-for royalties.

Test Your Idea Thoroughly

I've already discussed this, but it bears repeating. Business book readers are hard-nosed about what they expect from a book; they do not want to be entertained. They want help with problems that vex them. The idea you propose to write about should have worked for you, and you should have plenty of real-world examples to show how effective your idea actually is.

Better yet, your idea should have worked for others as well. The typical business book is no place for windy theory. From this perspective, consultants usually have a better chance at proving that their ideas work, because they have had the opportunity to use them in different and varied situations. The marketing manager who has built the better lead qualification mousetrap for the company that employs him or her has a sample of one. This does not mean that his or her business book proposal is not valuable; it simply means that the data to support it should be good and the author should be prepared to demonstrate that his or her ideas have legs.

Tell No One

Keep your writing to yourself. Vow that you will never show your writing to people who know nothing about your subject or who are not proficient writers themselves. You're going to need all the help you can get, but getting advice from people who are incapable of giving it can be terribly destructive. Free advice is worth just what you pay for it.

Backspace

Don't worry about someone stealing your book idea. A book idea only has value to a publisher when it is accompanied by proof of its validity and the promise that you can turn it into a book a publisher can sell. In all my years as an agent and an author, I've never seen an idea stolen by a publisher, large or small. However, I always kept careful and dated records of any ideas presented to publishers just for my peace of mind. I'd suggest you do the same!

Several years ago, a management consultant sent me a proposal for a book that was based on what I thought was an excellent idea. The author was proposing an adaptation of an old, but still valued concept, Management by Objectives. The idea was sound, and from what I could glean from the proposal, the author had the credentials and experience to do the book. However, the proposal itself was just plain awful.

I was intrigued enough to put in a call to the author. He had a very clear idea of what he wanted to do and explained it in terms that made me ask about the proposal. He explained that he had joined a local writers' group when he began thinking about writing a book. The group operated by critiquing one another's work. This group was made up of aspiring poets and those who fantasized about writing novels. In other words, none was in a position to offer this man any helpful advice at all, yet all had put in their two cents' worth. The result was the horrible proposal and an even more awful sample chapter. I asked him to send me his first draft, which he had written before he joined the group. It was good enough that, with minor tweaking, I was willing to take it on. The book was published a few years later. The point is this: if you need help, be sure to ask for it from people who are in a position to actually help you.

Be Honest About Your Commitment to Write the Book

Not only are there time schedules to meet, but there are quality standards that must be maintained throughout your entire book. An author I worked with years ago wrote two books a year for many years by just writing two pages a day. He did his writing on the train going into New York in the morning, and he edited what he wrote on the return trip at night. Two pages a day, five days a week, for 50 weeks, gave him 500 pages a year, and he never broke a sweat. If you think about writing this way, it is a lot less intimidating than the prospect of facing 500 blank pages. It enables you to work in manageable gulps. And it will help ensure that you deliver your manuscript on time.

We all tend to slip once in a while. If you lose a few days for one reason or another, make up the lost writing immediately. Putting off a day or two of writing now and then for a year can easily make you late in delivering your manuscript. Take schedules seriously. When a publisher contracts with you, that publisher knows almost to the day when they will begin editing, when they will do a set type, and even when the button will be pressed to start the presses. Slip a few days and you throw a real wrench into the machinery. This hurts you and it hurts the publisher.

Polish Your Credentials

Begin to establish your credentials that will interest a publisher. Publishers of books in all nonfiction categories are intensely interested in what authors can do to promote their books. The key question asked of the editor presenting your book idea at the acquisition committee meeting is usually, "Does the author have a platform?" In short, they want to know if you have a soapbox on which you can stand to help them pitch your book to readers. This is a contentious issue today, but it is a fact of publishing life. Even if you have a great idea and can write beautifully, unless you have a "platform," you will have a tough time getting a publisher interested in your book.

Publishing Tip

Begin early to line up people who will say good things about you. Don't be embarrassed about asking if you can quote something someone has said about you. If you are a blogger and you get positive comments on your blog, ask for permission to quote the person who commented about you. Don't promise anyone you'll credit them in an introduction or acknowledgments section of the book or give them author rights; just get permission to use the quote.

Start by listing the organizations to which you belong whose members might be prospective buyers of your book. This includes small local groups as well as larger national and international organizations. Check to see if any of these groups will promote your book or even consider a bulk purchase of your books to sell or give to members. The company you work for might consider buying copies for distribution to customers.

Next, start calling in any favors that could lead to your being asked to speak before groups of individuals who could benefit from the purchase of your book. And, of course, any media connections help enormously.

At this point, your job is just to assemble as much information as possible to include with your proposal. Gather names and numbers. The marketing and publicity people at the publishing house considering your book will need this information to bolster their decision to give your proposal a thumbs-up vote. You will probably be surprised at how many good connections you have when you begin to pull them all together.

Talk with Others Who Have Written Business Books

I have yet to meet, know, or work with a business book author who was not willing to talk with someone who was considering writing a book. That's the way they (we) are. Most are willing to help as long as it doesn't take a lot of time, and most are usually even willing to look at a few tentative pages and offer comments. Just don't send your entire manuscript or expect to have long, meaningful conversations about your book.

Most business book writers avoid getting involved with local writers' groups. You should probably do the same. Most local writers' groups are made up of people with artistic aspirations, rather than an interest in contributing to the body of knowledge in a specific business area.

Take a Few Laps Around the Computer

If you're like most first-time authors, your familiarity with the computer is probably limited to writing some memos, performing work-related tasks, and using your e-mail feature. And you probably think you are pretty good at it. There's a little more to learn, but you don't have to know how to touch-type. I have been writing books for more than 30 years and have never learned to touch-type. I use a few of the longer fingers on each hand in an almost random way. It just doesn't matter whether you touch-type or hack at it with two fingers. As long as you can record your words fast enough to keep up with your thoughts, you can hit the keys any way you want.

However, you should have a pretty good understanding of the way your word processing system enables you to manage, save, and edit your work. The main reason for this is that your publisher probably doesn't want you to submit your material on paper. Most publishers want your writing either on a CD=Rom or sent electronically.

Backspace

Whether you get a book contract or not, the one peripheral everyone should have is an external hard drive with a program that automatically makes copies of everything you store on your main hard drive. You may save your stuff regularly on your hard drive, but any of the major and minor glitches that these drives are prone to could mean that you have the material, but you just can't access it. And it could be that the Blue Screen of Death really does eat your manuscript. Either way, it's a disaster if you don't have a backup.

External hard drives are available with programs that can automatically record what you write on your internal and external hard drive. Currently, I use a Seagate unit that does this job for me. You can also get just a plain vanilla external hard drive and do the moves yourself. The moves in this case can be actually copying files from one drive to another or can use a backup program that condenses and compresses data to save you some storage space.

I tend to prefer transferring the actual files, rather than doing a compressed backup. It's just easier to get at your stuff if you have to. Most systems today have virtual hard drives. These are sections of your main hard drive that are partitioned and used to store material you put in the main section. If the crash you suffer is not of the mechanical variety, this is fine. But if the read-write head digs a trench in the oxide coating of your hard drive, you are sunk. It's your call, but I'd suggest that you go the belt-and-suspenders route and have an external data storage source that you can connect immediately to another computer, so you can keep on writing in case of a crash. Depending on the extent of the damage from a crash, you may need to take your computer to a repair shop.

Publishing Tip _____

I keep an old laptop as my back-up computer. If trouble arises, I can just connect my external drive to the laptop via a USB cable and still be able to work and get my e-mail. The laptop is slow, but it's a reliable old machine. I transfer new data at the end of every session.

Your computer may have a drive slot that enables you to write and rewrite to a DVD disc. If you have such a drive, you might want to use it to produce back-up discs. The discs are so inexpensive that it makes sense to use them in addition to any other back-up system you have. Just remember to follow the instructions for storing the discs. As permanent as the discs may seem, direct sun, certain atmospheres, and tools with sharp points should definitely be avoided.

Set Up a File Management System

Word processing programs are fantastic tools from a variety of perspectives. One of the most underappreciated, however, is the way they can store and manage your work. And one of the things people complain most bitterly about is filing.

The complaints are mostly the result of not having taken the time to understand the system and what it can do for you. Despite the program designers' use of familiar words (*file folder*, for example), most people just wing it and get in trouble all the time. If there is one thing you can do now, before your book contract arrives, it is learn to use the file system in the word processing system you work with. Just keep in mind that each word processing system is different. If you have been using Microsoft Word and your new machine arrives with Corel WordPerfect, you will have a lot of relearning to do, despite the designers' attempts to make the programs work with each other.

The Least You Need to Know

- The reviews of a book that competes with yours can often tell you more than you will learn from reading the entire book.

- Complete your research before you start writing.

- It's best not to show your work to those who don't know much about the topic of your book.

- Typing skills are unimportant, but filing skills are critical.

Part 2

Writing Your Proposal and Sample Chapter

A book proposal is the functional equivalent of any other business proposal. Its goal is to convince those who can publish your book not only to accept your idea, but also to see just how they can profit from a joint venture with you. Far too many good books are not published simply because their authors fail to convince a publisher of the worth of their ideas.

In the chapters that follow, you will meet the three people whose thumbs-ups are needed to see that you become a published author. More than that, however, I show you how a thumbs-down gesture from any one of these people probably means that you and your agent should start talking with another publisher. There are no tricks to this trade. It's all on the table, out there for everyone to see. The publisher wants to publish books that turn a profit, and if your proposal fails to make a convincing case, well, just read on and you'll see what I mean.

Chapter 5

The Proposal That Gets You the Contract

In This Chapter

- ◆ Why you must write your proposal to do more than interest only an editor
- ◆ Why ideas are often more important than great writing skills
- ◆ Why it's possible to pitch something "new and different" that has sold well in the past

A book proposal is a sales pitch. It's supposed to get a lot of people interested in you and your ideas and to help convince all those whose votes are needed, the publisher's gatekeepers, that your book should be on their list. That's a tall order. But that's the way book publishing works, and if you want your book published you have to write a gate-crashing proposal.

Nothing happens until the person at the first gate reads your proposal and *initiates* the in-house review process. At the second gate, your proposal will encounter a number of people who must give their *consent* for the process to continue. Then your proposal encounters the one person at the third gate who either allows the deal to happen or *authorizes* the sending of the dreaded rejection letter.

So when you don't hear from an editor for what you think of as an unconscionably long time, keep in mind that a lot of people are involved and that none of them are sitting around waiting for your proposal to cross their desks. Considering a proposal is a complex and time-consuming process.

The First Gate and Its Gatekeeper

If you or your agent has selected a specific editor to receive your proposal, it will move quickly to that editor's desk. If you haven't specified an editor, your proposal will move from the mail room to what is discouragingly called the slush pile. The slush pile is usually presided over by junior editors, whose responsibilities include making the first sort, deciding which editors should get which proposals. In some houses, those who read and sort are asked to provide their own brief comments. Whatever the process, your proposal for a business book will be given to an editor charged with acquiring business books.

A business book acquisitions editor will review your proposal from several perspectives. Although an acquisitions editor's interest centers on the content and editorial side of the acquisition process, she also reviews manuscripts for other factors that are important to the house. Acquisitions editors are familiar with most aspects of the publisher's program and can determine whether the proposal should be moved on to the keepers of the next level of gates. If, for example, the editor loves the idea of the book and thinks the writer is capable of handling the material but sees that all the charts and graphs needed to complete the book will be too costly, the proposal may move no further.

You might, then, think of the gate that the acquisitions editor controls as being quite broad. There's usually a fair amount of leeway when some aspects of a proposal might be questionable. Yet the gate can be narrow enough to stop a proposal cold if the editor thinks it has little chance of making it past any of the next gatekeepers.

Publishing Tip

If you already have a well-known person lined up to write a foreword, gatekeepers are impressed. If you have well-known people lined up to write cover blurbs, they can be even more impressed. A marginal proposal can often be moved to the starting line when you can produce endorsements the publisher recognizes and is impressed with.

Now, let's look at your proposal from an acquisitions editor's perspective. The following sections discuss some of the questions an acquisitions editor will ask as he or she reviews proposals.

Is It Appropriate for Our Publishing House?

With the exception of the publishers that publish in all aspects of business, most publishers are known for certain strengths. You wouldn't, for example, approach a publisher with a proposal for a marketing book when you know that the publisher has a significant presence only in the accounting field.

If you are submitting your proposal to just one publisher, you can be specific by relating the book you propose to the titles you know the publisher already has in print. But chances are that you are writing your proposal for more than one publisher and must be a little more general. Regardless, your proposal must make the case that your book is a good fit in the field, and any of the publishers who will see the proposal must see the fit quickly.

Is It Different or Exciting Enough to Work with the Current List?

As I have already mentioned, in the business field, there is very little published that is genuinely new and different, just fresh ways to look at and solve a problem. What makes an idea stand out is the author's way of seeing and solving these problems and proving the effectiveness of his or her ideas relative to what is currently in vogue.

Your proposal must make the point that you have something new, different, or maybe even revolutionary, and it has to convince the acquisitions editor that your idea has worked and can be rolled out to a large enough number of readers for the publisher to offer you a contract.

The acquisitions editor will have enough experience in the field to make the first decision to either pass or to recommend that the proposal move on to gatekeepers who bring book publishing expertise to bear on the decision.

The editor at the first gate will be knowledgeable enough about the subject to see the broad strokes of what you propose to write about. He or she will be able to take an educated guess as to whether your idea is viable and determine whether it fits in with the successful books on the publisher's list—or whether it is really a radical approach that could change established business concepts and make the publisher the leader in the field.

These are often tough calls to make, and this is why the review and consent of others is sought once the acquisitions editor is impressed enough with the book's ideas and overall potential.

Publishing Tip _____

If you have an idea that truly is revolutionary, think about publishing it quickly. The chances are that others are thinking the same thoughts. The zeitgeist is more than a hypothetical construct, and if you want to take advantage of the momentum, don't wait too long to write a proposal.

Is the Author Capable of Writing the Book?

Editors of business books are mainly looking for good ideas, and they want to know how clearly you can express yourself and your ideas, whether it's on paper or through someone else with whom you might collaborate.

If an editor likes your idea well enough but sees that you may not be able to go the distance with the material, chances are good that he or she will level with you and suggest some help. The editor may already have someone for you to work with or may give you the names and contact information of people who can help in the areas that need improvement.

If you have already decided to get some professional help, be sure to state that clearly in your proposal.

Does the Author Have a "Platform"?

An author with a "platform" is one who has an established identity that can be used to promote his or her book. The more visible or potentially visible you are, the more points you get when your proposal comes up for a vote.

Your proposal should include all press and other professional mentions you have that could be useful to the publisher's publicity people. Even if you are just a member of the local chapter of a national organization, mention it. The national office might be willing to go to bat for you when your book is published.

I have seen proposals for books that should have been published rejected because the author was not able to convince the acquisitions committee that he had what they wanted. Modesty may prevent you from telling all. Don't let this happen. Just stay on message and make sure that you talk about yourself in terms that relate to what you are doing at the moment and what you would be able to do for the book if the publisher decides to take a chance on you.

Can the Book's Publication Be Tied to Any Special Events?

Business-specific events that might be tapped by the publisher should be detailed. Major historical business events, as well as events that occur on some sort of regular schedule, should be included. And, of course, if you are part of any of these events, include all the details.

Keep in mind, though, that if you sign a contract today, your book will probably not be in print for at least a year or a year and a half.

Are There Bulk Sales Possibilities?

Suppose you propose to write a book about how you doubled the sales volume of your company in one year and that your company employs thousands of other salespeople. If there is any chance that your employer would be willing to buy books for all its salespeople, this should be mentioned in your proposal. If you can lock up a large enough order well ahead of the print date, you can usually negotiate very favorable deals.

There's More

I've only mentioned the major elements that most editors look for in a proposal. There are many others, and some that only you might know of. Be creative. Try to imagine what else in your field might make the publisher more interested in your book. If there are magazines that cover your field and you think one of them might be interested in acquiring the right to serialize some material from your book in regular issues, say so in your proposal.

Meet the Next Gatekeeper(s)

The next gate has several guards, and each must give his or her consent or your proposal will be returned without an offer being made. You may, however, be given the opportunity to answer some of the questions being raised. You probably won't hear directly from any of the other individuals involved, but their questions may be forwarded to you by the acquisitions editor. He has opened the door and has become your in-house advocate. Your editor has initiated the process and must get the consent of the other key players.

The Marketing and Sales Department

Every book that is ever proposed to any commercial publishing house must pass muster with the sales and marketing people. This means that your proposal must be as keenly marketing driven as it is editorially attractive.

Whether you are pitching to a publisher whose entire list is business books or a publisher that just includes business books in its overall list, pull out all the stops. Remember, your proposal is a sales pitch, and you are pitching to the people who will pitch your book to the booksellers.

The first thing the sales people will ask is for your opinion on which books already in print will compete with the book you propose. It is critical that you provide a comprehensive list of these books and, if possible, the sales figures for these books. Your agent may be able to help, but if you can't produce exact numbers, include information on the number of printings and revisions the competitive books have already racked up.

Publishing Tip _____

Don't hesitate to submit a proposal to a publisher even if you believe your book might compete with a title already on its list. But try to show in your proposal why someone who buys the existing book might also want to buy your book. You never know when a publisher might be looking for a new book to replace a title whose sales are slowing down.

The sales people also want to know if you or your employer, or anyone else, might be interested in buying a significant quantity of your book. At this point, specific commitments aren't necessary, but if you can offer any educated guesses as to how many books the publisher might be able to sell this way, you will make points with the sales people.

If there are any special sales possibilities outside of the obvious channels, be sure to include this information in your proposal. It's not unusual for some business books written for general business readers to be adopted as ancillary texts for college courses and specialized training programs. If this is a possibility, point it out in your proposal. It helps if you can cite examples of similar books that are being used this way.

The sales department will be asked to give an estimate of the number of books they think they might be able to sell in the first year. Every publisher hopes to recover all or most of its costs in the first year of publication. This doesn't usually happen, but it's the goal most often used when sales estimates are required for an offer to be made on a proposal. Keep in mind that a publisher can recover its costs in many ways, and sales to booksellers, whether they are online or in traditional brick-and-mortar locations, count along with subsidiary rights sales and periodical serialization.

The Legal Department

If the acquisitions editor's review turned up anything that suggested a legal review might be needed, your proposal will be passed to the legal gatekeeper. If the questions asked are serious enough and the legal people feel the publisher's risk exposure might be too great, your proposal might not make it through this gate. However, if the publisher wants the book badly enough, you will probably hear from the acquisitions editor about the legal department's' specific concerns.

If you are aware of any legal issues that might concern the publisher, don't try to hide them. Bring them up in your proposal and state what you think might be done to prevent any lawsuits. Be upfront about this. If a publisher wants the book, the legal department will prefer to see that you are aware of the concerns and being cooperative in addressing them, rather than trying to ignore them.

The Art, Design, and Production Departments

If your book is all words, and you have estimated the number of words you will probably write, all that is usually needed from the folks here is an estimate on the cost to take the book from manuscript to printed book copies in the estimated numbers the sales department has provided. Chances are that the sales department has been asked to give sales estimates for both hardcover and trade paperback sales.

If, on the other hand, your book requires illustrations to be made and the printing of more than just words, special estimates will be required. Some simple drawings and even some photographs don't add all that much to the production and printing costs. But if the book you propose must include a lot of complex graphics, special estimates will be required. You may be required to provide material that is ready to use for these. If you can't or choose not to provide the material, and the publisher still wants to do the book, it might elect to take on the work, but the publisher's costs will be reflected in the advances and royalties it will propose to pay you if a contract is offered.

Be sure to explain in your proposal just what you think will be required in terms of graphics and whether or not you will be able to provide them.

The Publicity and Promotion Department

Publicity and promotion are the tools most often used to sell business books, and the people you meet in this department will have a lot of questions for you. The more you can answer in advance in your proposal, the brighter your star glows in this department.

Every proposal should include biographical information that highlights the events and accomplishments in your life that can be used to promote your book. Running the winning touchdown for your college team may be very important to you, but unless you want to write a sports book, don't include it in your bio. As I have already mentioned several times, your "platform" will be a key factor in a publisher's decision to take on your book. Since business books are published to be sold nationally, or even internationally, your platform must be more than the accolades you got in the local paper for your speech at the chamber of commerce.

So what do you do if you really have a great idea but no platform? Here are a few ways some authors with good ideas have built platforms that lifted them from Podunk to popularity that caught publisher's eyes.

Join an Organization ... or Two

Almost all business fields are served by one or more associations that could give you national exposure. Check them out and join the one that seems to have the most national prestige. If there is a local chapter, join it. Most business associations publish member magazines, newsletters, and online information. An article in the Public Relations Society of America's magazine gives you instant credit. The same article in the local chamber of commerce's quarterly newsletter does little for you in terms of your goal of getting a book contract.

Volunteer to serve on national committees. Offer to speak at conferences and conventions. It's all well and good to work hard for the local chapter, but if you want that platform that so interests book publishers, go national.

Find a Mentor Who Can Take You National

You may be able to find a mentor in the association you join, but it's usually just as easy to find someone by doing it yourself. I'm sure that you read what others write about your field. And I'm sure that you can tick off the names of at least 10 of the big players in the field. You would be surprised at how willing many people are to help others on the way up. A simple letter to someone whose accomplishments you admire can often lead not only to help and advice, but also to a relationship that will give you the stature you need to get a publisher.

What is important here is that someone with a national image in your field vouches for your ideas and the potential for your book. If you are employed by a major national or international company and your book relates to your employer's business, chances are that you will be able to get the endorsement you need right at home.

The Last and Final Gate

This is the wild card in the game. There's always one person who has to make the final decision. Depending on the size and the structure of the publishing company, that person could be the president of the company. Or it could be one of the vice presidents, or it could be someone you'd never guess might have so much clout in the company.

Regardless of who this person is and what her title is, without her signature, contracts are not offered. Seems like something out of Kafka, doesn't it? You work your tail off on a great proposal, and all of the people on the acquisitions committee go to bat for you, but Ms. Big says no. Unfair? Perhaps. But whoever told you that this, or any business, has anything to do with fairness was dead wrong.

Okay, it's not as bad as that. Ms. Big is seldom the heartless beast you might think. But it can sure feel like that sometimes. So let's not get on the "poor me" kick, and we'll see just what can be done to get you through the next gate.

If you are using an agent, he probably knows all about the final gatekeeper and can tell you what to do with your proposal to enhance the odds of a positive response. If you are not using an agent, you should find out all you can about this person. This isn't easy if you don't have an agent. But if you have established even basic rapport with the acquisitions editor, you can probably get enough information about this person to tailor your proposal appropriately.

Every publishing company is different. In some, the path to the top begins in the editorial department. In others it may begin in the sales and marketing department. The path to the top in any publishing company usually includes a stint in a department where the final decision to buy a proposal is usually made.

If the final decision will be made by someone who rose through marketing, you know what you have to stress in your proposal. You can take the president out of the marketing department—to crib a cliché—but you can't take the marketing department out of the president. So although you have to convince everyone at the previous gates, you have to really put on a good show when you reach the last. And that show should be tailored to the gatekeeper's special interest.

Publishing Tip _____

If you can't get a handle on how the final gatekeeper might respond to your proposal, take a look at the company's backlist—the books it has published in the past few years, which readers of your proposed book might have read. You should be able to pick up a few threads that will give you a general idea of what gets through the gate.

Anything you know about this person's interests and behavior when it comes to making decisions on proposals will help you a lot. Your editor, your agent, or anyone you know who might have had a proposal accepted or rejected by this person should be contacted. Keep in mind that whether a proposal is accepted or rejected, you will only be told that it was on the basis of a collective decision. However, if you have been told that you have passed all the preliminary gates, you will know the decision was made at the last gate.

But what good does it do to know why a proposal was rejected? If enough people liked your proposal to move it to the top, you just might be able to resubmit with the revisions needed to get past the dissenting gatekeeper. If you really want to publish with a publisher that has taken your proposal to the final gate, it's worth the effort.

How Tightly Should Your Proposal Be Focused?

The proposal you give to everyone up to (but not including) the final gatekeeper can, and probably should, be written to appeal to that imaginary editor who works at all of the houses you may submit to. If you have one specific house in mind and you think you might have a good chance of publishing there, you should first do a proposal that is aimed at that house. You should know the titles the house has already published and you should include information in your proposal that refers to those books. You should also explain how your book will fit in with the existing line and possibly strengthen the sales of those existing books.

If you go this route, be sure to make it obvious that you are submitting your proposal exclusively to that one house. It will take time to hear from any publisher if you are a new author, but if you really want to publish with a specific house, focus your proposal and be prepared to wait a month or two. If your agent is known to the publisher, however, he should be able to get fairly quick attention to your proposal. It probably won't be an immediate yes or no, but just knowing that there is interest makes it worth waiting for the final decision.

If, on the other hand, you want to move more quickly and are not shooting for one specific publisher, then hit all bases evenly and get the proposals circulating.

The Least You Need to Know

- Your proposal must pass inspection at three different gates
- A good, salable idea is the key to getting the gatekeepers' attention.
- Regardless of how well written your proposal might be, if there is too small a market, you probably won't get an offer.
- Without a "platform," your chances aren't too good, but it is possible to create the kind of image that will get you past the gate.

Chapter **6**

How to Write a Convincing Proposal

In This Chapter

- How to write a proposal that gets immediate attention
- Why fewer well-chosen words outperform long-winded proposals every time
- A guided tour through the proposal that sold this book

Your book proposal is the main thing that stands between you and getting your book in print. If you have a good, convincing proposal, most likely you will get your book published. If you have a thrown-together, half-baked proposal, you can kiss those royalty checks good-bye.

In this chapter, I discuss how to write your proposal by letting you read the proposal I wrote to get the book you are reading published. You even get to read my original sample chapter. There have been some changes, but you should get the idea of how to write your own.

First, though, let's take a look at what your proposal needs to do.

The Lean, Mean Proposal Machine

If you talk to a hundred authors, you will find a hundred different opinions on how to write a compelling proposal. So consider this the hundred-and-first opinion, coming from someone who has written, revised, edited, critiqued, and ghosted more than a hundred book proposals.

While some writers go by the "more is better" theory, my preference is for the lean and focused approach. The reason behind this is simple. When you write a book proposal, you are writing advertising copy for your book, aimed at capturing the attention of the editor who just had a bag full of proposals dropped on her desk. You have very little time in which to convince her that the rest of the proposal is worth reading, so I believe the tightly focused proposal is most effective.

In short, you have to grab the editor's attention, make it easy for her to grasp the idea of the book quickly, and include enough material to move the editor to ask for more information or possibly a longer writing sample.

Think of your proposal as two parts: the idea pitch and the writing pitch.

The first presents your idea and the benefit it brings to the publisher and readers. It is the part that sells the book. Within your pitch, you should include sections detailing the title, the idea, the book, the market, the competition, the author, and the chapter outline.

Backspace

Many first-time writers try too hard to gain attention by writing in a style that is totally inappropriate for the job it is expected to do. Don't do this. Write your sample chapter as you would write it for the book. Don't try to write it to pitch the salability of the book. Just be yourself and you'll be fine.

The second part, the sample chapter, showcases your writing skills and convinces an editor that you know what you are talking about and that you can write clearly enough to do the job.

After you have captured the attention of the editor, you have very little time in which to convince her that the rest of the proposal is worth reading. And once you've pulled that editor through enough of your proposal, you have made the case for it to be set aside for a more careful reading.

Publishing Tip

Several of the books I reviewed for this chapter were based on the use of actual proposals. One book that I thought did this job very well was *Write the Perfect Book Proposal: Ten That Sold and Why* by Jeff Herman and Deborah Levine Herman (published by John Wiley & Sons, Inc.). Jeff and Deborah take readers through ten sample proposals and include their comments along the way. This is an excellent way to learn, and if this approach appeals to you, pick up a copy of their book.

This chapter is based on one proposal, the one I wrote to pitch this book. It was written with one editor in mind, Randy Ladenheim-Gil, executive editor of Alpha Books, the publisher of The Complete Idiot's Guide series. The proposal wasn't originally written for the series, however. I had envisioned it for the Alpha single-title line, which means I intended it to be a one-off title that didn't follow the series guidelines. With minor tweaking, I could have revised the proposal and used it to submit to other publishers if Randy had not been interested in it.

Randy, in her much admired publishing wisdom, saw the book as part of the Idiot's Guide series, based on the successes Alpha has had with other books on the subject of writing. All she wanted, then, was a revision of the chapter structure, which I did, and now you are reading the book I proposed.

The Title

Your first chance to get an editor's attention is with the title of your book. While perusing the shelves at your favorite bookstore, how many times has the title of a book caught your eye and caused you to pull the book off the shelf? Even if you are looking for a book on a particular topic, often the right title will catch your attention and compel you to read on.

Also, remember who you are writing for. The title of a book for business readers should not beat around the bush. It should make its point immediately and be directly relevant to what will follow between the covers. You can be creative, but don't be too cute or abstract.

I and most other agents agree that a book title should be as short as possible without sacrificing the impact of its message. If you feel you need to use more than a few words, think about using a short title along with a longer subtitle.

Your title should make a positive statement, even though your book may be about how to solve sticky problems. For example, a book about how to deal with sales slumps with a title like "What to Do When You Are in a Sales Slump" is doomed before a word is written. The same material, titled "Tested Techniques for Doubling Your Sales," makes the grade.

Publishing Tip

Yes, I know, some extremely successful book titles are clever and abstract. *What Color Is Your Parachute?* is a book title few will fail to recognize, and most know that it's about career planning. But you really take a gamble when you go this route. As good as *Parachute* is in this case, it might have been just another book if the author had used a different title.

The best way to come up with a good title idea is to do a search of all the books with which your book will compete. Ask yourself what it would take to get a reader's attention, given all the choices that are available. It may take you as long to come up with the few good words you need as it takes to write a chapter.

After you have what you think is a good idea, use it as your working title. For the moment, it describes the book you have in mind. However, as you get into your proposal and sample chapter, you will probably come up with plenty of other ideas. Keep an open mind. In fact, keep a list of every idea you have, regardless of how weird some may seem.

Of all the books I have written, none of them carried the first title I envisioned. Some I changed; some were changed based on suggestions from editors. Some titles were the work of the publishers' sales people, who knew more of what booksellers wanted than I did.

For this book, my original title was *How to Write and Publish a Business Book*. When it was decided that the book would be published as an Idiot's Guide, it had to carry the title now on the cover. Check the graphics on the cover and you'll see that, apart from the CIG line, it's still a short title that conveys exactly what this book is all about.

The First Section: The Idea

The first section of the proposal is the warm-up for your proposal. I call it "The Idea." This is the section that has to get the editor's attention as quickly as possible.

The information in it must be factually anchored, must relate to what the editor wants to see, and must be clear and unambiguous.

While "The Idea" is my name for it, it might help knowing that other proposals refer to this first section as the overview or mission statement. It should create a scene, present a problem, and suggest a solution.

Here, then, is "The Idea" I used in the proposal for this book:

> *According to an R.R. Bowker report published last May, there was a 12 percent increase in the number of business books published that year over the same period of the previous year. However, another report, published in* The Economist *at about the same time, took the steam out of this news by stating, "It's astonishing how bad most business books are." If I'm interpreting this correctly, there's a real need for a book to take advantage of this growth and to help people write better business books. I propose to write that book.*

> *Just about anyone can learn the basics of writing letters and memos from any of the hundreds of books already in print. But the typical business book author is not a writer by temperament, or by training. He or she is a businessperson with an idea to express. An extensive discussion of voice, verbs, nouns, and pronouns is a complete turnoff to the typical aspiring business book author. It's style, voice, pace, and focus where they usually go off the rails.*

> *Most important, however, the typical aspiring business book author seldom sees his or her book through the eyes of a publishing house marketing director. For most potential book authors, a "platform" is something to stand on, not the credits needed to promote a book. And they all vastly underestimate the commitment needed to write a good business book.*

> *Most business book editors turn down far more proposals than they ever buy simply because they see the problems they know they will face when the manuscript arrives. If they are fortunate enough to have a developmental staff or a source of good freelance editors, management quickly reminds them that the cost to turn a pig's ear into a silk purse is high. So what to do? Editors usually wrestle with the author from the get-go. What if there was a book that could help solve these problems? It doesn't exist, but this is your opportunity to publish it. Read on.*

The first paragraph quotes two respected sources and makes the points that more business books are being published every year and that many of them are poorly written. An expanding market and a need for the book are key points that would interest any editor.

In the second paragraph, I describe the typical reader and point out that other books on writing don't measure up to what a reader really needs; hence, there is a potential market for the publisher.

Another paragraph tells the editor what he or she already knows, that there is more work than hours available to do it, but that help is at hand in the book I am proposing.

The last paragraph builds on the others and ends with the exhortation "Read on."

Having created a scene, presented a problem, and suggested a solution, the next step is to describe the proposed book.

The Second Section: The Book

The title of the second section is simple: "The Book." It follows from the first section logically and doesn't bog down in superlatives. I hate to keep bringing this up, but if you could just spend one day in a busy editorial office and see the number of proposals that arrive, you would understand why I keep stressing brevity. Offers are made after editors and potential authors talk extensively, and the whole idea of a proposal is to get that dialogue started first.

> *Most of the books on writing an aspiring business book writer could choose from are big and expensive. I see this as a short book, coming in at about 65,000 words. I see it as a lower-priced evergreen, and most likely a trade paper original. This book could easily fall into the "other books you might want to consider" category on every Internet bookseller's list. As you know, this is the catbird seat for any publisher. My plan is to take the aspiring business book author on a virtual tour of business book publishing. There will be stops at the acquisitions editor's office. We will visit the editors, lawyers, and the contract people. And, of course, marketing and publicity will be a major stop on the tour. During each of these visits, I will present the information that is considered by most business book editors, agents, and publishers to be essential to a successful book. All of this will be based on my 30 years of experience as an agent and a published author and on the wisdom of many publishing professionals I have come to know. I can get impressive forewords and blurbs easily.*

> *The narrative style will be light, but the intent will be serious. Much of what I cover will be documented by specific examples. This will include writing style as well as how authors and publishers can work together for the profit of both. I will explain why some authors should seriously consider a good vanity publisher rather than waste their time trying to publish with a major house. My focus is to show potential authors that publishers need them as much as they need good publishers. It will be a reality check for the dreamer as well as a how-to guide for the person who writes the next best-selling business book on your list.*

Initially, I saw this book as a short book, about half as long as the book you are now reading. Randy, my wonderful editor, convinced me that a book of the length I originally proposed could not do justice to the subject. She was right. (Again!) But the proposal did its job: it got a discussion going with Randy, my agent, Ed Claflin, and me. The happy result is that this book is in print.

The second paragraph describes the book in terms of its journey from manuscript to bound book. The scenes are familiar to an editor, and the more comfortable an editor is with your material, the easier it is to make your points. Here's where many proposal writers go the bulleted copy route. There's nothing wrong with bulleted lists, except that they are boring. Just don't let narrative fantasy get in the way of what you are trying to say.

The main point is that publishers need good authors as much as authors need good publishers.

The Third Section: The Market

Yes, publishers do have marketing departments, but their major responsibility is that of marketing the books the house publishes, not researching the markets for books that are proposed to them. It's your job to provide current numbers and trends and to show that your book will sell well to the audiences you plan to write for.

It's critical that you not only provide the numbers and trends, but also that you cite your sources for this information. Chapter 16 shows you where and how to get this information, and how to present it.

The presentation style I chose for this proposal was a narrative, rather than something more graphic, because there are only a few critical numbers and trends to present. Charts, graphs, and checklists would have been overkill.

> *According to a report published in* The Economist, *November 1, 2007, "business books are soaring." The article continues, "Business books, it seems, are booming again." More to the point, and in support of my plan for the book outlined in this proposal, "There is also a growing demand from overloaded executives for shorter books." The article continues to describe how other publishers are planning to capitalize on this trend. The publishers listed include the Harvard Business School Press, as well as many of the traditional trade houses with business book lines.*

The Bowker report mentioned earlier stated that there were 9,006 new business book titles this year compared with 7,885 titles released for the previous year. Each one of these books had an author who could have been a prospect for the book I am proposing. Further, when you consider the ratio of books proposed to the number of books actually published, it translates to major numbers. No one, to my knowledge, has done any analysis on the real numbers, but if you consider the number of business books published relative to the number rejected, I'm sure you will agree that there's a significant market.

Even more interesting is a report published by BusinessWeek in mid-2006, which quoted an executive from the Wellesley Hills consulting group as saying, "The vast majority of the (business book) authors we surveyed—96 percent—said they did realize a significant positive impact on their businesses from writing a book and would recommend the practice." If ever there was an incentive to publish—and a talking point for your publicity people—that is it.

Actual numbers of books sold by individual publishers are difficult to get and even more difficult to trust. However, no publisher keeps publishing a category that doesn't make money. In my 30 years as an agent, I never saw a publisher drop a business book line. There were years when they expanded their lines and there were times when they cut back, but they continued to publish. The 12 percent increase in business book titles mentioned earlier has considerable predictive validity. Your market, if you publish my book, will be everyone who wants to write a business book. Most of them ultimately will not write the book they dream of, but they will buy the book on how to do it, just as those who dream of quitting their jobs and going it alone will continue to dream of having their own consulting businesses and buying books about how to do it.

Paragraph one cites an article that had appeared recently in *The Economist*, which stated that other publishers are publishing books for the same market identified for my book. A subtle hint is made that the editor reading the proposal might lose out if he or she passed on the proposal.

The second paragraph provides numbers that even surprised me. But who would question the number-one source of marketing information in the book industry, R.R. Bowker?

Then, in the third paragraph, even more confirming information, this time from another trusted source, *BusinessWeek* magazine. Note the exhortation in the last sentence, keeping in mind that an acquisitions editor must provide enough information to convince all the others who must give their vote to publish a book.

In the final paragraph, I drew on my 30 years as an agent and my earlier years as an advertising copywriter and agency owner. It may be a little over the top, but given that

I had already presented solid data from well-known and trusted sources, I took the liberty of suggesting that "everyone who wants to write a business book" will want this book. Don't do this unless you have first built a really strong case for your book. You can be forgiven for exuberance only when it's clearly documented.

The Fourth Section: Competition

The prospective publisher wants to know what your book is up against in order to gauge whether it will be able to sell your book. To make sure the publisher has all the information needed, you must list and describe the major books that compete directly, as well as indirectly, with the book you propose to write. Needless to say, your proposal must explain why someone would want to buy your book and not the competitor's book. You should also show why a competitive picture proves your point—that there is a strong market for your book.

While you want to make sure your book stands out from the competition, don't resort to tearing apart your competition. Instead, show how your proposed book is better than the existing titles and how readers will benefit from yet another title. Lacerating competitors is not the way to go!

> *In an article in the August 19, 2004, issue of* The Economist, *a writer said, "If you want to profit from your pen, first write a best-selling business book. In few literary genres are the spin-offs so lucrative." I was unable to turn up any books that will compete with the book I am proposing. However, I did turn up a fascinating book that makes my case quite persuasively. It's titled* The Business Impact of Writing a Book: Data, Analysis, and Advice from Professional Service Providers Who Have Done It. *It sells for a hefty $179, is a spiral-bound report, and is published by RainToday, a consulting firm that provides extensive data on the economic benefits of publishing a business book. RainToday provides back-up marketing services to authors. Speaking bluntly, anyone who shells out $179 to confirm what he or she probably already knows about the effect a book can have on his or her career or business will be more than happy to spend far less on my shorter book—which will tell them how to do it!*
>
> *The following titles are complementary rather than competitive. The lack of competition, however, raises an interesting question: Why hasn't anyone ever published on this subject? It could be that publishers think there is too small a market. But the data I have already presented shows a large and rapidly growing market. I don't have the answer. But the numbers are irrefutable. There should be such a book.*

How to Write a Book Proposal, Michael Larsen (Writer's Digest Books). Mike is a good friend, and you have every right to think that because of this my unqualified endorsement of this book might be tainted. But see for yourself. Read Mike and read the others. I think you will agree with me: his book is the gold standard.

How to Write and Publish Your Own Book, Kathleen Mailer (Aurora Publishing). This is one of quite a few books on self-publishing, and it is one of the better books. I do address the question of self-publishing in my book, and I think it does have a place under certain circumstances. There are no books aimed specifically at the self-publishing business book author, but this title can be helpful to the writer choosing this route.

How to Write a Business Book and Get It Published, Herman Holtz (New Ventures Publishing). Out of print. New Ventures was, I believe, a self-publishing imprint of Mr. Holtz.

101 Reasons Why You Must Write a Book, Bob Burnham and Jeff McCallum (self-published). There are some good ideas in this book, as far as it goes. The earlier mentioned report is far more persuasive because of the wealth of actual data.

Negotiating a Book Contract, Mark Levine (Moyer Bell). An excellent book and the book that was at my side quite often during my days as an agent.

I was able to find only one book that seemed to compete directly with the book I was proposing, and that was the one written by Herman Holtz. A thorough search showed that it was out of print and I was unable to obtain a copy. Each of the books found competed with portions of the book I was proposing, but there was no single book that took the same overall approach. Note that some of the books that did compete with portions of my book made the point I was making for the book you are reading. I was careful to show how the publication of each of these books made the case for the book I wanted to write.

There were few competitive books I could cite. However, fields like general management are both wide and deep. Anyone writing a book for this market would be well advised to do a thorough and carefully analyzed study of all the books that might compete with the book being proposed.

The Fifth Section: The Author

It's time to talk about yourself and present your credentials. Most inexperienced writers believe that the more they say about themselves, the better their case for a sale.

Don't leave out anything that would make your case, but forget about describing your term as senior class president unless, of course, you are writing a book about being president of a senior class.

> *I spent 30 years running a literary agency that I founded, James Peter Associates, Inc. The agency handled only nonfiction books, and a large portion of the more than 600 titles I sold were business books. I am the author of 12 books published under my own name with major national and international publishers and of more than 20 others as either the ghostwriter or collaborator. I have written college textbooks on marketing and advertising, general business books, and trade books on a wide range of popular subjects.*
>
> *Seven years ago I sold my agency, and I have been writing and editing ever since. I guess I'm lucky because all my working years have been fun. I continue to do the things that gave me the most pleasure during my earlier years, writing and editing.*
>
> *I have undergraduate and graduate degrees in psychology and marketing. I continue to take courses at Columbia, classes that I wanted to take but didn't have time for during my undergrad and graduate school years. It's fun being around bright kids and bright profs.*
>
> *I can deliver the complete manuscript six months from the contract date.*

I could have listed the published books I wrote that credited me as the author, but I decided that the number alone might be more impressive than the actual titles. As I had never written a book about writing, I think this was a wise decision.

I must admit that, since I've been in book publishing for 30 years, many of the editors who might have seen the proposal (had Randy decided to pass) might have recognized my name. Not that I am or ever was a big name, but publishing is a small world. So the bio was brief, but it left opportunities for any editor interested enough in the book to ask for more.

The Sixth Section: Chapter Outline

The chapter outline is a critical element. The outline that follows is the one I envisioned for the shorter book I originally planned. Note that this outline has changed since the original proposal. The point of the outline is to show that you have done your research and planning. It also shows what you plan to include. You've told the publisher how the book can sell. The outline shows that you know what needs to be included to make the sale.

Introduction

Acknowledgments

Chapter 1   *Before You Write a Word*

Chapter 2   *How to Write a Proposal and a Sample Chapter*

Chapter 3   *Selling Your Book to a Publisher*

Chapter 4   *Negotiating a Fair Contract*

Chapter 5   *Working with Your Editor*

Chapter 6   *Writing the Book You and the Publisher Want*

Chapter 7   *Working with the Publisher's Marketing and Publicity People*

Chapter 8   *Using Your Book to Enhance Your Career*

Appendix   *Sources and Contacts Every Business Book Author Needs*

This chapter outline was appropriate for the subject and the editors to whom the proposal might have been sent. A book about writing with obvious chapter titles was enough. However, a proposed chapter outline of almost any other book should be far more detailed.

Each chapter should be briefly outlined and a few paragraphs should be written to describe just what you intend to convey. Brevity is still important, but just as important is the information needed to convince an editor that you know what you are talking about, that you have something important to say, and that you will be able to write the book you propose.

The Seventh Section: Sample Chapter

Your writing sample is sort of like a screen test. If the editor has gotten this far into your proposal, he is probably half sold on the idea of presenting your proposal at the next editorial meeting.

If you are writing with professional help, this is the place to talk about it. It's a mistake to hide the fact that you are working with a pro. In fact, many editors breathe a sigh of relief when they see that a pro is on board. So say so if this is what you are planning to do. And if you have already connected with a writer, this is a good place to introduce her.

Everything that I included in my original sample chapter was eventually woven into this book, but because of the format of this series, that Chapter 1 that I submitted as a sample is not what you read. Changes and edits are eventually made, but your original sample chapter will likely be integrated into the book in some form.

Here is part of the original Chapter 1 I submitted as a sample chapter. If you look at Chapter 1 again, you can see how just this small sampling alone changed once the book was accepted and eventually edited and published.

Before You Write a Word

Any marathon runner will tell you that you don't prepare for long-distance running by doing sprints. The same advice applies to writing a book. Since you are planning to do some long-distance writing, I strongly suggest that you prepare very carefully before you write a word of your book. The guidelines and suggestions that follow should get you in shape. You're not entering the 50-word memo dash; you're planning to go the distance with a book.

Read the good writers first.

Read all the books you can get your hands on that cover the topic on which you plan to write. Read, not just for content, but for style. You're not cheating if you adopt the style of an author you admire any more than an artist is cheating who is inspired by the brushstrokes of a famous painter. When you find a business book writer whose style is comfortable for you, read his or her books several times and try to put your finger on what it is that has drawn you to the writer. Your readings after the first will be the most revealing. Content won't intrude, and you will see the author's nuance and style. It's best to do the follow-up readings immediately after the first. And do this reading armed with a pile of Post-it notes and yellow markers. In your own words, note what impresses you about the passages you highlight.

Pay particular attention to pacing. The positioning of long and short sentences and even long and short words can make the difference between dull and interesting writing. Book writers are seldom paid by the word, but those with less experience tend to overwrite as though they were. Brevity is not only the soul of wit, it's the soul of good business book writing. For now, just try to get a feel for what you think is good writing. If the author holds your attention and you are not easily distracted as you read, you can bet that the author you are reading knows what he or she is doing.

Read the reviews of other books published in your field.

Most ideas that are the subject of business books are extensions and enhancements of other ideas that have worked in the past. Improvements in any field are usually incremental and based on new ways of looking at accepted concepts. Most of these improvements can be seen as a continuum when you read what others have written earlier. You should read some of the critical books in the progression, but you can get a very real sense of your idea in this context just by reading the reviews of the earlier books. Reviewers' comments can often summarize the trends quite clearly for you. Not only will this help you focus your idea, it will give you critical marketing information to pass along to your publisher. It will also show you which publishers are doing books in your field and the kind of books that are chosen for review.

I'll save the comments for Chapter 9. This chapter is already way too long. But it had to be. Without a good proposal, your chances of seeing your book in print with a good commercial publisher are pretty slim.

The Least You Need to Know

- The main job of a book proposal is to get the ball rolling, not to make an immediate sale.
- Writing a proposal is as much a test of your writing as the salability of your idea.
- Your proposal should be written to sell your idea.
- Your sample chapter should showcase your writing skills or the skills of a writer or editor with whom you plan to work.

7

How to Find and Present Competitive Information

In This Chapter

- ◆ Using the competition to make your case
- ◆ Finding every book that competes with or complements your book
- ◆ The competitive secret weapon
- ◆ Writing your review for the strongest impact

There are two ways that other books will compete with the one you plan to write: directly and indirectly. Books that directly compete with yours are ones that cover the same subjects you plan to cover in your book. These are the books that are of immediate interest to publishers when they review your proposal. Currently, there are no books in print that cover the exact same topics as the book you are now reading.

However, there are many books in print that teach business writing, publishing law, proposal writing, or one of the other topics I cover in this book. Books that address individual topics covered in your book compete indirectly.

Someone who is already a skilled writer, for example, may know what makes a business book different from other nonfiction books and how to find a good agent but be looking for a book on proposal writing. This person might skip over your book because it has more information than she needs.

It's important for you to discuss both kinds of competition in your proposal, but you must emphasize those books that compete directly.

Where Most Business Book Proposals Fall Short

This may seem like a blinding glimpse of the obvious, but I can't begin to tell you how many proposals I've seen and rejected because the authors failed to provide the competitive information that I, as an agent, needed in order to make a strong case for a pitch to an editor. Many of these failures were the result of the author not carefully differentiating between books that compete directly and those that compete indirectly or of the author stressing books that were only marginally competitive.

First, however, let's look at the sources that will be most helpful to you.

Where to Look for Competitive Books

Your local library may not be a good source unless your library is the one located at the corner of 42nd Street and Fifth Avenue in New York City. In most parts of the country, however, local libraries are now part of regional systems. This means that you have access to many more books than you would if you looked only in the library nearest you. Most of these consolidated library systems have a composite Internet presence that allows you to search each library from your home computer and often even arrange for a book to be sent from a remote library to the one nearest you.

Publishing Tip

If your local library is large enough to employ a full-time reference librarian, make friends with him. Even though the books you might want and need may not be available locally, a good reference librarian can tell you who has them and how to get them.

The Internet has made the job of locating competitive titles a walk in the park compared with what it was B.C. (Before Computers). But just identifying a title that looks like a possible competitor and scanning its table of contents is not enough. You have to dip into the books that look competitive, and this can mean buying some if your library doesn't have the copies you need.

Professional and Trade Associations

Most trade and professional associations provide members information on new and older books in print that are useful in their work. Those organizations that publish magazines usually include reviews of recently published books in their current pages. And by now most associations have these reviews available to members online.

> **Backspace**
>
> Don't assume that everything you need will be in a professional association's files. Some associations tend to focus mainly on material that supports their cause and avoid filing material that doesn't. You might be able to remedy this by checking with associations known to have opposing views.

Check the organizations you belong to and see what they have. Some associations even have tie-ins with publishers and specialized booksellers to make books available to members at discounted prices. I'm not aware of any that have anything like a mail-in lending library service, but it pays to ask when you do your search.

Most publisher press releases sent to associations contain copies of the books they are pitching. You just might be able to borrow copies of those you need for a proposal review. If you like the book, buy a copy for yourself. Remember, you may be a published author yourself one of these days, and your royalties will be based on copies sold.

College and University Libraries

A membership in your college alumni association more than likely carries with it an active library card. If you are close enough to the campus, you just may have everything you need in your backyard. Many have their catalogues online, so distance may not be a problem. Even if you did not attend the university near you, university town-and-gown societies often make the library available to nonstudents for a small fee. However, remember that many titles in university libraries are held in reserve for students to read only on site. But for the purposes of gathering competitive information, you should be able to find what you need in an hour or two on site, especially if you have been granted Internet access to the library's list of acquisitions and know what you want before making a visit.

Reviews in Business-Related Periodicals

Business magazines are useful resources in testing your book topic. They also can help you identify your competition through their book reviews. While it might be impossible to get your hands on every magazine relevant to your subject, many magazines make their reviews available online.

Before I share some helpful websites, a word of advice. When you write your proposal, don't just rehash the review. Make sure you read enough of each book that you can make an honest and accurate comparison with the book you plan to write.

- *BusinessWeek*—Type this URL into your browser, www.businessweek.com/life style/books.htm, and you will not only have access to books reviewed in the current issue of *BusinessWeek*, but also to thousands of other reviews, all organized by subject to make your search even easier.

- *The Economist*—This is another excellent source of book reviews. You can get to them with this URL: www.economist.com/books/.

- *The New York Times*—You can access the business-related books reviewed by *The New York Times* at this site: www.nytimes.com/pages/books/. This will take you to their general book reviews. Just click on the "Business" tab, and you will have a wealth of information. In fact, at the time of this writing, 5,341 reviews of business-related books were available at this site.

Don't limit your search to just magazines and newspapers. Many of the world's major print and online business newsletters also provide the same services for the books they have reviewed.

Online Booksellers

There are quite a few excellent online booksellers you can use to scope out competitive books, as well as books that will help you support your case to a publisher. Each operates pretty much the same way; however, each has its own unique graphic presence and search system. I have selected Amazon as being pretty much representative of the way the systems work. Once you get the hang of using one of them, it's pretty easy to dig into any of the others.

Publishing Tip _____

In addition to the online retail booksellers, there are a number of excellent book wholesalers whose websites offer a wealth of information. If you type www.ingrambook.com into your browser, you will land on the site of the Ingram Book Group, a highly respected distributor. Using Ingram's site takes a little patience, however, mainly because it was designed to serve the needs of book retailers. It's worth taking the time to master it.

Let's say that you are planning to write a book on how to start a consulting business. The first step is to go to www.amazon.com. This will bring up the opening Amazon splash, which will give you a list of alternatives to choose from. In the Amazon search box, type:

starting a consulting business

This will narrow your search results from the approximately 1,867,454 titles that Amazon has available for sale to the more than 640 individual titles that it has available on the subject of starting a consulting business.

You could scroll through them all one-by-one, but you'd soon discover that many were published many years ago and are of little value to you today. So look to the right of your screen and find the "Sort by" window and select "Publication Date." The list will be automatically rearranged, starting from the most recent titles ranging down to those published many years ago.

Now you can begin scrolling and searching.

As you spot books that might be of interest, click either on the cover illustration or the title line and you will bring up a more detailed description of the book.

On the detailed description screen, you will see a list of choices you can make to get more information that will help you identify competitive or complementary books:

◆ Front cover

This is simply an enlargement of the thumbnail illustration of the cover that accompanies the basic listing. This, however, can be of some help because some show blurbs (endorsements) by people whose names and stature you might recognize.

- Table of contents

    This is an especially helpful feature. You can see just what the author has included and how the book has been organized.

- Copyright page

    Here you will find the name of the publisher and the date on which the copyright was granted. You will also see a series of numbers printed in reverse, such as 10 9 8 7 6 5 4 3 2 1. This is a history of the number of printings of the book. As successive printings are made, the number farthest to the right is erased by the printer. The number above indicates that the book is still in its first printing. On the other hand, these numbers, 10 9 8, indicate that the book is in its eighth printing. This, of course, is a sign that the book has been a very good seller.

    You will probably find a number of books with publisher names you've never heard of. This could be a sign of small presses and even self-published books. Self-published books account for a large number of books in print in this category. Many self-published books are excellent works that large publishers may have rejected because they felt there was not a large enough market to take them on. And, of course, there is some pretty awful stuff in print, too. So be careful, but don't avoid looking at books published by houses unfamiliar to you. You could miss an excellent bet.

- Excerpt

    Click on this, and you will get a sample of a few pages of the actual text. There's seldom enough to give you a real idea of the depth of the content, but there is usually enough to let you know whether the book is a slog or one you would enjoy reading.

- Index

    In many cases, all you will get with a push of this button is the first page of the index. Some excellent books are thinly indexed and some less-than-helpful books have indexes that go on forever. Even a one-page sample will give you the flavor of the book.

- Back cover

    There can be a wealth of information on the back cover of most business books, especially those published as original trade paperbacks. You could find a brief bio of the author, but most important, you are likely to find blurbs written by people in the field whose names you recognize. Keep in mind that these blurbs are written to help you decide to buy the book. The more prominent the names of those writing the blurbs, the more closely you should look at the books themselves.

Competition Can Make the Case for Your Book

If you are new to book publishing, you may be shocked by the sheer number of business books in print. You may be looking at a rather long list of potential competition. Now what do you do?

First of all, don't be intimidated. While there may be 10 books on the same subject you plan to write on, you just need to prove that no one else has written a book from your perspective and with your specific, unique ideas. But how do you know that your book is completely unique? It's time to read.

In order to complete a proper analysis of where your book fits in and why a publisher should consider investing in you and your idea, you have to read the books that are very similar to yours and skim thoroughly those books that might be close.

Classify Your Competition

As you read and take notes, you want to organize the potential competition into the following categories.

- ◆ Books that address a small portion of the topic you plan to write about

    Some of the best sources of support are the narrowly focused books that you uncover in your competitive title search. If, for example, you are writing a book on direct marketing, you will find many books that address just the creative side of the subject. It's easy to pay homage to the good ones and then show how you have picked up where their authors have left off. This neither denigrates the narrowly focused book nor adds to the weight of the competitive scene. It builds the case for your book and can make the case for your reader to look at the title you are referencing. One hand washes the other and everyone wins!

- ◆ Books that compete with yours, but are out of date

    As I have said, there are very few new topics to be written about, but there is a lot to write about that extends or modifies an existing base of knowledge. One good way to see what I mean is to read some of the management books that were published 30 years ago. They all dealt with the same subjects still being written about today, but they were based on existing norms, concepts, and needs. A 30-year gap gives you an idea of how radically some ideas have changed.

Now, think of the books that are being published on your subject. You just may have the one revolutionary idea that will change everything, but chances are that you are advancing the field in much smaller steps. It's books like this, yours and your competitors', that make progress in manageable steps and that intrigue those who publish your kind of book. So even if you don't have the breakthrough idea and your book will only advance the field by another small step, don't hesitate to seek publication.

Show that your book's starting point is where a recently published book ended and you will catch a publisher's attention quickly. Think this way and you will no longer see all those books in your field as competition but rather as stepping-stones that lead to your book.

◆ Books that compete directly with your book

Even those books that may seem to be directly competitive with yours can often be used to build your case. If you can build a strong argument that your idea or point of view contradicts that of another author, you could be in the catbird seat. It's not that easy to convince a publisher that your idea knocks that of another into a cocked hat. But it can be done if you really have the goods.

If you are a known and well-respected authority in your field, you're in good shape to do this. If you are not, it can still be done, but it usually requires the support of someone whose stature is at least equal to that of the author of the competitive book. If you can get an endorsement, or direct quotes to use in your text to support your point, go for it.

Even if you don't have the breakthrough idea, you can still get a publisher's attention if you write the book that either explains the concept better and more clearly or that puts an interesting spin on the idea that had not been thought of by the author or authors of the books that you feel might compete directly.

In the last few years, hundreds of books have been published that relate management techniques and skills to famous people. Some of the subjects were businesspeople, but most drew on the accomplishments of people in fields as diverse as royalty, military leadership, and even humanitarianism. Most of these books have been written by people whose skills and abilities included a lot more than just being able to write well. They are able to analyze achievements in widely diverse areas and relate their subject's judgment and actions to the problems that are faced in modern business. Many of these books are excellent and well worth reading.

The authors of these books draw from the accomplishments of well-known people and present them in terms of well-accepted management concepts. They are not presenting new ideas, but they are showing how accepted ideas in the hands of others can get things done. And there's usually a lot of room to take another author's notion of how a major figure gets things done up another notch.

Damning with Faint Praise

Never, never, never be nasty about a competitor's book in your proposal. However, it's easy—and usually a lot of fun—to criticize by just lobbing a faint compliment in your competitor's direction. Saying "This book, though well written, is not quite what we have come to expect from Mr. Jones" may infuriate Mr. Jones, but it sends the message you want to send to the person reviewing your proposal without appearing catty.

It's perfectly reasonable to point out the weak points of competitive books. However, you must be specific in your comments. Vague generalities just won't do. Whatever you say about a competitive book's failings, you must point out why and how your book will be better. Please, no superlatives, no brag and boast, just the facts.

If you, yourself, are one of your book's strong points, point this out, but do it with class. Better still, if you have quotes from others (not your family members, close friends, lodge members, or former high school teachers), get their permission to use them. Just make sure that they are right on point and not just the attaboys we all get, usually from people who want favors in return.

> ### Quote/Unquote
> "Nobody can be so amusingly arrogant as a young man who has just discovered an old idea and thinks it is his own."
> —Sydney Harris, American journalist

Launch the Secret Weapon

You might even be able to get some of the authors of the books you use to make your competitive or complementary case to help you make the case for your book. Most business book writers realize that no two books compete head on. They also realize that those who buy and read business books are usually looking for all the help and information they can get their hands on. And if they buy one book, the chances are very good that they will buy others—and one of them could possibly be yours.

A letter to the authors of one or a few of the books on your competitive or complementary lists asking for help probably won't go unread, and if they're well-worded, you could end up with a letter in return that could make the difference with an acquisitions editor.

Any such letter should begin with honest praise and the tacit acknowledgment that your book might be considered somewhat competitive. But when you point out that you are planning mostly to extend and expand on the author's ideas with appropriate credit, most will see that a mention in your book could lead to sales of their books. If you have ever wondered why seemingly competitive authors write glowing testimonials (blurbs) for the back covers of books that compete with their own, I don't think I need say more. It is an incestuous business, after all.

The Least You Need to Know

- ◆ You can usually find all the competitive information you need on the Internet.
- ◆ Books that compete with your book can help make your case.
- ◆ Never say a bad word about a competing book, just show how your book will be better.
- ◆ Authors of competing books are often willing to help you get published.

Chapter 8

Getting Help with Your Proposal

In This Chapter

- ◆ Choosing the right person to work with
- ◆ What you have to bring to the table
- ◆ Working together, working at a distance

Proposal writing is an art in itself. There are a few good books on the subject in print, and most of the writers' magazines address the subject regularly. Those of us who ghostwrite and collaborate on books are frequently called on either to write proposals from scratch or to at least lend a hand in their development. I discuss the roles of these freelancers in other chapters, but at this point it's time to get down to the specifics of who you should turn to for what and how to work with editorial and creative professionals.

Talk with Your Agent First

Apart from everything else agents do for their clients, they are a major source of advice and counsel, and they may even provide direct help when it comes to producing a proposal. If you have selected your agent wisely, she already knows the editors at the publishing companies that can and should publish your book. For example, she knows that editors at Publisher A may be more interested in proposals that showcase the author as a promotable property than those at Publisher B. This knowledge is power. It not only means that your agent can let you know what areas to stress in your proposal, but also where to not waste your time.

Few agents will ever send a proposal to an acquisitions editor without first providing some input. Depending on what they deem important, some may edit lightly and some may even rewrite portions of your proposal. Full rewrites are seldom paid for by the agent's commission and are usually negotiated separately. Most agents avoid what could be a conflict of interest and will not write proposals for clients they represent. Instead, they will suggest that you work with an independent freelancer. But what kind of freelancer?

If you have been poking around editorial websites, you are probably mystified by the different services that are available. Some people offer narrow and specific help and others claim to be able to do everything. Your agent should be able to give you a critique of what you have already written or explain the type of editor or collaborator you should consider.

> **Backspace**
>
> You and those who help you write a proposal may never meet. The phone, the fax, the Internet, and just plain snail mail are all you really need. As impersonal and cold as this may sound, face-to-face work sessions can be costly and much less productive than just a few e-mail exchanges.

There are two categories of people who can work with you on your proposal: those who can help you solve specific proposal problems your agent may have spotted and those who will either hold your hand while you write a proposal or actually write the proposal for you. This chapter is about these helpers, what they can do for you, and how to best work with each.

Let's first look at those who can help you fix or improve what you have already written. The editors you will meet in the next few pages appear in order of the type and amount of work your agent feels your proposal needs. We begin with those who can do the fine tuning of a proposal that is already in pretty good shape and then move progressively to those whose work is much more comprehensive.

The Copy Editor

Remember your favorite English teacher? The one whose gentle note on your term paper reminded you pronouns must always agree in number with their antecedents?

it an antecedent is? Ask a copy editor. Your copy
ges or simply point out where the work is needed.
, even those missed by your computer's spell-checker.
be flagged or removed with appropriate replacements

what you can expect from a good copy editor. He
e digit off the second time you quote the GDP for
it. Linguistic carts before linguistic horses will be cor-
thors claim to have mentioned earlier but were never
y editors. And when you mention that the CEO of
ion on the west side of town, an alert copy editor will
ing where, among the derelict buildings on the west

th the skill and depth of knowledge of the copy edi-
clients, on the right track.

et and they need to be near all their source materials.
ssing each individual point the editor raises. Most
e hour, and rates vary from place to place and from
ing a very specialized book, you might want to look
in your field.

-time jobs with publishing companies also do free-
his is especially true of copy editors with backgrounds
nal help is especially important. This usually means
editor 1,000 miles away. But this isn't a problem. In
of you. Any temptation to have coffee and a chin-wag
pretty much eliminated.

done elec-
ur copy
orrections
s. Each
note, correction, or query will be marked
by a brightly colored paper flag. Even on
the computer, changes will be highlighted

Publishing Tip

Always feel free to question a copy editor's changes or suggestions. But you better be sure you are right before you do!

and often followed by a note from the copy editor. It can be terrifying to a first-time author to see all those flags and their bleeding red ink or type, but it is this attention to detail that makes a good copy editor an author's best friend.

If you are at all unsure about your writing skills, one of the best investments you can make is in the services of a good copy editor to review and clean up your writing. You will learn a lot in the process.

The Line Editor

In the publishing business we often run into people doing the same work but being identified by different titles. A line editor is also called a manuscript editor. While a line editor may correct grammatical errors that she spots, this is not what line editors are paid for.

A line editor gets at what you are thinking, what you want to say, what you need to say, and how you say it. A good line editor adds nothing to the writing, but she makes sure that you say what you want to say and that you say it clearly and concisely.

The comments and questions you get from a line editor are aimed at keeping you focused on the subject, on the page, and on the ultimate purpose of the book. She will point out where you may have failed to provide information that is needed to keep the narrative on track and where you may have gone fuzzy. Also, she will point out where your tone of voice may be inappropriate and where the words you chose may be out of range for your intended audience. Inappropriate switches between passive and active voice are called out, as are vague words and unsupported claims.

Line editors quickly spot organizational problems. Mention the solution to a problem before you mention the actual problem and you may have some lengthy rewriting to do. And if you don't, a reviewer will surely spot your sloppy writing. Then, when your proud old high school English teacher reads the review she will be mortified. Don't let that happen!

Publishing Tip

If you have outlined your proposal thoroughly, give a copy of the outline to your editor. If the fee you are paying is based on an hourly rate, this advance information will help speed the work, especially that of checking consistency.

Most line editors do a first quick read of the material to get an overall sense of what to focus on in detail. If your writing is a jumble to begin with, most of your interaction will be at the level of putting things in proper order. This may involve some revisions and rewrites, but until there is a natural flow of ideas, it doesn't make sense to dig into the finer points of style.

This, incidentally, is where the most productive self-editing can take place. Avoid the temptation to correct spelling and grammatical errors as you do this read-through. Read what you have written to see if it makes sense and hangs together. Does B follow A? Is your narrative moving logically to the conclusion you are aiming for? Are there any stumbling blocks that can be converted to positive terms or just pruned from the text? You may be surprised at how much tighter you can make your writing by doing one or two rereadings of what you have written. But let a day or two go by between edits. Fresh looks almost always provide fresh insights.

How to Work with a Line Editor

You will probably have much more contact with a line editor than you will with a copy editor. If you have hired your line editor on an hourly basis, you already realize that chitchat could cost you as much as you might pay for a session with your psychologist or analyst and, as far as I know, there are no insurance plans that cover editing fees.

If you and your editor are working electronically, you will be exchanging comments and responses by e-mail. But if your material is on paper, expect to read and write a lot of handwritten marginal notes on the material you send back and forth. Write clearly and don't be afraid to ask your editor to do the same if her handwriting leaves you guessing about what is being said. "What do you mean by this?" is one of the most frequent questions a line editor will ask. This may seem like an invitation to begin a discussion—but the editor usually knows what you mean and just wants you to say it better. It's a kinder and gentler way of saying, "You could have been a lot clearer with this idea." Another shorthand note you will see is "Please clarify." Each editor has his or her own way to draw out meaning and enhance clarity. After a few pages of notes from your editor, you will probably get a feel for just how she works.

Line editors' queries and comments can relate to material as short as a single sentence or to an entire chapter. Comments on sentences are easy to deal with, but a "Where are you going with this?" that relates to an entire chapter means you might have a lot of work to do.

Quote/Unquote

"What the best of editors wish to be is the perceptive, demanding, energetic, and patient probers who can devote their particular talents and skills to the enterprise of working with authors to publish good books."

—Gerald Gross, *Editors on Editing*, Grove Press

It's tempting to get annoyed at "mere" editors who question the words you might have labored over and the thoughts you wish to express. Early in my career I had a client who resented an editor's comments and told her so. He basically said that he was the pro in his field and who was she to question what he did on the page. Without ire or even a trace or irony, the editor responded to the snotty author with a list of immediately recognizable authors in his field that she had edited. She concluded her note with, "And now shall we get back to work?" They did and the book was well received.

Working with a Professional Writer

There's hardly a field in which contract work is undertaken that doesn't have people whose job is writing proposals. Most of the major defense contractors employ highly trained specialists to do this work. There are probably as many independent writers and freelancers writing proposals for clients who want to build bombers for the U.S. Navy as there are writing proposals for authors who want to see their books in print. Maybe more when you look at the federal budget!

Some who write proposals do nothing but write proposals. However, it's more common to find professional collaborators and ghostwriters who write proposals as part of a total package that includes either collaboration or ghostwriting if the proposals they write lead to book contracts for their clients.

Getting to It

Collaborators, independent editors, freelance development editors, or consulting editors—no matter what you call them, these are the writing professionals who can help you get not only your proposal, but also, if you need it, your book written. Their help can range from a simple backup to being involved in writing each word for the entire project. It depends on the client's needs.

The Back-Up Writer-in-Residence

This relationship presupposes that you are comfortable with words and might even be able to pull off the entire book if you weren't doing a million other things. But you must be absolutely honest with yourself about what you can and what you can't do with words. Don't try to snow a consulting editor with "I can really do this myself, but I just need a little help," if you know that you have to revise your 10-word memos three or four times before you post them.

The first thing a consulting editor will probably ask you for is a sample of what you have already written. You might even be asked to submit a short piece of writing on some familiar subject. Yep, it's a test! But there's no pass or fail. The editor is trying to get a handle on just how much help you will need and what the nature of that help will be.

If it appears that your needs are in the backup, support, and rewrite area, your editor will explain what he or she thinks you need and what can be provided. Be wary of a consulting editor who doesn't review your work carefully first and who simply quotes prices and offers a contract. He or she may be the greatest, but a relationship based on only a cursory read of your work is going to be rocky. The smoother it can be made before any work begins, the better for both of you.

Most consulting editors have more than one book in the works at any given time. Therefore, the more that is known about the author and the need for help, the better able the editor will be to schedule work. So be upfront about your time availability and the dates on which material is to be delivered.

Working with an editor as a backup usually involves more than just submitting your material for review and comments. The work is usually more intense early on in the relationship, and as each becomes familiar with the work and schedules of the other, the interaction becomes less frenetic. It's a comfort-level sort of situation for both the author and the collaborator.

Fees, Charges, and Other Money Matters

Fees and charges for collaborating on a proposal and sample chapter vary greatly. However, no matter how the fees are stated, the professional you are working with has probably started from what he usually earns on an hourly basis. Because these numbers can often be high and intimidating to a potential client, quotes are usually stated as a total fee based on the consultant's hourly fee plus a guess of the time it might take to do the job. Most consultants charge separately for proposals and sample chapters. Here's a typical example based on a fee of $100 per page.

An average proposal, without the sample chapter, is about 40 pages long, which means that the fee should be $4,000. However, there is no such thing as average, and I have yet to meet a consultant who will not add at least 20 percent to his or her estimate to cover for unplanned expenses and time. So the price quoted is $4,800. Clients are seldom happy when they are billed for more than the estimate when work exceeds the estimate. And so the quoted $4,800 fee is not unreasonable. This is about where you will see fees quoted by most consultants as of the writing of this book.

That being said, I have seen estimates for a lot less and for a lot more. When should you go for cheap and when should you go for the gold? The question really is what you can expect for the money. A low estimate may not always signal a potentially shoddy job. The quote may be from a consultant who has written many proposals for books like yours and sees that he or she can do yours in less time than someone who might be less familiar with your subject. A low estimate can also signal a beginner who is either unfamiliar with prevailing rates or is lowballing you to get the job. Credentials will tell you something of the consultant's experience, but until you see samples of his work, you will never know whether the low price is what you really want or if the high price is worth paying.

Whenever I discuss a proposal project with a new client, I first send samples of proposals I have written and suggest that he or she show them to the agent involved. After all, this is the tool that the agent is going to use to sell the book. He or she will want the best, whether it's expensive or not, and will not hesitate to help to make a choice.

The sample chapter is almost always billed separately, even if you have already written the material and feel that all it needs is a tweaking. Whatever is needed, editing or research and writing, is either billed at an hourly rate or by the page. You should submit at least 30 pages of sample material with your proposal, whether it's all or part of one chapter or samples from two chapters. Assuming a $100 per page fee, a 30-page sample will cost $3,000. So the total quote for a proposal and 30 pages of sample material will run $7,800.

Publishing Tip _____

If the person you choose to work with on your proposal will also work with you on the book, he or she will probably deduct the cost of the sample chapters from the fee to write the book if the proposal is accepted by a publisher.

Most professionals who write proposals expect from one quarter to one half of the total fee up front, with the balance due on delivery of the finished work. You will be asked to sign an agreement, which few consultants object to your agent reviewing.

The Query Approach

A query is a pitch sent to an editor or an agent before you send anything else. It is not the conventional proposal pitch package. It's a brief package written to stand out among the pile of unsolicited proposals every agent and editor receives every day.

When you go the query route, you are using a basic two-step sales approach. The idea is to get an agent's or an editor's attention first. Considering that each get so many unsolicited proposals a day, a short, simple, and punchy query usually gets a read ahead of the other stuff. At least that's what many agents and editors have told me.

The query is actually a query package. That is, it includes a pitch letter as well as potential market data and enough information to tell a publisher that you are the right person to do the book. Keep the package to a minimum of material but a maximum of helpful information. Don't include extensive samples of your writing, but do mention and document your writing as it would relate to the book you would like to propose. Don't send more than one or two pages of your resumé, and limit that resumé to elements that would be meaningful to an agent or an editor. Don't include anything that you expect to have returned.

Your letter should pitch your book idea, not describe what you have included in the package. It should include a self-addressed stamped envelope for a reply. This is a query, and you won't be sending anything that should be returned, so an ordinary business envelope should be fine.

A simple form should be enclosed, which the editor or agent can use to reply. Give the reader several alternatives on the form, rather than just asking for a yes or no. But don't make this a long checklist. These are the items I usually suggest that clients include:

Would you like me to send you the proposal? I can send it as soon as I hear from you. Yes ( ) No ( )

Would you like additional material? Yes ( ) No ( )

What would you like me to send? _____

Would like me to phone you? Yes ( ) No ( )
Phone number and best day/time to call _____

That's it! Don't ask why the answer to the first question is no. Don't pitch anything else. And don't forget to include the editor's or the agent's name on the form. If you want real frustration, forget this and get one back on which the sender has not identified herself and you will really have reason to bang your head.

You can, of course, skip the query step and send your proposal along with a pitch letter. This proposal kit should state whether you want the proposal back and, if you do, you must include a self-addressed stamped envelope for it.

Despite my preference for using the query package, many writers still prefer to send the total package—pitch letter, proposal, and sample material. You'll be okay with either, but I think your chances are a little bit better with a well-prepared two-step approach.

There are as many ways to write good pitch and query letters as there are pebbles on a beach. I spent my early working years writing direct mail copy for book publishers and have a style that I think is the best ever. However, I can name a half dozen other writers with different backgrounds whose style is totally different than mine, yet all of us seem to have pretty much the same hit records.

So rather than continue to inflict my personal preferences on you, I can best help by telling you what not to do in your letters. Don't brag and boast. Don't make wild claims for yourself, your book, or its potential. Don't tell stupid jokes. Don't talk down to your reader. Don't use a lot of adjectives and adverbs. And—most important—don't forget to ask for the order!

Query by E-mail?

Agents frequently e-mail editors they know with brief pitches about projects they have available, but it's best for unknown authors to go either the traditional route of a query pitch or a complete proposal package. This will probably change as time goes by, but for now stick with paper and postage.

The Least You Need to Know

- You may be able to do it yourself, but help is available, whether it's simple editing or turning your proposal over to a pro.

- You can work with real professionals wherever you live, thanks to the Internet.

- If you choose a professional to write your proposal, consider one who will be available to either write the book or consult with you when you write it.

- Professional fees vary widely; the most expensive may not be the best, but the cheapest is often a bad choice.

Chapter 9

Writing a Winning Sample Chapter

In This Chapter

- How to select the chapter or chapters that will have the strongest impact
- Why you should write your chapter with one publisher in mind
- Why you must make a key point on every page
- How to handle controversial material to your advantage

A sample chapter should put you at least on second base. You don't have to knock the ball out of the park, but you do have to get the attention of the third base coach for a wave-in to home. Think of your acquisitions editor as that coach and you'll see just how important a base hit with your sample chapter must be.

Your sample chapter is like a movie screen test. It shows what you have to offer as a writer. It frames you in relation to the subject you propose to write about. Forgive me for mixing baseball and movie metaphors, but if your sample chapter fails to ignite an acquisitions editor's enthusiasm, your chances of acceptance diminish greatly—even if your subject presses the editor's hot buttons. This chapter will help you select which chapters to choose and how to write them.

Which Chapter to Choose

Your sample chapter doesn't have to be your first chapter. It can be any chapter you want. But you should choose not only one that proves that you know your subject, but also one that helps prove that you can write about it clearly and convincingly. You should also be able to show that you are bringing fresh material or at least fresh insight and an unusual approach to your subject.

Although book chapters are arranged in a logical sequence, each one more or less stands alone. So, for example, choosing to write Chapter 5 for your sample doesn't mean that you need to have the first four under your belt first.

Is There a Special Style to Use?

I usually suggest to my clients that they pretend they have been asked to write a white paper or a magazine article on the subject of the chapter or chapters they have chosen. It's a little fool-the-mind exercise that shifts the perspective from the challenge of writing an entire book chapter to that of just writing an article. Yes, I know, you're an adult and playing simple mind games is not for you. Humor me and try it.

How Long Should the Sample Be?

It's not the number of words that is most important but the way you use them and the impression you create with the words you choose. If you are doing a short book— approximately 65,000 words and 20 chapters—you should be able to give an editor enough of a picture of your skills and familiarity with your material with one or two chapters.

On the other hand, suppose you are planning a book of 120,000 words and 11 chapters. Your typical chapter would be close to 11,000 words long. That's a lot of words to write without already having a contract in hand, so a significant partial chapter will usually do the job.

You can forget the "rule" that you must include at least one entire sample chapter with your proposal. I and most of my colleagues agree that any more than 20 or 30 pages of double-spaced text would not only be a waste of your time, but also a burden on an editor or an agent who needs a good but quick impression of what you are doing and what you are all about.

Quote/Unquote _____

"It's my ambition to say in 10 sentences what other men say in whole books."
—Friedrich Nietzsche
"The most valuable of all talents is that of never using two words when one will do."
—Thomas Jefferson
"If you bring that sentence in for a fitting, I can have it shortened by Wednesday."
—Hawkeye, M*A*S*H

To put this in numerical perspective, 20 pages of double-spaced 12-point Courier text adds up to about 6,000 words.

Slice and Dice Your Sample Material

Remember, your sample chapter is like a screen test. You wouldn't read for the part of Hamlet as if you were trying out for a bit part.

Don't treat your sample chapter like this by choosing to use the easiest chapter in the book because you can get it done quickly.

What you choose to submit as your sample chapter offers clues to what an agent or an editor can expect from you if a contract is offered. An agent or publisher will be much more leery of you if you choose the easy stuff over the more difficult.

Take the time to review your chapter outline. Are there two chapters that deal with diverse material? Is there a particular chapter that examines some difficult topics?

You are more likely to impress not only your agent but also a potential publisher by choosing to submit samples from two very different chapters to demonstrate your versatility. Another way to impress is to submit a chapter that tackles tough stuff. You are bound to make an agent's day.

> **Backspace** _____
>
> I should note here that my preference for samples from two chapters, rather than one complete chapter, is at odds with conventional wisdom, at least from what some agents have told me. However, most editors I have talked with agree that as long as each section clearly demonstrates how the material is handled, samples from two chapters are fine. If you are working with an agent, see what she prefers and follow the advice given you.

If you are going to slice and dice, don't send a lot of short samples from many different chapters. Never send more than two or three samples from different chapters. Two 2,000-word samples can show an editor that you are not a sprint writer. Far too many magazine writers believe they can get away with sending a packet of their short pieces. It just doesn't work. Book writing is a marathon; magazine writing is the 100-yard dash.

Have a Publisher in Mind

Good public speakers will tell you that one of their keys to success is to picture the typical person in the group being addressed. They claim that this focus helps them speak at the appropriate level. It also helps them focus on the points that they believe most others in the group would want to hear.

Those who have written a lot of nonfiction book proposals will tell you that they usually write their sample chapters pretty much the same way. In some cases, they will write their sample chapters with an actual editor in mind. If they don't have a particular editor in mind, they will at least write to appeal to someone close to the typical editor of the house.

This may not be helpful if this is your first book and you have never met an editor from any of the houses on your list. However, most publishers make it easy for you to get enough information about their editors so that you can get an idea of what would appeal to most of the editors in the house.

It can take a little poking around on publisher websites, but most of the better business houses have biographical sketches of their editors right on the site. And some even include personal statements from the editors about what interests them and what doesn't.

This site has extensive information on just about every business book publisher in the United States. It can, however, be out of date at times. Two editors I know who retired four or five years ago are still listed as being active. This could be the fault of the keeper of lists at the site, or it could be because editors move frequently. Whatever the reason, this site will at least give you the names of most of the business book publishers you might want to contact.

Another way to get the information you need is to contact a publisher by using a toll-free number and asking them to send you information on their editors, their requirements, and what they might be looking for.

The editors' bios and personal statements can give you a pretty clear picture of the people you should be thinking of when you write your sample chapter. I think you'll find it pretty easy to scope out their interests and needs and be able to drop the key words and phrases you know will resonate in your sample chapter.

In addition to this focus, I'd suggest that you check out some of the books that the houses and editors you have selected have published recently. If you have access to a comprehensive library, you will probably find many of the titles in their stacks. Check them out for style and writing levels. If you are unable to find any, or enough to get a workable sample, check out the text samples that are available through many of the online bookstores. Most give you the opportunity to read a sample of the text on screen. It won't be as much as you would get if you had access to the books themselves. However, after you have read a few of the samples, you should pick up clues that will help you focus your sample chapter writing.

Showcase Yourself in Your Sample Writing

Your sample chapter should demonstrate your mastery of your subject as well as your ability to write clearly about it. As I have already mentioned, if you are working with a consulting editor, collaborator, or ghost-writer, be sure that you mention this in your proposal. And be sure that the person with whom you are writing has written the sample material you are submitting. Your proposal will showcase you as the subject matter expert and your collaborator as the writing professional.

Showcasing yourself in your sample chapter can be very tricky. Inject yourself modestly

> **Publishing Tip**
>
> Rather than blowing your own horn too obviously, mention that a prestigious group, of which you are a member, accomplished such-and-such wonderful things. Celebrity-by-association is a powerful tool, but don't overdo it.

whenever appropriate, but avoid bragging and boasting. And be sure to space your personal references widely. Your best bet is to show how you might have done something successfully. If you can show how your first attempt failed and what you did to rescue the project, you not only come off as humble, but you have a good approach for the typical case history. When you focus on the needs of your readers, you are on safe ground. When you focus on yourself, you're in trouble.

Make a Key Point on Every Page

Choose your sample chapter for its high-impact content. Write your sample chapter so that each page makes at least one important point. This doesn't mean that you have to change subjects from page to page, but you should structure your writing so that, as the topic you are discussing unfolds, key points appear in a rolling thunder kind of sequence. If you read much fiction, this notion should be pretty obvious. It's the build-up, the increasing tension, that leads to the point or conclusion of the narrative you are striving for. This is what carries readers of fiction, as well as nonfiction, from the first to the last page of a book.

It's not often that this can be done with most business material, and this is why you should pick a chapter with material that allows you to use this technique. Pick a chapter that has no excitement potential and the only thing you can count on to carry the day is spectacular writing. And even spectacular writing gets tiresome when no new points are made and no original conclusions are drawn. So pick your sample chapter carefully.

Most business books are seamless narratives, unlike the format of the book you are now reading. This gives you plenty of latitude in writing your sample to pace your material accordingly. It allows you to play with ideas and words in ways that can tap the techniques of fiction to capture an editor's eye and a reviewer's praise.

This isn't a lesson in fiction writing, but the idea of setting up and resolving conflict is one you might consider. If, for example, you are writing about a management technique that flies in the face of what has been done in the past, the best way to make use of the technique is to create a before-and-after situation. Set against the failures or excesses of a former system, the system you are describing takes on a coloration it wouldn't have if you approached it without the comparison.

This is an approach that should be used sparingly in business book writing. But if you have the material and can handle it, be sure to use it in your sample chapter.

Use Quotes from the Rich and Famous in Your Field

Quotations and endorsements from well-known figures stand out, especially if those quoted are making the case for the point you are arguing or the book you are writing. It's not as difficult as you might imagine to get known people in your field to provide you with usable quotes. After all, a person quoted is a person lauded. It's especially important to gather good quotes early on and to get them on the material you plan to use for your sample chapter. As agents and editors read your sample chapter, they will make immediate note of the names as possible reviewers, foreword writers, and back cover blurbers.

Be careful, however, that the quotes you use are not just transparent endorsements of your book. The quotes should support a particular point you are making in your sample chapter. Remember, editors and agents have seen it all, and they can spot reciprocal back-scratching in the blink of an eye.

Reach an Important Conclusion

Most business book chapters stand pretty much alone, but they should and usually do lead from one to another in a logical way. Any one of the chapters in this book could, with minor modification, stand alone as a magazine article. But all have been arranged to take you from knowing very little about writing and publishing business books to the point where you should be pretty confident in your ability to get published.

Your sample chapter, however, should reach at least one important conclusion. Unless it's the last chapter, it still has to lead in some way to the material that follows. But if you can include the resolution of at least one important issue in your chapter, you will have made points with the keepers of publishing gates.

As important as reaching one conclusion may be, your sample chapter should also hold out the promise of more good stuff to come. This could be something as simple as writing, "as you will discover in Chapter 7 ..." or as complex as building the case for the material to come.

Avoid Appearing Self-Serving

There are plenty of people who have enhanced their careers by writing books. Yes, this is self-serving, but well-written books that truly offer helpful information are quite useful, self-serving or not. However, when this motive is only thinly disguised, it's a fast trip to the rejection pile for the proposal.

Most business book authors use case histories to make specific points. And when a case history involves something you did, it's not inappropriate to mention it in your book. But your role should not be seen as a drumroll. Whenever possible, mention others who have participated in the story you are relating and give credit where credit is due.

Even if you have no personal case histories to mention, you can take advantage of some historical precedent by injecting your own comments relative to the subject about which you are writing.

Write to Attract More Than Just the Editor

Your proposal should grab everyone who has a vote on the acquisitions committee. The acquisitions editor is the keeper of the first gate, and the topics I have discussed so far in this chapter should help you write a proposal that will do the job. The sales, marketing, and publicity people are the keepers of the second gate. While they will be interested in how you write, they will be more interested in any information you present in the text that will help them sell your book. Needless to say, this information has to be injected with care. If fact, if you can include it so the others on the committee seem to "discover" it, so much the better. Here are a few suggestions for salting the mine for the other members of the acquisitions committee.

Those who are charged with promoting you and your book will be looking for all sorts of clues to help them promote your book. They are especially interested in people who potential readers would recognize as thought leaders in the field. Remember, most books are sold by publicity, not advertising. Suppose you were part of a team whose work you are citing in your book. If any of the people on that team are noteworthy, be sure to mention them, even if you had little or no real contact with them in connection with the project. The fact that you and they were on a team that produced something noteworthy establishes a connection, and a skilled publicity person can use that connection to your advantage. Don't be shy; it's done all the time. However, don't overdo it. "My very good friend, Bill Gates," could land you in an embarrassing spot if you and Mr. Gates only met once at the university cafeteria many years ago.

It's always best to first approach for permission the person whose name you are going to use in your text. Be sure to tell the person how it will be used in the text and, if possible, include the actual text you plan to use. Prominent names spotted in a sample chapter are bait in the water and will probably be used by savvy publicists. You owe it to your source to give him or her a heads up.

Write a chapter on economics in which you quote, with permission, Paul Krugman of *The New York Times*, and it will resonate immediately with your publisher's sales and marketing people. A book on management in which you quote any of the current gurus will immediately set sales people thinking about their next pitch to Amazon.com and all the other online and brick-and-mortar chains and independents. Just weave the names into your sample chapter without making it seem like a pitch to the publisher, and you will make many points.

Don't Avoid Controversy, But ...

When you get right down to it, controversy is what sells books. Your management system might seem to you to be head and shoulders above those presented in competing books. But there's no need to try to gain stature by bad-mouthing the competition. In fact, one of the most powerful rhetorical tools at your disposal is the damn-with-faint-praise approach.

The last thing an editor wants to see is a manuscript written in a hostile tone. You may feel like upending your competitor with a few well-chosen words, but don't. If you have ever watched any Senate hearings on television, you will have seen members referring to each other as "My distinguished colleague across the aisle." We all know that there are many other words the congressman or senator would prefer to use. But the irony of the accepted colloquialism is seldom wasted on readers and listeners.

 Publishing Tip _____

If you can get the author of a competing book to state that you have made strong points, even though he or she may disagree with you, you will make powerful points with editors and those who will read your book.

Discuss your issues about a competitor in factual terms. Don't let it get personal. In fact, the more generous you are with those with whom you disagree, the better your chances are of hitting that home run.

You Have Already Written the Book

Business books, and in fact most nonfiction books, are sold to publishers on the basis of a proposal, not by sending a finished manuscript. Don't be tempted to send a finished manuscript rather than a proposal and sample chapter. I've already mentioned this several times in earlier chapters, but it bears repeating here.

A proposal is a sales pitch. It's the format editors and agents are accustomed to dealing with. I'm sure that many excellent manuscripts never became books simply because their authors felt compelled to send everything, rather than just a proposal.

If, however, you have already written your manuscript, you have an excellent opportunity to choose the best chapter or chapters for your sample and to fine-tune your material. It's seldom a big deal to go over a chapter and cut or add material that will help make your case with a publisher.

Illustrate Your Points, Too

It's hard to do a business book these days without using a few simple illustrations. Charts, graphs, and tables make points graphically and they present data that might be difficult or cumbersome to describe in words. If you plan to use any illustrations, include a few samples with your sample chapter.

Be sure to say whether you will be submitting artwork in print-ready form from your computer, or whether special art will be needed. Unless special arrangements are made at contract time, it's the author's responsibility to supply all art in a form ready for the printer to use. If your book will involve many complete illustrations, your publisher may be willing to take on the job of producing the art or to provide either a grant or an advance adjustment that allows for the production of the material. These negotiations are best left to your agent, if you have one.

The Least You Need to Know

- Never send less than one or more than two complete chapters.
- Don't pick the "easy" chapter for your sample.
- Be sure that your sample chapter reaches an important conclusion.

Part 3

Finding an Agent and Other Helpers

Going it alone isn't easy. If the company you own or work for makes such great products, why does it find it necessary to hire salespeople? Literary agents, who work strictly on commission, are a necessary and important part of the publishing process, both for writers and the publishers who publish their clients' books. So are the independent editors, professional writers and collaborators, and literary agents whom you will meet in the section that follows.

I hope you are not shocked to learn that some books you have read and enjoyed might have been written—or at least heavily edited—by people whose names you will never know. There just aren't that many people out there whose armory of business skills includes writing along with creating great sales plans and developing financial or human resources ideas. You'd be shocked at how poorly some of these people actually write. But you'd never read past the first page of a book they write if it weren't for the help of an editor or a professional writer. We go behind the scenes in this section.

10

How to Find the Best Literary Agent for Your Book

In This Chapter

◆ Why publishers prefer to work with agents

◆ Why agency size doesn't matter: contacts count

◆ A good agent may find you first

You've come up with your idea, and you've written your proposal and sample chapter. Now what? Your book won't be published on its own. You need some help, and an agent is exactly what you need. An agent will help you find your way through the maze of getting noticed by a publisher.

An agent is your advocate with a publisher and your guide in getting your book published. Whether an agent works solo or for a large literary agency, finding the best one for you is key. In this chapter, we discuss what an agent can do for you and how to find one.

Most agents who handle nonfiction will handle business books. And there are even quite a few agents whose specialty is business and business-related topics. What you really need to know is the agent's success record with books like yours.

Thinking you want to represent yourself? I would advise against it. Most publishers won't even speak to an author unless he or she is represented by an agent. But if you really want to go it alone, I give you some pointers at the end of the chapter.

What Good Agents Know and Can Do for You

There were 276,649 new books published in the United States in 2007. That's everything, all categories. The number of titles published in the broad category of business and economics was 7,651. The number of general interest business books, the type you are probably thinking about writing, is estimated at about a thousand new titles. That's a lot of books, and the competition to publish them was fierce.

The authors of most of those thousand business books were probably represented by literary agents, and for good reason: it's not easy to convince a publisher that you have a good idea as well as the ability to write a book. Author representation is labor intensive, and those who are good at it have worked hard at establishing their reputations within the book-publishing community. You may have a great idea and the skills to write the book, but I seriously doubt that you would get to first base with a major publisher by trying to sell it yourself.

You don't know the editors who might consider it. If you got lucky and found an interested editor, you don't know the drill of negotiating a book sale, and you'd probably give away the store. There is a lot more to consider than just advance and royalties. All I can say is that most agents love to talk about how they sold a new client's book to an editor who had already turned it down when the author tried to sell it directly. If you have the time, give it a go. But don't say that I didn't warn you.

> **Publishing Tip**
>
> A good agent should provide editorial guidance, have solid connections with the best publishers for your book, know the current market trends, be capable of monitoring and managing your financial relationships with your publishers … and be kind and gentle when your book fails to make the best-seller list.

An agent's reputation—and livelihood—is based on his ability to spot writers with good ideas and to match them with the right publishers. It's no different whether the agent represents business book writers or those who write fiction. Most agents get their start as editors at book publishing companies and have a good sense of what works and what doesn't right from the start.

An agent's reputation with book editors is a door opener, but it's never a guarantee of a sure thing. However, most agents have working relationships with many publishers and they know what each house and each editor is looking for. This usually means that they have a far better chance of at least getting a few hearings on a project than you might as a new author sending your unsolicited proposal out directly.

How Literary Agents Work and Are Paid

Most agents work on commission exclusively. Some may charge for costly services, such as extensive duplicating, but very few work on a fee basis. The commission is most often 15 percent of all income from the sale of the published book.

A published book produces income in many ways, not just from the books you see in bookstores. Subsidiary rights, such as book club sales, sales of rights to foreign publishers, and periodical rights, can produce significant income. If you don't use an agent, you will either have to negotiate the sale of these rights yourself or grant your publisher the right to act on your behalf. When you grant your publisher that right, the publisher actually becomes your agent for all the subsidiary rights they sell to others. Some are very good at this; some are not. In most cases, you will probably give away money that an agent could have preserved for you. It's possible for subsidiary rights income to exceed the money earned from conventional royalties, so you can see that there is more to this than you probably imagined.

Agency Size and Specialization

Most literary agents are one- or two-person shops. Don't be surprised to find some major authors represented by small agencies you have never heard of. Size isn't all that important. It's the skills and contacts the agents have that are most important.

The Small Literary Agency

The smaller the agency, the more specialized it's likely to be. When you see a small agency that claims to handle literary fiction, chick-lit, thrillers, mysteries, and business books, be careful. It just isn't possible to do everything and do it well.

The typical small agency is one or two people, possibly with some full- or part-time clerical assistance. More than a few of these small agencies work from home offices. It just doesn't make sense to rent space when walk-in business is not encouraged and when most meetings with editors are done at the editors' offices. I worked exclusively from my home office for 30 years, managed the affairs of more than 80 authors, and was responsible for placing more than 600 books, all with major national and international publishers. An agent I met years back worked from his home on Nantucket. If you called and he was scaling the bluefish he caught that morning, he'd excuse himself and call back. What's the sense of working from home if you can't enjoy it?

Backspace _____

Writers, like everyone else, sometimes prefer to pass the buck when things don't work out as planned. "It's my agent's fault that my book didn't sell well" is a common bleat. If you are asking other writers about agents you are considering, listen carefully to both the praises and pans. Anything over the top in either direction should be taken with a grain of salt. Get the facts; skip the emotion.

Most literary agencies, large and small, are in and around New York City. The closeness to the major publishers helps, but it certainly doesn't deter some very fine agents who work out of California beach towns and Rocky Mountain aeries. The Internet has made it possible for agents, authors, and their publishers to work together without ever meeting.

You should think carefully about going with a solo agent who tells you he has 150 clients. I suppose it's possible to handle that many, and the agent may work night and day at it, but in general it's not a good sign. Most agents, both large and small, have a core list of heavy-hitter writers who get most of their attention, those whose ideas and proposals are geared to market needs and who deliver their manuscripts on time. Those clients who do books occasionally can be less reliable, but they still require some attention, too.

Business is your field, so you know the dangers of the 80/20 situation in which you get 80 percent of your business from 20 percent of your customers. Most agents float around that figure in terms of their ratio of very productive to less productive authors. The loss of a big client hurts. But when one of the B-list authors writes a winner and you had a hand in it, it's a great day to be an agent.

You can get a feel for where an agent stands in terms of her ratio of productive to less productive clients by asking to see a list of books the agent has placed over the years. You will probably see the same author names showing up regularly, surrounded by names of those clients who are less productive or on the verge.

The Big Literary Agency

The larger the agency, the more diverse the kind of work it does for its clients. However, the agents employed by larger agencies are pretty much specialists—just as are those who operate small shops—with a more narrow focus. If you are writing a business book and are represented by a large agency, you will be assigned to an agent whose specialty is business books.

What larger agencies can often provide is faster and more comprehensive coverage of the subsidiary markets for their clients' books. However, smaller agencies frequently work with independent agencies that specialize in handling these rights for other agents. The financial arrangements are such that the author usually nets the same amount from this arrangement as she might from having the work done by the internal department of a larger agency.

Some larger agencies are often nothing more than a group of independent agents working together and sharing support services collectively. Others are organized as any other company might be and the contact you have is on the company payroll. Whatever the structure, the key element is still that of editor connections and the ability to get your book placed with the best publisher.

Backspace

If you are planning to go with a multi-person agency, try to ensure that you will be assigned to one agent. The author-agent relationship should be close and personal. Bouncing back and forth between different staffers is not a good way to go. However, the larger agencies can provide emergency backup that a solo agent often can't.

The Lawyers Who Also Act as Literary Agents

Your agent may happen to have a law degree, but I'm talking here about those whose main work is the practice of law, though they also represent some of their law clients as a literary agent. Lawyers who work this way are more than likely specializing in the law relating to intellectual property.

The need for legal representation is slight for most authors of business books—unless you are planning a heavy-handed rip-off of someone else's work. If your agent happens to have a law degree but his card says "literary agent," you might have a two-for-one opportunity. Just make sure that if he offers legal advice, you know in advance if it will be billed for and if so, how much you will be charged. Negotiating a typical business book contract doesn't require the assistance of an attorney. Any good agent does it all the time.

Where to Find the Best Agent for Your Book

The best place to begin is by contacting the AAR, the Association of Authors' Representatives (www.aar-online.org). Full disclosure: I was a member of AAR for many years when I was an active agent. AAR members agree to a rigid code of ethics that you should appreciate. All members are professional; this is not an organization for agents-in-training. Acceptance for membership requires complete documentation of full-time professional work as a literary agent. In short, a lot of what you should discover about any agent you might consider has been handled by the AAR membership qualification process.

Quote/Unquote

"The AAR (Association of Authors' Representatives) believes that the practice of literary agents charging clients or potential clients for reading and evaluating works (including outlines, proposals, and partial or complete manuscripts) is subject to serious abuse that reflects adversely on our profession. For that reason, the AAR prohibits its members from charging reading fees."

—AAR website (FAQ page)

This is an excellent reason for checking first with AAR when seeking representation.

Literary Market Place (*LMP*), the major source of information about the book publishing business, also includes extensive lists of sources who act as literary agents. Most libraries have copies of *LMP*, although you may not find it in the open stacks. It's a very helpful tool for librarians and they often keep it with their own professional sources. However, most are willing to let others use it.

Many of the magazines published for writers either publish directories of agents or include listing information in the pages of their issues.

Cut to the Chase

The sources I've just discussed are reliable and helpful, but there's a quicker way to find the perfect agent for your book. Almost every author includes a long list of acknowledgments in his book. That list almost always includes gracious thanks to the author's agent. There, now you know the name of an agent who handles the kind of book you want to publish. All you have to do is go to one of the directories for the agent's contact information and you have a hot lead. You might want to ask the agent if she is an AAR member or at least abides by the standards set by the association. A search of the AAR member directory on their website will tell you whether or not an agent is a member.

Contact Other Authors

Okay, so maybe the author of the book you admire didn't acknowledge his agent. It may be that he didn't use an agent, but you'll never know unless you check it out. Write the author and ask if an agent was used and whether he might offer a recommendation. Most authors who are pleased with their agents' work will not only give you contact information, but also may forward your request to their agents. You may hear directly from the agent if your idea seems to have legs.

If you are unable to get the author's address, just drop a snail mail note to the author, addressed by name, care of his publisher. It may take a little time for the publisher to forward the mail to the author, but most will do it.

If the author doesn't acknowledge his agent but sends kudos to the editor, a note or a phone call to that editor will probably get you the name you need. If you are lucky enough to get the editor on the line, don't waste his or her time—just get the agent's name, say thanks, and get off the phone.

Establishing Contact with an Agent

Once you have determined which agent seems to mesh with your work and aspirations, you have to get her attention. The typical solo agent gets between 20 and 30 unsolicited queries a day. Yes, a day! I can't imagine what the mailroom of the larger agencies looks like each day after the mail deliverer leaves.

Given this kind of competition for an agent's attention, you can probably see why it's best to follow the guidelines for queries that most agents agree with:

◆ Write a query letter first.

Describe the book you plan to write in no more than one or two pages. Include information on the market you envision for the book. Include current information on the size of your market. Tell why you are qualified to write the book and why you feel it is important that you write it.

If you lack the credentials to write the book alone, tell what you plan to do in order to produce a salable manuscript. If you are already working with a writing or editorial professional, include the name and qualifications of the person.

Backspace

The freelance help you use should have specific book publishing credentials. Experience in your subject matter helps but is seldom the key factor in the selection. Listing your high school English teacher, as good as she may be, is not the way to go if you are planning to work with someone at the developmental editor, collaborator, or ghostwriter level. An editorial professional already known to editors in your field adds to the strength of your query.

Do not send this query letter by e-mail! Use the United States Postal Service or one of the overnight services if you are in a hurry. And be sure to enclose a self-addressed stamped envelope for a reply. Your letter should have all your contact information, including your e-mail address and telephone number, just in case the agent wants to get back to you quickly.

◆ Do not try to contact by telephone.

Most of an agent's routine business is done by telephone and the Internet. If you manage to reach an agent and he doesn't tell you to send a written query, make it short.

◆ Send queries to several agents simultaneously.

Multiple queries are okay. But once an agent asks to see your material, stop the querying. If your query letter has been persuasive enough and several agents have responded, send the requested material to only one, but contact the others and let them know that other agents have shown interest. Most agents aren't put off by being put on a list. If the first agent passes on the idea, he may be making a mistake, and the next agent on the list might spot it.

◆ Send exactly what the agent asks for.

Book proposals should be written in a standard format. Don't try to wow the agent with stylistic and graphic gimmicks, colored paper, zippy typefaces, and all the other stuff loaded with your word processing program. You read all about proposals in Part 2.

◆ Relax; it could take weeks to hear back.

Once an agent has shown interest and you have responded with what she has asked for, you will hear back, but it will take some time. It could take a month or more. If your proposal is for a time-sensitive book, make that very clear in the material you send. And if you haven't heard in five or six weeks, it's okay to get in touch. This time an e-mail is usually fine.

◆ What if you are turned down?

One of the reasons for showing proposals to agents one at a time is that you get an opportunity to discover problems with your project that you might not have anticipated. An agent who writes back rejecting your project will probably tell you why. Take these comments seriously; other agents will probably see the same flaws. If the first agent hasn't asked for a revised proposal and just said no, do what has to be done with your proposal and move it on to the next agent who has expressed interest.

◆ What if the agent says yes?

Once an agent has agreed to take you on, the search should end. Unless you are a personality and can command a mega-advance, don't try to play one agent off on another. If later on you discover that the relationship is not working out and your best efforts to get it or keep it on track fail, you can agree to disagree, end the relationship, and move on to another agent. I discuss this situation in some detail in the next chapter.

An Agent May Find You

Agents are constantly on the lookout for people with ideas that could be turned into books. Agents, like publishing house acquisitions editors, read widely in the fields they cover. Many attend conferences and association meetings in which members speak and give presentations. In short, agents are always on the prowl. I found about half of the 80 authors I represented when I was an agent by reading widely and contacting those who wrote articles and those who were written about by others.

A call from an agent will probably seem vague at first. He will mention how the contact came about and ask some general questions before even mentioning representation. A call from an agent should not be considered as an implicit offer of representation. An agent will try to take your measure, just as you should try to take the agent's measure. Of course, if you are already represented, tell the agent up front. An ethical agent will apologize for the intrusion. If the agent's call intrigues you, do whatever he suggests or requests to get to the next step.

Doing It Yourself

You may actually have the time and some of the relevant experience to act as your own agent. If you do, give it a try. You will probably discover, however, that most of the major business book publishers really prefer to work with authors who have agent representation.

The editors in these houses know that the proposals they get from good agents will have been tightly pre-qualified. Any agent who dumps everything she has on an editor goes on the return-without-reading list. And many editors who do find an occasional good proposal in their slush pile will often contact the author and recommend that she secure the services of an agent.

Publishing Tip _____

Do yourself a favor: before you try to go it alone, talk to an agent, or better yet, several agents. I have only hit the highlights in this chapter, and while a good chin-wag with a few agents still may not convince you that an agent is the best way to go, it will certainly give you more information about representing yourself.

Even though they know they will probably have a tougher time negotiating a contract with an agent than they will with a neophyte author, editors recognize the benefit of the professional relationship. A third party, your agent, comes in handy in many ways other than just getting the best deal for you. Would you know what to do if the first half of your manuscript was rejected and the second advance payment were to be cancelled? An agent would!

The Least You Need to Know

♦ There are agents who specialize in representing business book authors.

♦ A good literary agent works strictly on commission.

♦ A good agent knows how to sell, handle financials, interpret contracts, and edit manuscripts. And he or she should be able to be your personal nudge when the publisher is slow paying royalties.

♦ A good agent has well-established contacts with the publishers who can best publish your book.

11

How to Work with a Literary Agent

In This Chapter

- ◆ Three major criteria for making an agent selection
- ◆ Eight questions you should ask an agent before signing up
- ◆ Don't worry if your agent doesn't return your calls immediately

In the previous chapter, I discussed how to find an agent for your book. This chapter is your guide on how to choose and work with an agent. As I have said, there are good agents and there are not-so-good agents, so don't rush to sign up with the first agent who expresses interest in your project. Given that there are, at any given time, thousands of writers looking for agents and that there are far fewer agents, there's plenty of room for nefarious practices. Most agents are scrupulously honest but are often tarred by the same brush as the dishonest agents. It's harmful to start any evaluation from a cynical perspective, so please look for the best in people, but be very aware that there are some agents who should be avoided.

Hiring an Agent

Let's think of the agent qualifying process as a series of filters. Anything that gets stuck in your filter is something that should be questioned. If the answer you get doesn't feel right, find out why. Don't be afraid to ask the agent for answers, and don't allow yourself to be stampeded if the answer is not what you feel you should hear. Going with the wrong agent will at the least set you back in terms of time and at the worst could cost you some money. Being with the wrong agent could even affect your reputation.

There are three areas to consider: honesty, competence, and reputation. Let's first look at the question of honesty.

The Honest Agent

Literary agents are a lot like manufacturers' agents. They represent the sale of their clients' products on commission but often provide help and guidance along the way without charge. Therefore, any agent who asks for a reading or evaluation fee is to be avoided.

When extensive work is needed on a manuscript, a good agent will suggest that the author get professional help. Most agents have lists of freelance editors they have worked with or know by reputation. An agent who pushes a particular freelance editor is to be suspected. Most agents will give clients a list of several editors and insist that the author make his own decision. And you should be free to make your choice of anyone, regardless of whether the agent knows the person. An agent's goal is solely to get a manuscript that is salable and an author who is a pleasure to work with.

A good agent reports all financial activity to his client regularly and on time. Most publishers pay royalties twice a year. Publishers issue statements to authors' agents whether or not any royalties are due. Good agents not only send royalty checks on time, they also send all reports on time, whether or not money is due the author.

Most agents will work with authors either on a per-book basis or on a contract basis. I never had a contract with any of the authors I represented during my 30 years as an agent. I looked on the relationship as one in which both I and the author had to perform our work successfully or we should consider parting. The relationship, however, was memorialized by having a simple clause included in the publisher's contract for each book placed. The clause identified my firm as the agency of record and stated the fiduciary responsibility of the agency to the author.

There is probably nothing wrong with an agency requiring its clients to sign a general contract, as long as you know exactly what you are getting into. It's far too complex a subject to get into in this book, but if you feel you need advice, talk with an attorney who has publishing experience. Your neighbor the real estate attorney is not the one to ask.

Backspace

Good agents don't run writing "contests," they don't offer any paid-for ancillary services, and they don't charge to evaluate a publisher-offered contract.

The Competent Agent

There are no tests or licenses required to become a literary agent. You could hang a sign on the door and be in business immediately. And this is the way many of the most successful agents of today got into the business. However, they brought some solid experience with them that prepared them for the work. Most were editors at publishing houses, some worked in sales and marketing at publishing houses, and others came from other publishing-related areas.

Most editors negotiate the contracts for the books they acquire, and they usually play a fairly active role in the publisher's marketing development and planning activities. So by the time they decide it's time to do something else and being an agent gets the nod, they are already on pretty familiar territory.

In addition to being able to offer competent editorial advice, a good agent has his eyes on the trends in the publishing business as well as the fields in which the publisher publishes. He should have some knowledge and experience in handling your subsidiary rights and some experience in licensing and publicity.

In short, your agent should know enough about everything that relates to your relationship with a publisher that he can negotiate a fair contract and act as your representative if trouble arises. But, most of all, your agent should be able to find the best publisher for your book and negotiate a deal that is fair and beneficial to you and your publisher. It's not an easy job, but most agents who make it say that they wish they'd become agents sooner and that they would never go back to whatever they did before.

The Reputable Agent

You may not have to even ask the agent you are considering for a list of authors she represents and a list of books placed. She will probably have the lists in hand if you meet in person or will send them immediately by e-mail or snail mail. An agent's history and client list is the best guide to what she might be able to do for you.

Most agents aren't into glitz and glossy presentations. In fact, the glitzier the brochure, the more suspicious you should be. Substance trumps style in this business. An agent who represents familiar, major authors in your field is likely to be a better choice than one who represents authors you've never heard of and has a brochure that takes your breath away. This goes for splashy websites as well.

Publishing Tip

Most agents will give you the names of editors with whom they have working relationships and some will also let you talk to current clients. If a current client declines to talk with you, it's not necessarily a sign that the agent should be avoided. As you should know by now, writers are pretty private people.

As I mentioned earlier, membership in the Association of Authors' Representatives is granted only after careful vetting. However, there still are many very fine agents who are not members and never will be. There are joiners and there are nonjoiners. What more can I say?

Ask These Questions

When meeting with an agent, ask the following questions:

- How long have you been an agent?

  Time in the field loosely translates into experience. You don't survive very long working on commission if you don't have the proper experience.

- What did you do before you became an agent?

  Publishing-related experience is very important. Anyone who is going to take charge of your writing career, even if you are planning only one book, should know what he is doing. Academic background is less important than you might think. Although most editors majored in English in college, you will find a wide range of academic disciplines in the ranks. My undergrad and grad degrees are in psychology, but before I started my agency, I had written eight books and spent a few years writing direct mail advertising copy for book publishers. Beware of the dreamer, however. Being a literary agent is a serious business.

◆ Do you handle all rights, or do you work with sub-agents?

A good solo agent with a manageable client list can handle all primary and subsidiary rights for her clients. However, a solo agent with 150 clients who claims to be able to handle everything is either a super agent, a liar, or a badly deluded individual. Larger agencies usually have specialists for the subsidiary rights work, such as movie deals. Your business book will probably be passed over by Steven Spielberg, however, so you may not have to worry.

◆ Who within the agency will be my agent?

If you are considering a larger agency, chances are that your initial contact will not be the person who will actually do the work of representing you. Make sure you have a bio on the agent and try to meet or at least talk on the phone with the person before you say yes. The agency's reputation may be great, but you may be assigned to someone who is also representing novelists and poets. You want a business book pro in your corner.

◆ Do you want a full contract or are you willing to work book-by-book?

Most agencies are willing to work with authors either way, even those who seem rather insistent about wanting a firm contract up front. I'd suggest that you hold out for a book-by-book arrangement, at least at first. When you have more publishing experience under your belt and you see what the agent can and cannot do for you, then is the time to talk about a contract that binds you and the agency till death, or a lawsuit, pulls you apart.

◆ What provisions are available in the event of the agent's death?

This question is more important if you are working with a solo agent. Her death could tie up the payment of earned royalties unless proper provisions have been made.

◆ What are your commission rates?

Most agents work at a 15 percent commission rate for all work sold domestically. The rate for co-agented books, foreign sales, and special sales to organizations other than book publishers is usually 25 percent. Some business books are published by companies other than conventional book publishers and there may be no royalties involved, so the higher rate is justified.

◆ Do you discuss all offers with your clients?

This is a given for most agents, but it pays to ask. A publisher making a smaller offer than another could actually be the better publisher to go with. Advances are important, but so are royalty rates, subsidiary rights potential, and many other things. You should have all the elements of all offers before you make a decision.

These are important questions to ask every prospective agent. However, keep in mind that most agents won't have the time to answer them unless they have already shown an interest in your work. So don't shoot yourself in the foot by bringing them up until you are well along in any other discussions of representation.

Getting Down to Business

Once you have signed on with an agent, the real work begins. Assuming the agent was intrigued by a proposal you sent, the next step is polishing the proposal and getting it ready to send to editors. Getting the proposal right the first time is so important that I have devoted an entire part of the book to it: Chapters 5–9.

If your new agent thinks your proposal is close enough to working, she will probably either touch it up or provide suggestions for you to do the touch-up yourself. Listen carefully to the agent's suggestions. Book editors get so many proposals every working day that anything that varies from a generally accepted format is probably not going to get much, if any, attention. Your agent knows the drill. Don't get picky about what you may see as clever and creative when the agent suggests something else. Clever and creative can get attention, but it is content and style that gets the contract offers.

The early days of the relationship will probably be fairly intense. The agent probably sees a book that should be sold quickly and she probably also sees some pretty heavy lifting for you. Time is important. Publishers usually publish seasonally; that is, they have four lists a year. If the agent is shooting for a list that is closing soon, you and the agent will get to know each other very well very quickly. If this is not the case, the relationship may seem quite casual. Deadlines drive the business!

 Publishing Tip _____

Keep in mind that your agent represents quite a few clients, all with projects in different stages of development. It's a juggling act, so don't be too upset if your calls aren't returned immediately. A quick, short e-mail will often bring a faster response, and usually a more considered one, if you have a specific question.

An early intense relationship usually ends quickly once your manuscript has been delivered and accepted by the publisher. Don't get nervous or upset when the phone call and e-mail frequency drops considerably. You have not been forgotten. The agent serves many clients, all at different stages of their career development and all at different stages of the books and proposals they are writing.

Unless your agent has suggested a specific topic for your next book, it will be up to you to start sending him or her your ideas. Don't get into full proposals; short notes describing the book you are thinking about and the size of the potential market will be more than enough to get things going. The responses you will get from these notes will probably be short and terse, totally unlike the encouraging words you got when working closely on the first book. Don't take this as a sign that you have lost your agent's attention. If you have, for whatever reason, most agents will bring it up.

The author-agent relationship is a very close one. You are working together creatively and financially, and apart from a marriage, it doesn't get much closer. Just remember this—the agent needs you as much as you need the agent.

The Offers Pour In

Well, they may not exactly pour in. Trickle is more to the point. Your agent will share all offers with you and give you some idea of the benefits and drawbacks of each offer and the publishers who make them.

Big publishers sometimes make awful offers, and little publishers sometimes make great offers. The difference seldom has anything to do with you personally; it's almost always a factor of the number of books the publisher thinks it might be able to sell. If a small publisher has some successful and related titles already in print, the offer might be better than that of a name publisher who might be looking at a market in which it has only a minor presence. Your agent will explain all this, and he should be able to do this in terms of what you might expect to earn from each publisher.

Sadly, too many authors grab the offer with the higher advance or royalty and end up losing money on the deal. A good agent, who might seem to be pushing a favored publisher, is probably not doing that at all. He is pushing for the publisher that will earn you more money. When the publisher earns more, you and your agent both earn more money.

The Contract Arrives

Most publishers use "boilerplate" contracts that they have developed over the years and offer as standard. No two publishers' contracts are the same. While they all cover the same ground, each does it differently and with different requirements and stipulations. If your agent has done books with the publisher before, she will know what to look for initially. I say initially, because it's not unusual for the publisher to change just a few words in the contract that make significant changes in their agreements. They might be missed in a cursory review. And because the agreements are no longer on preprinted forms, but stored in a computer and used as needed, a careful reading is necessary. A word here and a word there can be changed without having to make very visible marginal notes, as had to be done when preprinted contracts ruled.

Even if your agent reads the contract and explains it clearly to you, you should read it, too. Don't rush through. Read it slowly and make sure you understand what is said in each and every paragraph. It's a step to take carefully, asking your agent questions as you go along. Agents are anxious for their clients to understand contracts and their ramifications. It makes it easier for them to handle your affairs when they are sure that you know what the contract you signed is all about.

Backspace

Some book publishers' contracts are long and complex; others are deceptively short. Long contracts tend to nail down everything; short contracts, of necessity, are quite vague. Size does matter—read every word, especially those in shorter agreements. They leave a lot to the imagination and interpretation. That interpretation could involve a costly legal fee if you have troubles later on.

Once you and your agent have agreed to everything and you have signed, your agent will return the contract to the publisher. Make a note of when your first advance payment should be due and drop your agent an e-mail a week or two before, reminding him or her to make calls to the publisher if necessary. Chances are that the agent has already begun the nudging process; after all, he or she works on commission and doesn't get paid until you get paid.

Working with Your Agent While You Write Your Book

When all the front-end stuff has been completed and your first advance payment has been made, you probably won't hear from your agent unless you make the call. This doesn't mean that you can't call your agent anytime, but make sure that you have real issues to discuss. As I said, agents are editors, salespeople, publicity people, contract folk, and friends when you need a friend. But please keep in mind that your agent represents many other authors and time really is money for him or her.

In general, if you have editorial questions as you write, you can get in touch with your editor. Most are really helpful people who are concerned about their authors and the books they write.

If you run into serious writing problems, your editor or your agent may suggest that you seek professional help from an outside editor. Your publisher's editor is mainly responsible for keeping the book on track and for maintaining the editorial standards set for the book. It's assumed from the sample writing you submitted with the proposal that you will be able to deliver an acceptable manuscript. If things don't work out, you may have to get help and pay for it yourself. I discuss writing with a collaborator, and even a ghostwriter, in Chapter 12.

But for now, keep in mind that you will be expected to turn in half the manuscript by a given date. If you fail to meet the schedule or deliver unpublishable material, you will either have to get help or the contract will be cancelled and you will have to return the money.

If the first half of your manuscript is acceptable to the publisher, you will receive the next advance payment. As with the first payment, it will be made to your agent and your agent will remit it, less his commission.

Writing the second half of the manuscript is a repeat of the first half, only it usually goes faster and more easily than the first half. Again, once the editor accepts and the check has been cashed, your agent will vanish as you work. Don't take this personally; he is always there if needed.

Delivering the Manuscript

Very few publishers want manuscripts printed on paper today; most want and some insist on a manuscript in one of the many different digital forms. Alpha, the publisher of this book, wants only electronic submissions. Your agent will tell you all about your publisher's individual requirements and can usually help you if you get snagged on any of the formatting issues.

If you have been submitting material chapter by chapter, the final chapter and any associated material, such as introductions and appendixes, will constitute the completion of the manuscript. At this point, your agent should request the balance of the advance. Some publishers will pay the balance at this point; others pay only when galley proofs have been read and any changes that have been requested have been made. Unless the editor is asking for any fix-ups or additional material, your job is done—at least for the moment.

Most publishers will submit proof pages for you to read. Spelling is not what they want checked; they want to make sure that everything is as you wrote it and they are giving you a final look at what will be put between covers. This is not the time to make major revisions, unless, of course, events have taken place that make what you have written irrelevant. Heavy rewriting at the proof stage is not going to make you popular with your publisher, and there may even be dire consequences. Don't even ask—I shudder to think of them!

Sales, Publicity, and Marketing People Will Show Up

Before your book has been printed, you will probably start getting calls from the sales, publicity, and marketing staff of publisher. They will be assembling the promotion package for your book. Your agent can be a big help here by suggesting ways to promote your book that may have never occurred to you. This is a critical phase, so do your best to be helpful.

 Publishing Tip _____

If you plan to do any publicity for your book by yourself, be sure to coordinate with your editor or your publisher's publicity person. For one thing, it's a waste of time and money to duplicate the effort. For another, it makes you and the publisher look like a gaggle of amateurs.

If you have any contacts who can help promote your book, put them in touch with your agent or your editor. Publicity is what sells business books. Advertising helps grease the wheels, but publicity is the main tool.

The Books Arrive

Most publishers send a small quantity of books to authors as soon as they are printed. The quantity is stipulated in your contract. If you want more copies, they can usually be bought from the publisher at the conventional bookseller's discount. However, if you would like to have a fairly large quantity of books and are willing to commit to a number in advance of the publisher's printing schedule, it's usually possible to negotiate a price based on a mark-up of the publisher's total production costs. Check with your agent about this at the time you negotiate the contract.

The Royalties Roll In

The publisher will make royalty payments directly to you if you are not represented. If you do have an agent, the publisher will send the checks to your agent, in your agent's name. Upon cashing the check, the agent will forward you a check, less the agency commission. Subsidiary rights income is usually paid at the same time. Your check should include a statement from the agent as well as a copy of the publisher's statement of your account. If you have any questions regarding the publisher's statement, discuss them with your agent, and your agent will take up any problems with the publisher.

Your Next Book

If you have an idea for another book, now is the time to start discussing it. Chances are that your publisher will want to wait to see how your first book sells before getting into any serious discussions about your next book. And unless your contract calls for you to offer your next book to your publisher before offering to it to another, you might want to think about another publisher.

If your first book sells well, there is a good chance that you can get a larger advance for the next one. But you usually have to ask for it, and you may have to do some negotiating to get it or to get better royalty or sub rights terms. Here, again, is where your agent comes in really handy. Most authors prefer to write, not to negotiate. Most agents get a rush from the negotiation process, so turn your agent loose and stick to your keyboard.

I've only hit the highlights in the process of working with an agent. I wouldn't work without one. Remember, I was a full-time agent for 30 years. Now in semi-retirement, I continue to write books; but I would never do it without a good agent at my side, and my good agent is Ed Claflin.

The Least You Need to Know

◆ Good agents are very selective in the clients they choose to represent.

◆ Your agent is your sales rep, your editorial consultant, your financial consultant, your legal advisor, your publicity and marketing guru—and your friend when all goes wrong and nobody else will listen.

◆ Agents like to help writers build careers, so have more than one book in mind when you talk with prospective agents.

◆ You don't have to sign a contract with an agent that gives him or her the rights to everything; most will work with you a book at a time.

12

Ghostwriters, Collaborators, Freelance Editors, and Book Doctors

...blished

... if and when you need it

...nd what kind of help will be most

♦ How to work with editorial professionals and how they are compensated

♦ Whether or not to share the credit

Most definitions of the word *author* include a reference to someone who creates or originates something. By that definition, a songwriter is an author, as is an inventor, a designer, and even an architect.

A *writer,* on the other hand, is most often defined as one who writes books, scripts, columns, manuals, and just about anything else that uses words one way or another. Only the entries for *writer,* which include long lists of synonyms for the word, include the term *author.*

To the point—authors may be writers and writers may be authors, but to be an author one does not have to be a writer.

The authors of many books you may have read may never have written a word of what you read. However, you would not have benefited from the author's thoughts and ideas if it had not been for the help of someone whose skills were used to provide you with the book you enjoyed. You may have even read some of the books I have written as the ghostwriter.

Why Some Books Are Never Published

Every business book editor is looking for good ideas. If the ideas are accompanied by evidence of good writing skills, the editor has struck gold. Sadly, that doesn't happen often enough for most editors to take the long and leisurely lunches that are glamorized in the movies. The VPs and editors-in-chief of even the biggest publishing companies have sandwiches at their desks more often than you might imagine. A good idea well expressed is really a rare commodity.

However, when an editor spots a proposal with a good idea that needs some work, he will probably see what can be done to turn the idea into a readable book. The editor usually starts by expressing some interest and suggesting that the author make some revisions to his proposal. If the revised proposal has what it takes, a deal might be made. If it doesn't, and the editor still likes the idea, the editor may suggest that the author find some professional help. That help could range from simple editorial guidance to the use of an active collaborator or even a ghostwriter. Publishers seldom provide that help themselves; they usually give the potential author the names and qualifications of a number of people who can help. It's then up to the potential author to make the choice and to make appropriate financial arrangements. Publishers provide in-house developmental editing and copyediting of an author's completed manuscript, but it's up to the author to first provide a manuscript that is acceptable by conventional publishing standards.

Keep in mind that I am talking about commercial publishers, those who usually offer cash advances on signing a contract and royalties upon successful sale of the published book. There are, however, private publishers that do offer all of the services, from writing through marketing and distribution of books. These houses are often unjustly maligned, snidely called "vanity publishers," and looked down upon by those whose books have the name of a famous publisher on the title page. This is a big mistake. Many independent and private publishers do excellent work and provide readers with material that would otherwise never find its way into print.

Publishing Tip

It may seem confusing for an author to work with two editors, one at the publishing house and an outside freelancer. Keep in mind that the in-house editor is mainly responsible for reviewing an author's writing for publisher acceptability, while a freelance editor is the author's working partner to ensure publisher acceptability.

Do It Yourself or Get Help

Whether to do it yourself or get help boils down to taking a good look at yourself and asking, first, if your idea is strong enough to interest a publisher. If it is, are you capable of writing the book yourself? If you feel you need help, are you willing to listen to and work with someone whose comments might be at odds with the praise your high school English teacher heaped on your term paper? Be honest with yourself.

It's corny, but it resonates—time really is money. You may actually be a good writer with a good idea. But if you get megabucks-an-hour for your consulting service, it probably doesn't make sense to write your own book. You won't come close to earn anywhere near your fees from your book, unless it turns up some spectacular client for you. And if you really aren't comfortable writing, it's going to be even worse.

Backspace

The advances paid to business leaders you read about in the papers are unusual, to say the least. Behind some of these advances you are likely to find that the leader's firm might have negotiated a pre-publication sale of a large quantity of books to be given to customers, prospects, and others whose influence can be felt in special places. This makes it a lot easier for the publisher to up the advance ante, so be impressed, but not too impressed.

Let's look now at each of the services that are available and see how you might work with each and what you might expect to have to pay. Note that I am using the term *author* to refer to the content person, the expert. I use the word *writer* to refer to the word person, editor, collaborator, or ghostwriter, the one who helps the author one way or another to produce a salable book.

How to Work with a Freelance Editor

If you are looking for a freelance editor, you will quickly discover many people doing the work but calling themselves by different names. For example, a development editor and a content editor do pretty much the same thing. So rather than focus on titles, I discuss editors by the services they provide. If you feel that a freelance editor is what you need, discuss your needs in functional terms. Telling an editor you need someone to check your spelling and grammar will get you what you need, but asking for content or developmental editing won't necessarily. Apart from the functional differences, the cost differential can be substantial, so pay attention!

In the Beginning ...

If you write reasonably well, you may just need some touch-ups. Someone who edits your material for spelling, grammar, and minor stylistic issues will probably be the right choice. Better yet, hire a pro to do it for you. This kind of editing is the least expensive of all the editing processes. Remember that a clean manuscript or proposal can make a big difference in an editor's enthusiasm for your project.

> **Backspace**
>
> Beware of your computer spell-checker and grammar program. Just pushing a button to accept the spell-checker's choice can lead to everything from disaster to some good laughs at your expense by your publisher. And never automatically accept the grammatical suggestions your grammar program offers. Most of these programs seem driven to insert semicolons where commas will do perfectly well.

The Next Level

The term most often used to describe the work done beyond the basics is line editing, so I'll use it. A line editor cuts surplus modifiers and tightens the language that dampens the impact of your ideas. You can take a quick pass at this yourself by looking for all words that end in *-ly*. Any that can be eliminated without altering the central meaning of the thought should be cut.

A line editor will also cut clichés such as "like there's no tomorrow" from your writing. Line editors cut redundant words and phrases from your text and are truly happy when they can slash away at a mixed metaphor. They are especially watchful for inappropriate switches in tense and for words you dragged up from the thesaurus that only a Rhodes scholar would recognize.

Line editors do a lot more, but these examples give you an idea of where most people make awful blunders in their writing and can use help.

The Big Picture

Called content or developmental editors, the people at this level work to improve manuscripts substantively. Whether this person is a freelancer or an employee of your publisher, she is a collaborator in every sense. If you are unsure about your writing, it's best to seek the help of a developmental editor from the beginning of the project. Halfway into a book is not the place to start over if it just isn't working, and a developmental editor can help you avoid that problem.

Good developmental editing fixes foggy writing, maintains the author's focus, clarifies ambiguities, and upholds the tone of the overall writing. It also helps authors to organize and structure the book, individual chapters, and even paragraphs. Most authors recognize and accept development editing graciously, except when an editor suggests removing favorite phrases and sentences an author thinks of as gems.

Depending on the needs of the manuscript and the nature of the working relationship, a content editor can do rewrites directly or simply point out where the writing might need help. The content editor's role is flexible, but there needs to be a good understanding between client and editor at the start or there will be problems. The main subject to be agreed upon is whether the editor is expected to do the rewrites or only provide comments and suggestions for the author to follow.

Publishing Tip

If you are unfamiliar with writing and book publishing, it's tempting to think of these editorial processes as distinct from one another. They can be, but more often than not, the lines are blurred. You may be able to find an editor who will correct your spelling as well as be able to tell you that you have to start Chapter 3 over again. I have yet to meet a developmental editor who would not correct a problem of tense in a sentence if he spotted it, even though it may not be part of the job.

How Editing Is Billed

All editing can be charged for by the word, by the page, or by the hour. It can even be done for a flat fee if the editor has a clear enough idea of what will be involved. It's useless to give you real numbers because they vary so widely that even an average can be misleading.

After you decide which editorial process will be most helpful, shop for estimates. There are plenty of editors who advertise their services and post their fees on the Internet. Check out those who seem interesting and review their price ranges. It's a mistake to make buying cheap your sole criterion for selection, so look first for editors with qualifications that impress you. If you know people who have used editors, get their recommendations. Word of mouth is the most effective means to find someone, and the publishing people you work with are a great place to start. You can also ask to see what projects the editor has worked on or samples of his or her work. You can also research an editor's name online to find projects he or she has worked on. Most editors are willing to tell you something about the work they have done for other clients, so you can get a feel for their skill sets, experience, and credibility.

Editorial projects, if they are lengthy or will be long-term project assignments, are usually billed at agreed-upon stages. The most common unit of billing for book editing is by the chapter.

Editorial work is labor intensive, and most freelance editors who work on book manuscripts are usually on tight deadlines. They are usually friendly and enjoy a good chinwag as much as anyone else. But try not to get a colloquy going during working hours, and don't drop in unannounced. I once heard of a very successful freelance editor who moved to the backwoods of Maine just so he could work in peace. Of course, the beauty of that part of the country must have played a part, too.

How to Work with a Freelance Collaborator

There are two types of collaboration. When two or more content experts work on a book together, it is a professional collaboration. Generally speaking, when one author is seen as more important than the others, her name is listed first on the cover and title page of the book. Each of the collaborating authors brings his or her specialized knowledge to the project.

The other type of collaboration is one in which the content author works with a professional writer. The writer usually brings at least a basic understanding of the material to the project, but her major contribution is to make the author's work readable and enjoyable.

Professional writers who collaborate with content authors have been responsible for some of the best nonfiction best-sellers you may have read. The few content experts who have the skill to write their own books are rare and often celebrated by both their publishers and their readers. But this doesn't mean that those whose writing skills are not sufficient to turn their material into interesting books should be demeaned in any way. Collaborating is a symbiotic relationship that benefits everyone. And it shouldn't evoke any embarrassment if you feel that the assistance of a professional writer would help you produce a better book.

The Collaboration Process Works in Many Ways

Collaborations are structured to make the best of each person's skills. The lines here are as blurred, just as they are in the editing processes I just described. In most collaborations, a book contract already exists, so there is a goal in sight and the publisher's editorial suggestions have been discussed and agreed upon. Starting a collaboration without some solid focus is a recipe for disaster for all involved. Here are the types of collaboration that can be most productive when a business book is the subject.

◆ The writer writes everything from the author's notes.

   This type of collaboration is usually undertaken when the author needs some help but really has more of a problem with time. Most professional writers who undertake this type of collaboration will insist on having all the research material in hand, along with the author's outline or at least a clearly thought-out plan for the book. If a publisher has acquired the book, the author's proposal should give the writer a clear idea of what is expected. I should mention that the proposals for many books that will be written with collaborators are also written by the collaborator, so jumping into the project is usually not a problem.

   It's very important for the author and the writer to see eye to eye on everything very early on. Differences of opinion can be resolved when only a few chapters are involved, but this becomes a serious problem when the author sees nothing of the project until the writer delivers the finished manuscript. Stage-by-stage approval is the best way to keep the lawyers at bay.

◆ The writer and the author work closely together.

This may surprise you, but many authors and their writer collaborators never meet. There are many reasons given for this and most have some validity. But it does beg the question of practicality: how can two people undertake a project as complex and personal as writing a book and never meet? From my perspective as a collaborator and a ghostwriter, time is a major factor. Most of the writers I know feel the same way.

It was far more difficult to work closely when we had to depend on just the telephone, faxes, and the postal service to communicate. However, the Internet and e-mail has made collaboration at a distance far more practical, and I think it has resulted in better collaborations and better-written books.

Whether you and your collaborator work face-to-face or never meet, it's important to be in touch regularly. Resolve minor issues and problems early and quickly.

◆ The author does the rough drafts and the writer does the final writing.

Here we are into the blurry area again. If the author's drafts are really rough, a collaborator is usually needed. However, if an author can produce a reasonably good draft, all that may be needed is the services of a good developmental editor. One way to help you make the best choice is to talk with your editor at the publishing company that has bought your book. You can trust the judgment of most book editors to steer you in the right direction.

How Collaboration Is Billed

Unlike editing, most collaboration is not billed by the word. Most collaboration is billed by the hour or by the page, chapter, or book. It is mostly a matter of what both parties are comfortable with, the size and complexity of the project, and the deadlines involved. Again, actual numbers will be misleading. You can, however, get an idea of what collaborators charge by checking book collaborator websites. Be sure to check qualifications at the same time.

How to Work with a Ghostwriter

The line between heavy collaboration and ghostwriting is the next blur you will encounter. It's generally assumed that all research is provided to a collaborator, while a ghostwriter will provide some or maybe even all of the research. As with collaboration, the details of a book that is ghostwritten should be fully discussed and agreed upon by the author and writer before any work is undertaken.

> ### Publishing Tip _____
>
> Many years ago I was asked to talk to a local group about my ghostwriting work. One person showed up, so I suggested that we just chat rather than go through my prepared spiel. He agreed and I quickly discovered that he thought of ghostwriters as people who write about ghosts. Maybe some do, but when I explained that I'm called a ghostwriter because I write books for people who have something important to say, but who don't have the appropriate writing skills to do it themselves, he was shocked. "You mean (name withheld) might not have written (title withheld)?" he asked. When I told him it was possible, he just shook his head, got up and left. I wonder if he has ever read a book again after that shattering experience.

Most professional ghostwriters see their work less as art and more as that of an artisan with very salable skills. In other words, we have become accustomed to steady, predictable, and often quite rewarding work. Many of us write books and other materials that appear under our own names, and others are quite content to live well in the shadows of the authors for whom we write books. We are an interesting bunch!

The actual work is done on much the same schedule as that of collaboration. Once the author and the writer agree on all the details of the project, the ghostwriter usually submits material to the author one chapter at a time. I can't overestimate the necessity of the author reviewing and approving material as it is written and reviewed. Enormous amounts of time and money can be lost by both parties if a start-over is needed after a lot of work has been done but not reviewed and approved.

How to Find a Ghostwriter

Most authors discover ghostwriting when a publisher's editor discovers them and suggests a book project. The main job of a book publisher's acquisitions editors is to scout people who are doing interesting things that they feel others would like to read about. In many cases, these people are simply not qualified to write a book. If the acquisitions editor really wants a book from the person, she may either give the author the names of some qualified ghostwriters or the names of some literary agents who can undertake the process of author development as well as management and screening of ghostwriters.

Both agents and editors regularly work with ghostwriters and collaborators. Good editors and good agents are not financially obligated to the ghostwriters or collaborators they suggest. Yes, there are always some who give all the others a bad name, and the best way to discover who they are is to poke around the publishing blogs. But if an editor or an agent thinks highly enough of what you do and also feels you might need some help, investigate everything. Publishers and agents don't waste time. Agents work on commission, so there is nothing in it for them until they sell your book. And unless an editor thinks a book you might write with help will make money for his employer, you won't be hearing from him either.

How Ghostwriting Is Billed

Depending on the research needed and how much the ghostwriter is expected to provide, ghostwriting can be billed by the word, chapter, or book. However, it's more common for the ghostwriter to estimate the time and effort needed and to provide a client with a firm fee for the complete job. These fees are usually stated with some caps on work to be done. If the work turns out to take longer or requires more effort, a ghostwriter expects and usually contracts for additional compensation.

Most new authors try to offer the ghostwriter the advance and part of the royalties as compensation. However, unless the author has a top name that is sure to get a lot of attention, this offer is usually turned down. Other than for projects that are sure to make a lot of money, most ghostwritten books are contracted with the author for a fee payable in thirds. The first third, which is usually not refundable, is paid upon signing of an agreement between the ghost and the author. The second third is paid when half the book is written, and the final payment is made when the manuscript is completed.

Ghostwriting contracts usually contain options on the author's next ghostwritten book. Some include clauses that call for bonuses for the ghost when royalties reach an agreed-upon amount. I discuss this in more detail in Chapter 17.

> **Publishing Tip**
>
> It's not uncommon for the ghostwriter to be included on the contract the author makes with the publisher. There are some good reasons for this and some good reasons to avoid it.

The economics of having a book in print reveal that even though a ghostwriter's fee will probably exceed the amount of the advance, it would be impossible to create the attention that a book gets any other way without spending a significant amount of money. The publisher's advance offsets that cost, so the net cost of the exposure is a lot less than you might imagine.

Working with a Book Doctor

Book doctors have all the skills of good editors, collaborators, and ghostwriters. However, the traditional book doctor does not do any major writing for his client. A book doctor reviews material at any stage and offers suggestions for improvement to the author. The suggestions often include rewrites to show the author just what the work would look like if his suggestions were followed.

Book doctors provide written reports to their clients and will often talk extensively with them directly or by way of the telephone. These consulting services are billed by the hour, and most book doctors charge either by the page or by the word for their assistance.

Book doctors work with clients at any point in the development of a book. It should be noted, however, that fiction is usually submitted to agents and publishers as a complete manuscript, while nonfiction is almost always sold on the basis of a proposal and a few sample chapters. Either way, book doctors can be very helpful.

Jerry Gross, one of the better-known book doctors working today, says that a book doctor for a nonfiction book is best used after the first few sample chapters have been written, but before anything has been shown to a publisher. He says, "It isn't easy to get an editor's attention a second time once a proposal has been rejected. A book doctor works to give you that initial edge."

Most book doctors work either on a per-page or an hourly rate basis. Some will quote you a flat fee for a project, but only after they have done their own internal calculations of the time they will spend on the project. Again, quoting current rates will be counterproductive. Check the Internet and you will get a picture of the range of skills offered by book doctors.

But Whose Name(s) Will Appear on the Cover?

Editors, book doctors, and ghostwriters are generally happy enough to have their clients offer a few words of thanks in their acknowledgments. But there is a growing trend among collaborators of wanting to share some cover credit. It's hard to say why this is happening, other than inflated egos, which are as much a part of book publishing as they are in any other field where individuals are on public display.

I will be taken to task for this, but I believe that it's usually a mistake to include a collaborator's name on a book unless the collaborator is working with the author from a content perspective. Business books are written as much to promote the author as they are to provide information for readers of the books. Business books are reviewed in the business press, and when they have popular appeal, they are reviewed by the general press. It detracts, I believe, from the credibility of the author to acknowledge someone who did not directly contribute to the content.

> **Backspace** _____
>
> Most of my ghostwriter and collaborator colleagues are well enough known to publishers that we seldom have fewer than two or three projects in the works at any given time. Most of my colleagues prefer to have a simple "thanks" in the acknowledgments. As long as our names are spelled correctly on the checks, we're happy!

Some publishing company publicity people share this view. When booking authors for radio and TV gigs, they are pretty much forced to include any writer or collaborator named on the book. And when the two appear on the tube or radio and the author sounds great and the collaborator doesn't, the whole thing falls apart. If the collaborator is banking on part of the royalties, she should seriously consider whether a name on the title page is worth what might be lost if a gig doesn't materialize because of concern over the performance of the collaborator.

The Least You Need to Know

- ◆ Professional help is available in many ways.
- ◆ You can work with the best editors and collaborators even though they may be thousands of miles away.
- ◆ The cost of professional help can be greatly offset by the advances and royalties offered by commercial book publishers.
- ◆ Most editorial professionals will agree to total anonymity.

Chapter 13

Working with a Co-Author

In This Chapter

- ◆ Twelve tested tips to help you define your book clearly
- ◆ Deciding on how to credit authorship
- ◆ Deciding how to split the money
- ◆ Using Management by Objectives to guide the collaboration

Maybe you haven't come up with your idea by yourself, or maybe your book needs more research than you can do by yourself. It's time to discuss co-authors.

Depending on who you talk to in the publishing world, you will probably get a variety of definitions for co-author. Here, though, I am using the term specifically to describe a person who is a full-fledged co-author, a content expert and not necessarily a professional writer.

While you and your co-authors may have the same ideas and purpose for your book, no two people have the same writing style, and a book written by two or more people, unless someone carefully watches over it, can be a mess. One author writes in first person and active voice, for example.

Another prefers third person and passive voice. This may seem like a minor issue, but I'm sure you have quit reading more than a few books because of problems like these. You may not know passive voice from active voice, but you knew something was wrong and it kept you from finishing your reading.

For this reason, an additional person is often brought in to watch over the book. This person is usually responsible for writing the book from the authors' notes or for melding the styles of the authors into one readable manuscript.

If you are at all familiar with the handbooks that exist in most fields, which are the work of dozens of the key people in the field, you probably know what I'm talking about. One chapter is a pleasure to read and another is unreadable because they didn't have that one person to tie everything together.

This chapter is about heading off the problems two or more people have when writing together. It's preventative medicine. My prescription: read this twice carefully before writing with others and be sure that your co-authors do the same. And the prescription label I would suggest is this: Warning! Writing a book with others can cause good friends to become mortal enemies.

Define the Project Clearly

In most cases, two people who decide to write a book together have a lot in common right from the start. They may work together, they may teach together, and they may have even been heading toward the same conclusions, even though they may have never met. But there is a common interest and each sees the other as sharing part of the load and participating in the overall project.

Remember the old movies in which the kids in the neighborhood suddenly see that they have a common interest and one says, "I know, let's put on a play"? They all think it's a great idea and then all hell breaks loose. There's your model!

When you and your potential collaborators get the idea to do a book together, the euphoria grabs everyone. Then, unless you do what I'm suggesting in the rest of the chapter, you will have more than your share of problems. But enough warnings! You're adults and you don't behave like kids on a playground.

Yeah, right!

> ## Quote/Unquote _____
>
> "If you have an apple and I have an apple and we exchange these apples, then you and I will still each have one apple. But if you have an idea and I have an idea and we exchange these ideas, then each of us will have two ideas."
> —George Bernard Shaw

Here are several questions to help you define the book you want to write and set guidelines for how you and your collaborators work together.

♦ Who are the readers you want to reach?

   Because most popular business books have a how-to undertone, this is resolved almost automatically. If you are writing a book on sales lead qualification, your audience is not corporate presidents and CEOs. The way you answer this should allow you to get a pretty good idea of the size of the audience, which you will have to know when you pitch your book to a publisher.

♦ What is the main message of the book?

   You and your co-authors must agree on this right from the start. Writing at cross purposes is not what your publisher wants because this is not what readers want. You may disagree on some aspects of the subject, and putting your disagreements in front of your reader is seldom a problem. But make sure that, regardless of how you disagree, you and your co-authors agree on the key premises.

♦ Is this a project that is equally important to each of you?

   Later in this chapter, I discuss sharing the burden, but for now it's important for each co-author to know where the others stand in terms of commitment of time and effort. If one wants the book in print quickly and the other is indifferent about the publication date, things will get sticky.

♦ Who will be the lead author?

   Generally, the first name to appear on the title page is considered the lead author. However, when two or more people of relatively equal stature agree to write a book together, the decision as to whose name comes first can disrupt long-standing friendships. There are no rules that will help you make this decision. I do, however, advise that once the decision is made, it shouldn't be changed. When you and your co-authors agree to the sequence, move on and write the book. You can request in your publisher's contract that both names always be set in the same size type.

- How will the work be apportioned?

  It's not a good move for co-authors to share the actual writing of the book. No two writers have the same style, and when writing is shared, the result is usually awful, even if both authors by themselves are good writers. There's plenty of work to be done; so decide up front who will write and how the other work will be apportioned so that everyone has the same workload and essentially the same contribution to the book. If all authors want to write, consider working with a third person, a silent wordsmith who will take material from each author and rewrite or edit it so that the manuscript is cohesive and consistent throughout.

- How will you solve disagreements?

  No two or more people can write a book without disagreeing about something. Recognize this from the start. First, agree not to fight and then decide how differences will be resolved. Most disagreements are about either content or style. If, as I suggested earlier, you all agree on who does what, this should not be a big problem. The problems, then, usually boil down to who is producing on time and who isn't. If you have your schedules in place, unless the offending writer has a legitimate excuse, everyone knows what has to be done.

- How will the money be split?

  The easiest way is to simply state that the income from the book will be apportioned equally among all the authors. Keep in mind that if you are working with a freelance writer or editor he may be working for a fee, rather than a portion of the advance. But when two or more content experts are writing together, it's rare that the division is done any way other than by equal portions of the total income. Total income means everything—advances, royalties, grants, and all subsidiary rights income.

- Who will manage the money?

  Don't have all the income sent to one member of the writing team with that person spreading the wealth to others. Apart from the issues of trust that can pop up—even among the sophisticated types who write books—the issue of taxes will become a problem for all. If all the money goes to one author, that author must report the total amount on his tax return, then expense out the individual amounts to the others. It's far simpler to have your agent do the splits directly and handle the tax reporting.

If you are not working with an agent, your publisher can handle the splits, sending the money as agreed upon in the contract. Don't think of this after you have signed the contract, though. With good reason, publishers really hate to revise contracts once they are signed.

♦ What would happen if one or more of the co-authors can't follow up?

> **Publishing Tip** _____
>
> When you use an agent, the publisher will make payments to that agent and report the payments to the IRS. The agent will then make individual payments to collaborating authors and report the individual payments to the IRS.

This becomes a major issue if one of the collaborators fails to or is unable to do what she agreed to do to produce the book. It could be cause for the publisher to cancel the contract. The only thing I can suggest in this case is that all the authors named in the contract have all their material in place from day one so that any question of failure is not based on lack of content. If the person in default was the one who agreed to do the writing, another person with equal writing skills must be brought in. The number of issues that can come up in this area are many, far too many to address in this short chapter. But this is an issue that does come up from time to time, and I urge you and the others with whom you write a book to agree on individual bailout plans before a word is written.

♦ Who owns the copyright?

When two or more people write a book, the work is seen as a joint work and all authors are considered joint copyright owners. This is pretty straightforward, but the collaborating authors must agree to how each author is permitted to make use of the material covered by the copyright. It's not as easy as it might seem to come to terms on these issues because the use of the copyright usually involves money—and you know what that can lead to. Whole books have been written on this subject, so anything more than a warning is not really possible at this point.

♦ What about expenses?

Money causes problems in most relationships, including co-authorship. In addition to deciding how the expenses should be shared, you might want to think about how they will be paid. I have known a few authors who have set up checking accounts together just for the payments. When the account runs low, each contributes the same amount to bring the balance back to some predetermined working level. One author usually keeps the checkbook and does the paying but keeps the others informed of all the transactions.

◆ Who handles the promotional responsibilities?

In most cases, co-authors are booked together for radio, TV, and personal appearances. If there is any reason why one and not another should be booked, decide and make sure that your editor passes this information along to the publisher's publicist.

Writing Your Own Collaboration Agreement

I strongly urge you to create a collaboration agreement before you do anything else. Whether you are best friends or just meeting for the first time, it's important that all agree on one another's responsibilities and rights, such as the copyright ownership, the division of money, and even whose name is first on the title page. If there is a lot at stake, get help from a lawyer, but be sure that he specializes in publishing law. Most agents, however, can help you with this as part of the service they provide with their representation.

Backspace

You can write your own collaboration agreement, but be sure that whatever you put on paper is witnessed by a person who is not part of the agreement. Also be sure that you have all signatures notarized.

You can find an excellent collaboration agreement in Jonathan Kirsch's must-have publishing law book. It's a trade paperback, so not to worry about what you may know about the price of leather-bound law books. The title is *Kirsch's Handbook of Publishing Law for Authors, Publishers, Editors, and Agents*, and the most recent edition is available from the publisher, Silman-James Press, as well as from Amazon, Barnes & Noble, and just about any online bookseller.

Writing as a Team

If you have discussed the previous questions and are comfortable with your answers and the answers given by your co-author(s), your next hurdle is the actual writing process. It's difficult enough for one person to write a book for the first time, but it gets even more difficult when two or more people collaborate.

I have met very few people who actually write together. That is, by actually meeting and putting words on paper or in a computer face to face. Most of the productive collaborations I have seen and been involved with are the result of one person being made responsible for the actual writing and the others providing the back-up help, such as research. Watching two or more people sitting in a room and trying to string words together is like watching a bunch of people trying to put together an order to phone in to a take-out restaurant, using a menu printed in a language none of them understands.

Whether you actually meet or do it without meeting, style must first be agreed on by all. Your publisher may have a style manual or at least a fairly comprehensive style sheet for authors that will solve many problems right away. If not, be sure that you and your co-authors read and understand Chapters 18 and 19.

You are writing a business book, so I'll assume that you understand how flowcharts work, or you are at least familiar with the basics. Most well-structured collaborations that I have seen usually go very well once all agree to the process. And the best way to ensure agreement is by using the basics of the Management by Objectives process.

There are many good websites devoted to the subject that will bring you up to speed on the process. In a nutshell, however, the system requires each participant to state in writing how he or she will make specific contributions to a common goal. Once all agree on the steps and how they will be accomplished, each signs off on his or her own part and gets to work. It's one of the best of the collaborative general management systems and is particularly well suited for a project like a collaboratively written book. One of the major benefits of Management by Objectives is that because of the prior commitment feature, problems that arise during the writing can usually be resolved a lot more quickly.

 Publishing Tip _____

Management consultants like to say, "What gets measured gets done." This is good advice for two or more people collaborating on a book. If you all agree on what you must produce and measure it regularly, it's easy to lay it on a slacker who may be holding you back.

You may not need to meet face to face to write, but you should meet regularly to review what each author has been doing and to judge the overall progress of the book. If you are near enough to each other, set a schedule to meet regularly—and stick to it.

If you are not that close, talk on the phone or use an Internet chat service. If you do have the opportunity to meet face to face, both authors should make notes and checklists of work that needs to be accomplished before the next meeting. If you meet on an Internet chat loop, everything you say to each other can automatically be saved. You will both have identical records of the chat, so there's no room to weasel out of doing what you promised to do because you can't read your notes.

The Least You Need to Know

- More than two people can collaborate on a book.

- You should have a firm written agreement with your collaborators, but you or your agent can create it.

- Management by Objectives techniques can be used to identify potential problems and to solve later problems.

- It's often easier—and even more productive—for two or more people to collaborate by e-mail or phone than face to face.

Part 4

Finding a Publisher and Negotiating a Contract

Even if you work with an agent, you need to understand how the publishing business works. The easiest way to do this is to walk through everything that has to be done to find the right publisher, make a convincing case for your book, and negotiate a contract that works for you and for the publisher. A publisher expects you to bring a lot more to the table than just a good idea and a publishable manuscript.

The chapters in this part guide you through the critical issues of a typical book publisher's contract, and they outline the responsibilities you and your publisher have to each other. I hope you come away from this part with a better understanding of everything a publisher does.

Chapter 14

Business Books Are Different

In This Chapter

- ◆ It's not just content that makes business books different from all other books

- ◆ One factor common to all business books

- ◆ Biographies of businesspeople often sell as well as the better how-to titles

- ◆ Very successful business people continue to read the start-your-own-business books, always hoping for some new ideas

Whether you have found an agent or are planning to go it alone, now is the time to start looking for publishers who might be interested in your book. An agent can really be helpful here, because he or she should know which publishers are making the strongest market in the area in which you are planning to write. If you are going it alone, this chapter will help you pick the appropriate category in which your book fits best, and it will show you how to identify the publishers that should be interested in your book.

Reader expectations are mainly what differentiate business books from other books. If you want a time-killing book on your next flight, you'll probably read a thriller, a romance novel, or maybe something a little more enlightening. If you want to learn how to write and publish a business book, you are already reading a how-to book on the subject.

Where, then, do those memoirs written by business leaders fall? And how about the relatively new genre in which authors talk about their personal enlightenment through business experiences? And, of course, there are books that are read for specific enlightenment, such as how to do something that will get you promoted, add untold riches to your checkbook, or even make you a better account executive for having followed the author's suggestions.

Simply put, some of the books you see in the business section of the bookstore would not have been there a few short years ago. Now, however, right next to *Principles of Marketing* you just might find *Zen and the Art of Micromanagement.* It has become a lot more difficult to describe a business book in just one or two sentences.

Books not written specifically for business readers have become strong sellers in other bookstore sections. And some books you would never have guessed would appeal to business readers have had good runs on the business section shelves. Much of this cross-selling is usually serendipitous, so it's best for our purposes to stick to the narrower definition of a business book as one that is written mainly for businesspeople. Note the weasel word "mainly." If the book you are writing just might have some potential for cross-selling, be sure to discuss this possibility with your agent and editor to see just how much attention you should pay to the elements that might help it sell on other shelves.

What follows are general descriptions of and comments on the most widely read categories of business books. Your book may cover more than one category, and you may have even dreamed up a category that I haven't thought of. But keep in mind that all business books, whether specifically written as how-to books or as biographies of famous business leaders, have one common appeal: readers hope to learn something from reading them. Why read a biography of a famous banker whose life may have really been quite dull when you could have read an exciting biography of the first man to climb Mount Everest? You want to learn what the banker did to become successful so that you might try it yourself, that's why. So regardless of the category, keep in mind that your reader wants to learn something.

Leadership Books

The simplest definition of a leader is one who has followers. This, however, does considerable disservice to real leaders as well as the category of books on business leadership. After all, someone has to be in charge. Whether that person leads by force of personality or by encouraging those who follow to exceed themselves in whatever they contribute to the activity, leaders are necessary.

This means that a more comprehensive notion of leadership is called for, and that seems to be embodied in the latest buzz phrase: thought leadership. There is more to this notion than just another way to sell books or run businesses. If you are paying attention to the current crop of leadership books that draw their strength from popular and famous figures, you will have seen that whether they were generals, philosophers, or executives, those whose ideas have been applied to business are also considered to be thinkers. Only a fool leads troops into battle without a well-thought-out plan. And any CEO who embarks on a major market development effort without a thoughtful plan is also a fool.

Alan Axelrod, author of many of the current best-sellers on leadership, told me, "I work from a very simple premise: it is good to learn from the best. I look at history's most successful, most innovative, most inspirational, most productive leaders, and I try to distill from their lives and careers the lessons of their approach to leadership. History is a vast treasury of ideas—of free ideas. I charge for the service of gathering them, sorting through them, finding the most useful, and presenting them clearly in a book."

You may have read some of Dr. Axelrod's books. They include *Patton on Leadership* (Prentice Hall), *Revolutionary Management: John Adams on Leadership* (The Lyons Press), and *Winston Churchill, CEO* (Sterling). He has written more than 80 books.

Career Planning and Management Books

This is a major category for most business and general book publishers. The category includes a wide range of subjects, and most publishers are generally quite receptive to good ideas in this field. Books on job searches, writing resumés, writing cover letters, and handling job interviews are generally the most popular. There are quite a few books that try to cover all these subjects between one set of covers, and some of them have been perennial best-sellers that have made their authors quite wealthy. There are publishers that specialize in the subject, but most general trade book publishers have at least a few titles and some have extensive lists that cover all aspects of the field.

Most career-related books are written for readers who are seeking help in planning and managing their careers. Some publishers do books for career planning specialists, including psychologists, guidance counselors, and others who work in the personnel management and human resources areas.

This is a good category for writers with a background in business-related human resource management and college career counseling who have developed systems for career planning and development with proven results. It's especially helpful to be able to illustrate points with actual case histories.

Writing a book for those seeking career guidance and those offering it requires the writer to have good subject-related credentials. The general media has a healthy appetite for writers on this subject, and with the right credentials and an unusual angle, you could find yourself on a major TV show. You can be especially appealing to media bookers if you have already had some media exposure and have some relationships that can be exploited.

It's not easy to convince an editor that your career planning system is the be-all and end-all of the field. An editor who has done books in this field has probably seen it all. Your proposal has to be laced with solid examples of how your approach works and has worked for others.

Publishing Tip

You should be able to write reasonably well, mainly because readers look not only for the quality of your ideas, but for the conviction with which you present them. A great idea with middling writing is about as welcome to an editor as a terrible idea that is presented in sparkling prose.

If you do have the great idea but are shaky about your ability to write about it, there are a number of good professional writers and ghostwriters who can help.

One of the nice things about books on careers is that if they sell well initially, their publishers tend to keep them in print, often publishing revised editions every few years. Be sure that you or your agent looks carefully at the language in your contract that covers revisions and updates. I talk about it in Chapter 17.

Sales and Sales Management Books

Every successful salesperson has a secret technique! This is another hot category, and general trade publishers as well as those whose interest is only business are always on the lookout for their next sales star title.

There's one thing that makes this a tough category to crack, however, and that is that not every technique works in every field—despite what the authors claim. This usually means that the broad category of sales, which is large, becomes fractured into smaller categories. And the smaller the market, the less likely a publisher is to make a good offer or even a poor offer. A book on sales lead follow-up would appeal to just about every salesperson, but a book on sales lead follow-up in the pharmaceutical field has a very limited appeal. Your proposal should be laced with real and well-documented examples of what your system can do and information on the size of the specific market it applies to.

Publishing Tip

Recent management trends stress that everyone in the company should sell. Not that an accountant's job depends on her bringing in sales, but when an opportunity presents itself, the accountant and any other staff person should make an effort. Books on selling for non–sales people are generally good sellers if the ideas are good and specific case histories are presented.

Up the ladder a bit, but in the same general area, are books on sales management. The same problem exists here, but it's not quite as rigid a qualifier. Managing a force of people selling valves is not that different from managing a sales team selling just about any other industrial product. Specific product knowledge can be picked up on the job. If you have managed a sales team selling valves, you can manage another team selling just about anything in the fluid control field. But let me assure you that if you have a book on how to sell only valves, you are not likely to find a publisher who will be interested, unless it is the publishing division of a valve trade association.

Books About Marketing

I could have included this with sales, but there are enough books published under this heading to consider them separately. In very broad strokes, sales is a tool of marketing, and marketing is most usually defined as discovering customer needs, figuring out how to satisfy those needs, and then either producing products to satisfy the needs or maximizing the benefits of the products you already have to satisfy those needs. Salespeople carry out the plans of marketing people.

Books on marketing range from high level, laced with quantitative exercises, to low level, which focus on the everyday issues of just about any business of any size. Most deal with some aspect of marketing planning and implementation. As you might imagine, the audience for marketing books is smaller than that for sales books. And the number of publishers who publish books in the field is correspondingly smaller.

> **Quote/Unquote** _____
>
> "Marketing is not only much broader than selling, it is not a specified activity at all. It encompasses the entire business. It is the whole business seen from the point of view of the final result, that is, from the customer's point of view. Concern and responsibility for marketing must therefore permeate all areas of the enterprise."
>
> —Peter Drucker

Few general trade publishers who do business books will have many titles in print on marketing. And those that they do have tend to fall more into the area of reference titles. There are a number of marketing handbooks in print, and the ones that succeed early on are usually revised regularly and kept in print for a long time.

All this having been said, there have been some notable successes in the field of marketing, but they tend to be gimmick-oriented. I dislike using that word, because many of the books I'm thinking of are excellent. If you want to write a book about marketing, I'd suggest that you read or least become very familiar with the books that have been published in the last few years. If you can show that your idea builds on the strengths of those books that have been successful in the past, you could have a good case.

Advertising and Public Relations

Books about advertising tend to focus on specific advertising functions such as copywriting, graphics and design, and the creative management processes. There are books on the management of advertising and how-to books on subjects such as how to make money in freelance advertising or starting and running your own advertising agency. All of this generally points to smaller markets in which larger publishers seldom have a big interest. There are the exceptions, of course, but if this is your field and you want to write a book for those in the field, be sure that you can convince a publisher that there is a large enough market to warrant the publication of a book.

> **Quote/Unquote** _____
>
> "I have always believed that writing advertisements is the second most profitable form of writing. The first, of course, is ransom notes"
>
> —Philip Dusenberry

Books on public relations shake out pretty much the same way as books on advertising. Public relations is a tool that can be used by local retailers as well as international corporate giants. One book seldom fits all, and the segmentation of the market usually makes it difficult to get a publisher interested in a book on the subject. Again, if you have a good idea and can convince a publisher that there is a market, go for it.

Books on Entrepreneurship

This is wide-open territory, and there is hardly a general trade publisher or specialized business publisher that doesn't have a presence in this field. Books published in this category tend to focus either on specific businesses or on entrepreneurship in general. "How to start and run a pet shop" as well as "how to be the entrepreneur you always wanted to be" anchor the ends of the range in this field.

It's a strong field for most publishers, both those that specialize in business books and those that publish in other fields as well. There is hardly a person in someone else's employ who doesn't fantasize about being his own boss at one time or another. In case you ever wondered why you see start-your-own-business books in bookstores at vacation destinations, it's because that's when the fantasy usually peaks. Who wants to go back to the office when you could run a guesthouse on Nantucket? Smart publishers beef up their list of these titles for their spring and summer lists and cut back for the fall and winter lists.

Books that do better than most are usually written by people who have done it themselves and who can tell enlightening as well as entertaining stories about how they did it.

The general category of self-employment and entrepreneurship is pretty much a year-round category for reference-type books in the field. Years ago I wrote a book for Prentice Hall about 100 businesses that could be started and run with less than $100. It seemed to sell well in all seasons. It was more of a reference book than an inspirational how-to. It could be done on $100 back when that book was published!

As I write this, the markets have tanked, banks and automobile manufacturers are being bailed out. Unless my experience in previous nasty economic times fails me, books on self-employment and entrepreneurship will be a good category in all seasons for quite a while to come.

Publishing Tip

If there's one thing that makes books on starting and running your own business sell well, it's well-told case histories. There is a strong fantasy content to this category, but the best and most successful of the genre tell stories well and deliver on the facts and figures.

Books on Consulting and Starting a Consulting Business

This is a subspecies of entrepreneurship book, but it deserves separate attention. Most people with executive jobs who think about going it alone don't think about running a gift shop. They dream about using what they know from years of training and experience to consult with those who can benefit from their knowledge. Some pretty big consulting firms were started as a one-person shop by some of these people. And more than a few make a better than average living as solo consultants in fields where they once toiled as someone else's employees.

The books on this subject done by general trade publishers tend to be how-to books and insist on well-told case histories that support the author's perspective, without pitching the author in some ghastly brag-and-boast mode. It's an excellent category if you have the right idea and the credentials to do the book. Because these books need to maintain a steady upbeat tone and a style of controlled enthusiasm, manuscripts are often heavily edited or silent collaborators are used to do the job.

Quote/Unquote

"It has been said that a consultant is one who borrows your watch to tell you what time it is."

I have been unable to trace the source of this quote, so I apologize in advance to the person who coined this phrase. It could also be said that a consultant is a person who borrowed your book on how to be a consultant and now tells you how to run your business.

There are many good examples of books in this category that continue to sell well year after year. If you are researching books in the field, check for the original copyright and look through those books that have been in print for a long time and have gone through more than a few printings and revisions.

Books on Personal Finance, Investment, and Retirement Planning

Books on how to make money by investing and how to save for retirement are perennial favorites. This is an excellent category, but publishers usually demand that the authors they sign up for books be able to promote their books very aggressively. Usually the authors need to have strong connections that will help with the promotional effort. The TV and radio shows that thrive on guest interviews love well-connected writers in this field. This means, conversely, that if you don't have the connections, you will have a tough time finding a publisher—even if you write well and have really discovered the keys to the investment money chest.

Quite a few of the books published in this area are dreamed up by the publishers themselves, for authors they currently publish who have made their marks on radio and TV. They are usually variations on the themes of the authors' earlier books and the promotion of the new title depends heavily on what has resulted from the author's earlier efforts. If you can get going and known in this category, you can keep pretty busy with new books and revisions of your earlier books.

Retirement books are perennial favorites. Again, you need what publishers call a "platform": connections to media or organizations that will aggressively help you promote your book. There's hardly a general trade publisher that doesn't have at least a toe in this big pool. There are some organizations other than book publishers that publish extensively in this field, too. So don't limit your search for publication just to the usual suspects. With the right idea for a book on annuities, you just might interest one of the annuity investment firms in taking on the project in order to promote their wares or to give away to existing customers.

Speaking, Writing, and Other Communications Skills

You are reading a how-to book on writing and publishing a business book. It has a narrow focus, but there is a significant audience for it, mainly because it's well known that careers can be made and promotions gained with the publication of just one successful book. However, careers can be made and promotions can be gained by writing far fewer than the 120,000 words my publishers asked for in this book. Books abound on memo and general business writing, whether they are how-to books or collections of actual letters and memos that can be copied or adapted for all occasions. There are books on how to write articles for business magazines and websites. What has always amazed me is that the books on public speaking did so well long before any form of inexpensive reproduction of the human voice existed. But thrive they did. Now there are CDs and tapes—believe it or not, they are still used—to instruct in the art of public speaking, and their sales can be quite good. Again, however, to be of interest to a publisher, the author should have connections with some network or organization that can help boost sales. And the author should have the voice of authority to pull it off in the audio accompaniments.

Probably more popular than books on how to give speeches are books on how to write them. It's not a huge market, but most of the successful books in this area are collections of compiled speeches that can be used or adapted for many different occasions or books of quotations related to specific areas that buyers can apply to their own speeches.

Until the Internet arrived, books with collections of memos and lines to use to construct your own memos were very popular. They still are, but they have been somewhat overshadowed by books on how to be even briefer in e-mail messages.

Attaining Personal Success

The business book slice of the general category of personal self-improvement usually draws on tested concepts that focus on specific business situations. Some of the books in this category are actually quite good and very helpful. However, because this is an evergreen market, every year sees dozens of new entries in the field that come and go very quickly.

This is a very competitive market, so be sure you have a good new idea or a clever twist on a tried and true one. Also, it is very difficult to get an editor's attention if you don't have some fairly significant media connections. Testimonials from names readers might recognize can help you make a publisher take notice.

Publishing Tip

One way to get a publisher's eye is to write articles for business magazines that cover the field in which you work. Most book editors scout these magazines looking for authors who have ideas and who seem to be promotable. You may hear from an editor before you even think about writing a book.

If you are on the seminar or sales-meeting circuit doing self-improvement or motivational programs, publishers get interested. These programs are often well attended by people who usually buy books and other self-improvement material. It's often possible to place an order for your book before the publisher prints the book and get a price that is even lower than it might if you got the author or bookseller discount.

Corporate History

There are a number of professional writers who specialize in this area, and there are a few small companies that focus on documenting corporate histories, from researching and writing to illustrating and printing. It's a field of business writing where you will compete with people who write professionally.

However, if you work for a company that has an interesting history and you have the research and writing skills, a word in the ear of the CEO just might land you the job of writing the company's history.

If you are able to land the assignment from your boss and the company has a history that would be of significant interest to people other than past and present employees, think about discussing the project with a traditional book publisher. In addition to producing an edition just for the corporate sponsor, such a publisher might be able to find an audience for the book with general readers as well.

Susan Shelly is the author, co-author, and collaborator of many books, in fields as diverse as health, personal finance, business, and corporate history. She has worked on books detailing the histories of companies like Aramark and Vanity Fair Corporation. And she has written for smaller organizations as well. I asked her about her corporate history writing and she shared these comments with me.

> "Spending time in corporate America is a nice change of pace for someone who primarily works from a home office, but even more fun is the experience of being part of a team that actually produces corporate histories from scratch.
>
> "Recently I was asked to write the history of a prominent drug and alcohol rehab facility located near my home in Pennsylvania. But the facility was looking for a finished product—not just a manuscript. To that end, I teamed up with friends Ted Niemczyk and Tracy Hoffmann, who own a graphic design/web design firm near my home and who possess the capabilities to design and lay out a book. We founded Company Heritage Books (www.companyheritagebooks.com) and produced from scratch a coffee table–style book telling the story of the facility. The book was well received. As a result of that book, we were chosen to produce a fiftieth anniversary book for an area university and now are working on several other projects."

What is especially interesting about Susan's experience is the way one thing led to another.

Business History and Businesspeople

This is a popular category, and with the right idea you may even have a few publishers bidding for your book. However, in that case, you probably have some very good and impressive credentials. So don't set out to write the history of American banking unless you really know what you are talking about and are a really an excellent writer.

Well-written business histories that have a wide appeal and some drama are always of interest to general publishers. A history of the Great Depression of 1929 should not be attempted; there are too many in print, and most of them were written by authors whose skills and reputation would probably overshadow your work. However, a story of the Depression told from the perspective of one of the major figures of the times, shedding a different light on common perceptions, would surely get a careful read from most editors.

If this approach interests you, pick a topic and research it, looking for a figure who is either tragic or heroic, and write your book about or from the perspective of that person. This, of course, is only one way to look at business history. Look for elements in the history of the subject you have chosen that challenge conventional wisdom, and be sure that your book has a point and a point of view.

You are less likely to be turned down for lack of a "platform" with a book like this than you are for any of the other business categories. But you will have to convince the publisher that you can maintain high writing standards throughout. And, as with any other book proposal, you will have to be able to prove that there's a substantial market for the book you propose.

You might even get started by looking at the titles and subjects that a few of the publishers you are considering have already published. A publisher with more than a few titles on business in Silicon Valley would be more interested in your idea for a book about the guy who "really" invented the Internet than some others might.

Biography is a popular publishing category. Find a good story, prove you can write it well, and do solid research, and you could be on your way a lot more quickly than if you tried to compete in the more popular categories. However, don't try to do a biography of a really famous businessperson, even if a biography has not yet been written. Get some experience and credentials first. Find a very interesting person who has made headlines but has yet to have a book written about her.

Business Reference Books

Business reference books are an interesting category. It may seem boring to write or compile a book of quotations or encyclopedic references (a term book people use to describe books that continue to sell well long after their initial publication), but good reference books can become very strong backlist sellers, books that publishers keep in print forever and that continue to earn royalties. Business references run the gamut from pop stuff, like quotes for all occasions, to serious reference books that are used in just about all business areas.

There are publishers that do nothing but reference titles, and just about all general publishers have lines of reference books or at least a few reference titles that are in their catalogs year after year.

Some reference books require regular updating of entries and others are never changed. Some are published in paperback format and others in expensive hardbound editions. If there is a reference needed in your field, think about doing the book. The absence may be because there is too small a market or because someone just never thought of it. Check it out.

Other Types of Business Books

The books described in the previous pages are the more popular types of business books, the books that first-time authors are most likely to consider writing. Here are some other categories that you might want to consider.

♦ Economics books

Books on economics are more likely to be written for professionals or students. However, every so often some economist with the skill to pull it off writes a book on economics for the rest of us. Some are funny, some are serious. If you have the knowledge, the skill, and the right idea, talk with your agent about it.

Tom Gorman's *Complete Idiot's Guide to Economics*, published in 2003, has had three printings in the five years it has been in print. Check the copyright pages of other economics books and you will probably see the same story—steady sales, additional printings, and occasional revisions. It has been said the one book that has outsold all books in other categories has been *Economics*, a college textbook by Paul Samuelson. Many have tried to cut into his pie, and some may have come close, but he still reigns as the king.

♦ Books for business students

This is a huge field, considering that business is taught at community colleges, at state and private colleges and universities, and by most of the many universities that offer M.B.A. and doctoral-level degrees in business.

In addition to publishing the textbooks themselves, there are many opportunities to publish ancillary books. I can personally attest to the strength of this market. An ancillary text on marketing that I wrote for McGraw-Hill continued to pay me significant royalties for more than 20 years.

- Books on business ethics

  This is a relatively new category and I can't report on the strength of sales of the titles in the field. My guess is that there are enough sales to keep the books in print, but I don't think you will get rich writing on this subject.

- Books on global business

  This is a growing category of books, but unless you have an idea that will work for a rather large audience, it can be a difficult market to crack with the larger publishers. There are, however, smaller publishers, both in the United States and abroad, that specialize in books on this subject. An agent should be able to locate good contacts for you.

The Least You Need to Know

- No matter how high people rise in business, most continue to read books on working for themselves.

- There are many different types of business books, but all, including biographies and even company histories, either directly state or subtly imply some kind of business "secret."

- Each type of book requires a different writing style.

- Your topic may not interest a big publisher because of a limited market, but there are enough smaller publishers serving limited markets that if you have a good idea and can do the book (with or without help), you will probably find a publisher.

Business Book Publishing 101

In This Chapter

- Publishers need you as much as you need them
- Good publishers will nurture new authors who have potential
- The publishing process can be frustratingly slow, but it's a careful and deliberate process
- Most business book advertising is a waste of money

As you learned in the previous chapter, popular business books are published by general book publishers that publish in a wide variety of categories. However, some publishers' claim to fame is a narrow focus on business books. Recently, some of these specialized business book publishers announced that they were entering the general market with books that ranged from popular health to history and politics. This could mean that business book publishing is weakening or it could mean that publishers see opportunities in other fields. However you look at it, the number of new titles in the business book category every year is always impressive, as the following numbers show.

2005: 7,885

2006: 9,006

2007: 7,651

You can read just about anything in these numbers, but doing so won't tell you much. However, it's probably safe to assume that this is simply diversification and market forces at work. This chapter details what a good publisher should bring to the table. The next chapter details what a publisher will look for when it considers publishing your book.

One of your agent's jobs is to know what is going on internally at various publishing houses. For instance, how many books on a particular subject a publishing house has in the pipeline or where the editor who would be a good fit for you is transferring to.

Partnering with Your Publisher

Getting your book published is not a one-sided proposition. The simplest way to look at this is that you and the publisher are entering a partnership. You want the best partner (to handle editing, publicity, and sales) as much as the publisher wants the best partner when it accepts your proposal (your idea and writing talents).

Whether your publisher is a general publisher or a specialized business publisher, the process of acquiring and publishing a book is pretty much the same from house to house. The difference between publishers is generally accounted for by the skills of the individuals with whom you work, the emphasis your publisher puts on business books, and your type of book in particular.

It's tempting to think that a publisher that does nothing but business books might be better for your book than a general publisher that does business books along with other categories. This could be true, but it is not necessarily the best way to go.

The publisher who does nothing but business books might have far too many books on your subject in print and could be trying to strengthen its presence in another area. When marketing is hot, for example, books on finance might get shortchanged. It's not difficult to get a sense of this problem by just looking at your category in a publisher's catalog. If you know your field well, you will see quickly when a publisher is slicing a category thinner and thinner. And, of course, most agents should be able to give you some insight beyond that which you find between the covers of the catalog.

Publishing Tip _____

Most publishers prefer to have an agent in place when negotiating a contract with an author. If you have pitched your book yourself, and an editor has shown interest, she might suggest that you find an agent before proceeding.

Editors seldom suggest the name of just one agent. Rather, they will give you a list of agents and tell you to interview them all and make your own choice. Some will suggest that you contact AAR, the Association of Author's Representatives, for its list of members. There is no collusion here.

Many of the items in the typical book contract favor the publisher—however, most are negotiable to one extent or another. Agents know what to look for and how far they can push with each publisher. No publisher is going to point out where they have wiggle room, though very few will actually cheat you. Agents keep everyone happy and honest, plus a lot more.

If you have an idea of the kind of advances a particular publisher has been paying for books in your category and the advance offered you is especially low, this might mean that your book is not high on the publisher's list of priorities. Obviously, a higher than normal advance offer sends quite the opposite message. Again, here is where a good agent can help. He or she should know what is happening within the house and be able to advise you appropriately.

Types of Publishers

More than a few good university presses also produce excellent lines of general books, which often include the more practical type of business books that you might be considering. The bigger university presses can often be as competitive when bidding for books they want as some of the better commercial houses.

There are excellent reference publishers whose titles are sold at the trade level. They might consider your manuscript if it meets their criteria. If your book is one that has a small audience, it may be worth self-publishing or working with one of the subsidized presses. The better of these presses usually make good efforts to place their books with the outlets that cater to readers of books on the subject you write about.

All of this might lead you to think of writing your proposal to appeal to all. After all, if it could sell in the reference market as well as in the general trade and even academic market, it might seem to make sense to cover all the bases. This is not the way to go. As I have already mentioned, book proposals should be tightly targeted.

Publishing Tip _____

A quick way to see who is publishing what is to head to Amazon.com, open your category, and scroll through the titles already in print in your field. But stop at each title, click on the copyright page of each, and make a note of the publishers' names. Most will probably be familiar, but when you spot something unexpected, check out the publishing house on the Internet. You may be surprised.

Quite a few of the better-known general trade publishers also have scholarly imprints that might be appropriate for your book. W. W. Norton and St. Martin's Press are excellent examples of presses with interests in diverse fields. Why not? If the scholarly houses like Columbia University Press and Oxford University Press can do trade books, why can't others do scholarly books? They can and they do some very fine books. The point? Keep your options open—wide open!

There are far more options than you might have thought of if you have not had any contact with the publishing world.

Now, let's follow a proposal from acquisition to publication and see just what a publisher does to turn your idea into a book and to sell the book it publishes.

The Acquisitions Process

Whether you or your agent submitted a proposal to a publisher, or a publisher contacted you about a book idea an editor had, the first person you will more than likely meet is an acquisitions editor. In some publishing companies, this person might be called a sponsoring editor or possibly a commissioning editor. In larger houses you will find editors working within limited specialties, such as business. Really large houses might have editors whose specialties are within an even narrower scope, such as marketing and sales. Acquisitions editors in smaller houses have a much broader reach.

If there's one group of people I admire in book publishing, it's acquisitions editors. To be successful, they must have clear strategic vision, not just the ability to judge good writing from bad. They must be able to build on the existing successes of the house they work for and still be able to break new ground. They must be able to "do the numbers," explain them clearly to agents and authors, and yet still keep a sharp eye on their employers' bottom line.

They must have extensive relationships with many sources outside the house, such as agents, distributors, bookseller chains, and the companies and organizations from which their next best-selling author might emerge. And, on the inside, they are the consummate consensus builders. It's their job to go to bat with sales, marketing, production, publicity, and finance people to turn your proposal into a contract. They are usually the people you or your agent will negotiate with if the decision is made to make you an offer. So when an editor doesn't return your call as quickly as you think it should be returned, have a little patience!

On average, most acquisitions editors buy between 15 and 20 books a year. The books they buy are from authors they already know and work with and authors they don't know yet but might like to work with. They do this while managing the internal affairs of the 20 books they bought the previous year, which are in various stages of delivery. It's not an easy job, but I have met a few who so love their work that they have declined promotion offers to management-type jobs.

The acquisitions process itself varies widely from publisher to publisher. In most cases it involves regularly scheduled meetings with all or most of the people who might be involved with the book if it were acquired. This can include marketing and sales, publicity, production, legal, art, accounting, and, of course, other editors. Your proposal will have been circulated for everyone to read before the meeting. If the editor presenting your proposal is especially interested in making a case for your book, he might invite you or your agent to make a brief presentation at the meeting. If everyone has done their homework and all questions have been answered to everyone's satisfaction, decisions are made there and then. If there are missing numbers or some expressed doubts, the proposal might be tabled until the next meeting, when the sponsoring editor would be expected to resolve the issues.

Acquiring a book is a rigorous and thorough process mainly because everyone has an interest at stake. If the editor signs up too many books that do not earn out their advances, or if marketing and sales fail to get the attention the book deserves from their key accounts, or if production forgets to include the cost of paper in their estimate, jobs can be in jeopardy. And your book may impress everyone, but the budget for the projected release date could be strained and your proposal can be passed over.

> **Backspace**
>
> The acquisition process can be frustratingly slow. Just to have been presented at an editorial meeting means that your proposal has more going for it than the hundreds (yes, hundreds!) of others that arrived the same week. Don't push. It is a buyer's market.

This may be more detail than you wanted to hear. But the more you know about what happens, the more you will realize just what a group of people went through to get your book accepted. And if your proposal didn't fly, you should know that it wasn't for a lack of trying.

The Developmental Process

Once a book is bought, it is usually scheduled at the acquisitions meeting for a specific seasonal list. Most new authors are given a year to submit a final manuscript. Depending on the confidence the editor has in the author's ability to write, the book may be scheduled for delivery in smaller and more frequent submissions. Experienced authors are usually expected to submit their material in two stages.

With a year to write, the publisher then usually needs another six months to complete all the final editing, production, and printing and binding processes. This means that you probably won't see your finished book for at least a year and a half after you sign the contract.

After you sign the contract, it will probably take at least a month or two for your first advance payment to arrive. No one is holding the money in a secret high-interest Swiss bank account, so don't wait for the money to arrive before you start writing. You have a firm delivery date and your contract probably has a clause that invokes some pretty nasty penalties for late delivery. Keep in mind that while you are writing in real time, the publisher is investing money in materials, time, promotion, and sales efforts well ahead of the completion of your manuscript. Miss a press date and the cost to print your book could go out of sight. You don't want to know what happens then! Payments, unless arranged otherwise, are usually made upon acceptance of half the manuscript and upon submission of all of the material.

The editor who sponsored your book will remain your contact editor throughout the developmental process, but you will be meeting and working with others along the way. The first editor you will probably hear from is a manuscript editor. This editor's responsibility is for style and clarity.

The next person will usually be called a copy editor. A copy editor's scope and responsibility will vary from house to house, but in most cases you will get comments in the form of questions and you will be expected to respond with changes yourself. You may get a short revision or rewrite from a copy editor, but the change usually will be accompanied by an "Okay?" from the editor.

You may also hear from a line editor. This editor's job is to read your material for clarity as well as to fine-tune the pitch and rhythm of your material. Line editors are not fact-checkers, but when they spot something that seems questionable, they will usually query you. Don't assume that because a line editor asked about a few points that he or she is doing all your fact-checking. That is your responsibility.

Backspace

A publisher's editor is not going to hold your hand as you write. You will get general comments and instructions up front and you will be expected to take them seriously as you write. Don't turn your relationship with an editor into long discussions on style and craft. If, by the time you have delivered half your material, you haven't heeded your editor's comments and suggestions, you could find yourself in trouble. Your contract calls for the delivery of "acceptable" material. That word is defined by the instructions you were given initially, so pay attention.

If you need more than copy editing, you may hear from a developmental editor. These editors take a broad look at the way written material works. Their comments are directed more at simplifying complex material, organizing material for structure, maintaining a logical narrative flow, and eliminating material that adds nothing to the text. Most of their comments will be in the form of longer, more searching notes to you. A developmental editor may rewrite and revise some of your material as a means of showing you what is expected, but don't expect a developmental editor to rewrite all your material.

It's not likely, but you might hear from a managing editor who has questions about the scheduling of your material. You might even hear from an indexer. But that's about it.

The Acceptance Process

Then, when all the various editors have had a chance to review your manuscript, you should see your marked-up manuscript for your final approval before it goes to type. It's probably rare today, but you might actually get this on "real" paper with editors' notes on the sheets and on attached paper flags. However, it's much more likely that you will get your manuscript back via e-mail with all comments done electronically, but fully visible on your computer screen. You can't imagine how much better this is than the old paper system. In fact, I am writing this paragraph as I review all my editors' comments. Ginny Munroe, one of the best development editors I have met in a long time, called my attention to this missing material. It takes a pro to keep a pro on track—thanks, Ginny!

Your contract will probably state that your advance payments are due upon the acceptance of your material, not upon its delivery. If you have been delivering satisfactory material all along, you should have received the progress payments stipulated in your contract. And unless you dropped the ball before the goal line, final acceptance should follow almost as quickly as the earlier advances.

> **Backspace**
>
> By the time you finish your manuscript, you'll probably have an idea for your next book that you're dying to lay on your editor. Do it, but be aware that unless you are a big name, your editor probably won't make a commitment until she knows how well the book you just wrote sells. You can, however, ask for a "placeholder," informally committing the editor to giving you first crack at the idea in the event someone else submits a proposal similar to yours. I have never asked for any signed agreements on these and have never had a publisher renege on the verbal commitment. You may be less trusting than I!

Upon acceptance by the publisher, your manuscript is turned over to design and manufacturing people who are responsible for turning your manuscript into printed books. You may never have any contact with the people who do this work, but you will be hearing from sales, marketing, promotion, and publicity folks.

The Marketing, Advertising, Promotion, Publicity, and Selling Processes

Here again we run into words that mean different things to different publishers. As you must know by now, the term *editor* means whatever an editor or his or her employer wants it to mean. You will find the same thing happening when publishers talk about how they sell the books they publish. But however they use the terms, they all sell books pretty much the same way.

Before I get into the details of all this, it's important for you to know that long before you have finished writing your book, the publisher has already begun to crank up the selling machine. As long as you meet your halfway mark with acceptable material and appear to be on course for an on-time delivery, the publisher will probably start writing catalog copy for your book and may even have some preliminary meetings with its sales force for feedback that can be used in the campaign.

This is a rollout process that allows for some slippage. However, if you don't deliver on time or deliver an unusable manuscript, all hell will break loose. If the publisher has to take your book off its scheduled list, not only will all enthusiasm for your book evaporate, but it could mean anything from outright cancellation of your contract to moving your book well into the future, where it will certainly not be treated with the respect it might have had earlier.

If I seem harsh, I mean to be. On the few occasions when clients of mine dropped the ball, it was my responsibility as their agent to make things work. In some cases, clients had to hire, at their own expense, editors or writers to do quickly that which they had failed to do. In others, where contracts were cancelled, I had to resolve contractual and financial issues that the authors never thought would hit them. Whatever happened, it was ugly. So, please, meet your deadlines!

Now, let's take a trip down the hall to see the sales and marketing people. Let's drop in on the marketing manager first.

Marketing

Most publishers organize all their sales, publicity, and promotional activities under the umbrella of a marketing department. As well as overseeing these activities, marketing people are usually responsible for the research and planning that is needed to make intelligent forecasts of the future. You may find marketing people working very closely with editors to determine where their company's best efforts should be centered. You may even find some larger companies doing some market research or contracting with outside companies to do it for them.

In years past, before marketing assumed the responsibilities it now has, editors acquired books they liked and thought would be important to readers. Upon publication, a sales force took the books to the field and by their efforts made the market for these books. Contemporary publishing is more market-driven, in that a publisher's output is more keyed to a perceived need than the idea of selling what the publisher wanted to publish. There still are heated discussions as to whether a publisher should be market-driven or content-driven. Simply said, should a publisher do books people want or should a publisher be the arbiter of what book buyers should have? I only bring this up because this is a book about business books, and I thought you might like to see that publishing is much the same in many ways as the production and sale of everything from fashion to factory machinery.

Publishing Tip _____

A publisher once told me that the simplest way to talk about marketing in publishing is that rather than wait for a best-seller to be dropped at the doorstep, a company can now take positive steps to make one happen. This does a great disservice to all the great acquisitions editors who proactively sought authors long before the term *marketing* was invented. But it does explain why publishing is not that different from other businesses today—despite how much we may want to protest.

Chances are that you will have little or no contact with people in the marketing department, but you will be in contact with people from each of the departments that report to the marketing department.

Advertising

Depending on how they sell their books, some publishers will have extensive advertising departments; others may have none. Years back I did a number of books with Prentice-Hall that were sold directly through mail-order advertising. Prentice-Hall not only had a huge advertising department that included some of the best copywriters and artists in the business, but also had its own printing plant that did nothing but print the complex mailers used to sell individual titles very successfully through the mail.

That was then. What little actual advertising is done today is done mainly to satisfy an author with enough leverage to get what he wants and to publicize the name of the publisher in the bargain. Advertising, in most cases, just isn't cost-effective in the general book business anymore.

Publishing Tip _____

If you go to some writers' conferences, you may hear speakers urge attendees to hold out for an advertising budget in their contracts. If this is your first book and you aren't a celebrity of some sort, forget about it. You should, however, at least get the publisher to outline the promotional path it has planned for your book. Ask where you might fit in and be able to help, especially with publicity, if you belong to any organizations whose members might be interested in your book.

Most publishers who still do some advertising focus on the media that reach the book-selling people, not the reading public. *Publishers Weekly* and the regional and local book trade journals get the bulk of the publishing ad dollars. Money is sometimes made available to book chains that do their own advertising and promotion.

While using conventional advertising may not get your book sold to the general public, publishers have found that actively promoting your book will ultimately get your book into the reader's hands.

Promotion

Most promotion is aimed at the retail level. If the publisher thinks you have a winner and wants to push things harder, special promotions may be arranged, such as purchasing end caps—those stands promoting a single book that are placed strategically at the ends of bookstore aisles. Shipping boxes that open to form book displays and hold quantities of books are called *dumps* and are most often seen near the store checkout. Window posters, shelf talkers, special bookmarks, the list is endless. But this is where money is best spent on building sales for your book. Magazine and newspaper advertising just doesn't drive enough traffic to a store to buy your book. But money spent to attract those who are already in the store to your book is far more effective.

Publishers will occasionally offer promotional assistance on a cooperative basis to individual bookstores as well as to the large chains. These deals usually involve the store running ads in local publications advertising a special promotion, such as a discount price if the buyer brings in a copy of the ad. Ad costs may be shared or paid for entirely, depending on individual situations. This kind of advertising often does well, but just advertising a book alone in a newspaper or magazine is usually a waste of money.

Other incentives for retailers to stock your book in depth include special quantity discounts, two-for-one offers, and similar techniques. I could describe lots more promotional approaches, but if you visit bookstores, I'm sure you are aware of most of them.

Publishing Tip

Money spent on advertising to build retail traffic is nowhere near as effective as money spent on in-store promotions. The audience has already identified itself as being interested in books. When newspaper ads include coupons and bring-this-ad-discounts, the results can be better.

Publicity

Depending on you, your book, and your targeted audience, money spent on publicity is often the most effective way to promote a book. If you have been around book publishing, you are probably aware of the question every editor asks a potential author whose proposal seems interesting: "Tell me about your platform." The editor wants to know whether you are promotable and if you already have any media connections. The more promotable you are and the better your media connections, the brighter the bulb burns in your editor's head.

Not every author will benefit from an appearance on *Oprah*, just as not every author will benefit from being the subject of a feature story in a magazine whose readers are devoted to porcine husbandry. Your publisher's publicity person, or an outside consultant the publisher may engage for your book, will research and narrowly define the media available for your book and how to best approach getting coverage by that media. This could include radio, TV, magazines, newspapers, and other interview opportunities. Needless to say, a major source of publicity for just about any subject can be found on the Internet, on the special as well as general interest sites.

Once the strategy has been defined, the publicist will begin making media contacts as close as possible to the publication and book availability dates.

Publishing Tip _____

If you need coaching and media training, your publisher may offer it, but unless you have what the publisher sees as an immediate heavy-hitter status, you will probably have to get your own training. There's nothing more disheartening than to see an author with a superb book on a major network show make a mess of an interview.

Not all publicity involves the high energy of TV or even talk radio. Some of the most productive business book publicity I have seen resulted from contacts with print and internet media that was set up by a publisher's publicity people. If enough of the respected columnists in your field get a buzz going, with either brief mentions in their regular columns or with features written specifically for your book, you should be able to count on royalties early and often.

Backspace

Be aware that your publicist may go out to the media with a story that may not seem all that closely related to you or the subject of your book. Trust her! Media pitches must hit at an appealing news angle. Once a contact is made, you will usually have plenty of opportunity to make the points you want to make. Your publicist should coach you in the best ways to handle the segue to your topic.

Keep in mind that publicity exposure is totally in the hands of the media. Any attempt to control placement and timing will probably result in your story being dropped. Do what your publicity person tells you to do and do it when it has to be done.

Book tours are usually reserved for high-profile authors and are usually keyed to book signings at major bookstores and appearances on local media. If you aren't offered a book tour, don't make a fuss—unless you really like taking late-night flights, doing early morning tapings, and spending your evenings in motel rooms of smaller chains located in the outback of the area covered by the media coverage scheduled for you. If you get any speaking engagements, most will probably be within easy travel distance of your home. It really is rare for the author of a typical business book to be offered a tour or book signings. Most of the productive media will be print- and Internet-based.

Book reviews for business books are among the more productive ways to get attention for your book. If your book does well, it will probably be reprinted with quotations from favorable reviews on the dust jacket.

A poor review, however, can kill a book very quickly. Years ago, a book I wrote on how to set up and run a house advertising agency got excellent reviews from quite a few newspapers and business magazines. However, one reviewer missed the point completely and his review was in a key publication. Needless to say, retractions are never printed and the book languished during its initial printing. The book did sell well eventually, but it took time for it to catch on and to overcome the effect of one reviewer's misperception of the goal of the book.

Print publicity usually carries the implied weight of the publication that carries it. Radio, TV, and personal appearances have a short-term effect. While it may make you feel good to appear on a nightly business TV program, the same effort spent on print usually has a more enduring effect.

Sales

Your publisher will include your book in its catalog for the period during which it is launched. These catalogs are for the use of the publisher's sales people and for the distributors and wholesalers who call on the book trade. Most publishers do four catalogs a year.

Some publishers have their own sales force to call on the book trade; others may use independent reps and distributors. Most will work with independent distributors, no matter which method of selling they use, in order to have local supply on hand for the retail booksellers.

General interest business books seldom are carried by small independent bookstores, unless the author is a local or if there is a known interest in a book in the area. So it's a good idea to alert your local bookstore about your book. The store might do a book signing or do other added promotions.

Online booksellers often are able to make significant sales in areas served mainly by small independents. Customers are able to find a wide array of books they can't find locally.

If you are connected with an organization that might be interested in buying a quantity of your book, you can usually arrange with the publisher to give you the booksellers' discount price. And if you can get a firm commitment for a decent quantity before the print date, you should be able to negotiate a pre-publication sale that can be significantly less expensive than even the traditional bookseller price. Publishers usually ask for a deposit up front and ask for a signed purchase order, which binds you to pay when books are printed and delivered. Your agent is probably accustomed to these negotiations, so leave them up to him. A price based on the publisher's cost plus a markup can be significantly less than a cost based on the publisher's retail price less a discount.

The Least You Need to Know

- Business book publishers are as interested in seeing you succeed as you are.

- Don't expect miracles—but they do happen often enough to make this business fun and profitable.

- Your editor may speak softly, but she carries a big stick—listen carefully to what is told to you.

- Publicity and promotion sells business books—the two people you want to know well at your publisher are your editor and the publicity person.

Chapter 16

What a Publisher Expects You to Bring to the Table

In This Chapter

- Why ideas often trump writing ability
- What your "platform" is and why you must have one
- How editors decide whether to trust you or to reject your proposal
- Why an editor may be looking at your second book before you write your first

Anyone who has been in book publishing for more than a few weeks has heard this story, but just in case you haven't, I'll tell it. A first-time author whose proposal has just been turned down manages to get the editor on the phone. In as polite terms as his feelings of disappointment will allow he asks, "But just what are you really looking for?" The editor replies, "I'm looking for authors with new ideas that have sold very well in the past."

As silly as this may sound, it's not all that ridiculous. After all, just what is an idea? An author I work with summed it up nicely, saying, "An idea is my concept of what needs to be said in my book. It's the result of my thinking about a problem in a creative way." He was talking about a book he wanted to write about sales management.

Sales management! If ever there was a subject that has been overexposed, sales management probably is it. Nevertheless, it's an area that is constantly changing and calling for fresh ideas. So something that sold well in the past—how to better manage sales—sells well and fresh ideas will continue to be published. So the editor wasn't really being funny, was he?

This is a long way to get to the point, but the first thing a publisher's acquisitions editor really wants to see is fresh ideas that have sold well in the past. Second, the editor wants to know whether you can carry the load and, third, the editor hopes that you have more than just one book in you. It's every acquisitions editor's dream to discover writers who can write quickly and continue to produce successful books for years to come.

Getting to Know You Personally

Our jumping-off point here is the call you get from an editor or your agent telling you that your proposal has made it past a publisher's preliminary gatekeepers. The editor is responding to some aspect of your proposal and would like to know more about your idea and more about you.

At this point, the editor is probably most interested in confirming what he has seen and likes in your proposal and in getting answers to some questions the proposal has raised. This is usually the easy part. Validate the numbers you cited, confirm the authority of those you might have quoted, and convince the editor that the premise of your proposal will be taken seriously by readers and reviewers. Then comes the screen test!

Publishers today want more than good ideas and good writing; they want authors who can take the show on the road. Good writers and thinkers now have to be good performers as well, or at least they have to be well-connected people. The how, why, and why not of this is still debated endlessly. The fact remains, however, that your book stands a much better chance of being published if you are capable of taking an active part in its promotion than if you aren't or won't.

The celebrity factor is as important in business book publishing as it is in publishing books on pop topics. An interview by a *Wall Street Journal* editor is the business book equivalent of a *Rolling Stone* interview with the author of a book on the rock star du jour.

The first element of your screen test will involve some questions from your agent or editor, and the word *platform* will turn up early in the conversation. Despite our years of exposure to words well written, we in the book trade still fall victim to the tyranny of clichés and idioms. In this case, the word *platform* has come to stand for anything and everything you can bring to the deal that will turn a publisher's modest efforts into a raging success.

Publishing Tip

Publishers think of your platform more in terms of ongoing efforts than just random guest spots on radio and television. They are looking for something more stable, such as your being on a radio show producer's A-list whenever an expert on a special news event is required. If you are regularly mentioned in the columns that cover your field or are a regularly featured speaker at major programs in your field, you get good marks. Writing a local history column in your hometown weekly newspaper won't help much if your book is about crisis management.

This doesn't mean that you must be prepared to launch your own publicity program, book tour, and lecture series. But if you could do it, you'd see that even excessively Botoxed rigor would turn to a smile on your editor's face. But just what does an editor mean when he asks you about what you can do and what connections you might have?

Connections

Do you have connections with any media that would help promote the book? If you have written articles in magazines that cover your field, their editors might be willing to review your book or even suggest an article based on the subject of the book. Keep in mind that any publication that values its image of objectivity will never guarantee anything but a fair review. Any attempt to pressure a magazine editor or reviewer will do far more harm than good. But if you have a connection and can make the introductions and be willing to take whatever comes, most publishers will accept that. And so should you.

Backspace

Don't jump the gun, no matter how well connected you are with any media sources. Timing is critical in all publicity and promotional efforts. The editor will want to know that you are not going to gum up the works and that you fully understand and appreciate the need for careful planning and timing of these efforts.

Do you belong to any associations, groups, or organizations whose members might be reached by mail or e-mail? If you can supply names and addresses of a large enough number of individuals, any publisher would be missing a good bet by not promoting to the list. School alumni associations? Professional groups? Fraternal organizations? Military or veteran groups? You might even be able to get attention from groups to which your friends and relatives belong.

Your Other Activities

Your personal and professional history will be of considerable importance to your publisher. The interested editor will have an abbreviated resumé taken from your proposal and will want you to fill in the details. Even your hobbies and off-work activities will be of interest. A good publicity person sees more in you than just someone who has written a book.

Going Beyond Your Resumé

It's surprising how some of the things you have done but don't consider worth mentioning when you talk about your book might really prove valuable. Anything even remotely related to some sport can be turned from a dusty memory into an exploitable experience by an astute publicity person. There's hardly a management guide written these days that doesn't include a mention of the author's experience as a footballer or a curler and how it informed his award-winning theories of management. If you don't know what curling is, ask any Canadian.

Your Image

Because most authors are expected to take a fairly active part in the promotion of their books, a publisher wants to know early on how you come across in public, especially in extemporaneous situations like phone interviews. If you are working with an agent, your agent will probably have already given the editor a pretty clear picture of what to expect and not to expect. And if you have had any telephone conversations with your editor, he has probably made some notes already about your ability to handle yourself clearly and unflappably.

One way to bypass this hurdle is to send along audio or video clips of any presentations and interviews that make a positive case for your presenting abilities. Be aware that your sense of a good appearance may be colored by a dash of ego. Most agents are quite capable of helping you evaluate yourself and the material you might want to send to an editor. I can assure you that it is better to send nothing than to send clips that show you nervously reading a speech from 3×5 note cards in the meeting suite at a local Motel 6, even though you may think they look great.

> **Publishing Tip** _____
>
> We all have nervous tics that give us away when we are anxious. I thought I was immune to this human frailty until I saw a tape of a presentation I gave at a client's annual meeting. There I was, scratching the top of my head whenever I hit a rough moment. How do you respond to tight spots? Try to find out before you send out any tapes that make it look as though you are swatting flies.

Your Work Habits

It doesn't take long before an experienced editor can sense whether you will need constant hand-holding or whether you can take instruction and pretty much work independently. You may even be a great writer and need little or no help from an editor. But if you show an inclination toward a need for a pen, phone, or e-mail pal, an editor will get nervous. This is seldom an automatic disqualifier, but it can become a problem.

Most business editors work regularly with CEOs of major corporations on their memoirs as well as with consultants who see their books as career launching pads. Few will talk about the others they edit and are currently editing. They rarely gossip. So it's not necessary to be defensive if your credentials are slim or aggressive if you see yourself as a master of the universe. You and your editor will just be working partners, and if you can convey this attitude early on, you will have made points that could help turn your proposal into a contract offer.

Just remember, your editor wants your book to succeed just as much as you do. One of the elements of an editor's performance review is an evaluation of the books he has signed that made money for the house and the number that didn't.

Your Potential for More Books

You don't necessarily have to show potential for future books, but if you can, it does help make the case for the book you are currently presenting. If you compare book publishing with just about any other business, you will quickly see that publishing's up front effort and expenses are enormous. Every new book is a separate investment of time and money. Therefore, every editor looks for authors who can be developed to become "house" authors, people with whom they can work to build future successful projects. (There are contractual issues you should understand here and they are discussed in Chapter 17.)

There are a number of advantages to building a relationship with one publisher for most or all of your work. Once an author and a publisher have done a couple of books together, the publisher often suggests ideas for books it would like to publish with the author. Good publishers are not interested in imposing on the relationship, and the books suggested are most often the full property of the author, as is defined by copyright law. There are publishers who do work-for-hire deals with authors, but this is not an issue here.

As with all situations, there are also disadvantages. The most often cited is that of not seeing what other publishers might offer for a manuscript that you feel obliged to do as a "house" author. There's nothing wrong with having your agent test the waters for you. In fact, it's good business to get some occasional feedback from your publisher's competitors. Remember, however, the publisher has the same option open to it.

Getting to Know You Professionally

Although editors of business books hope the people they sign up to write books will bring good skills to the table, expectations are seldom as high as they might be for most other nonfiction books. Business book authors are seldom professional writers. Most write books about what they do and have done. Sales managers write about managing sales. Human resources people write about finding, training, and developing their employer's human capital. Some write extremely well, while others have difficulty writing anything coherently.

Publishing Tip

Don't try to be creative with your proposal. Try to write clearly, convincingly, and honestly. Lucid writing is the essence of good business writing. Your agent may be willing to let you look over some proposals her clients have written that made the grade.

Editors always hope the person with the great idea will be able to write clearly about it, but if the idea is good enough, they are often willing to take a chance with someone who can't write very well. But this doesn't mean that poor writing will be published. It means that either the editor or other editors on the staff will take an active hand in developing the manuscript or that they will encourage the prospective author to work with outside professional help. In Chapter 12, I discussed in some detail the process of working with freelance editors, collaborators, and even ghostwriters.

If you wrote your proposal yourself, the editor will have a pretty good idea of how you write from the material you submitted. If you had professional help with the proposal, do not try to play it off as your writing. Be honest about the extent of the help you had and about how much help you plan to use to write the book if you are offered a contract. It is nothing to be ashamed of. In fact, it is seen in a very positive light by most editors. They know that the idea they liked will be well presented in the manuscript, and they know that they are not going to have to waste a lot of time dragging you through freshman comp to get your material to a publishable level.

Your Research Skills

Most business books require a fair amount of research. This research may be based mainly on your own files and material, or it may require you to do a lot of archival searching for other information. Either way, you have to impress the editor with your command of the skills needed as well as your attitude toward the integrity of the data you search and report. Nothing sinks a book faster than sloppy research. Get one review in which the reviewer spots that you were off by 1 percent on the gross domestic product of some small country, and all your other data will be seen as questionable.

If your book calls for a fair amount of research, your editor will probably ask you some pretty specific questions. While there is an awful lot of good material on most subjects posted on Internet sites, there is also an awful lot of misinformation floating around the Net. Be sure to convince the editor that any Internet searching you do will be only a small part of your overall research strategy and that any Internet data you plan to use will be confirmed by other sources.

Libel and Plagiarism

I'm sure that it comes as no surprise that your editor will ask some very searching questions about how you plan to handle sensitive material and how carefully you will avoid any issues that might open you and your publisher to questions of plagiarism. Regardless of your intent, if you libel someone or use someone's material improperly, you will expose yourself and your publisher to the wrath of a thousand lawyers. At least that's what it seems like.

Backspace

Make sure you understand the indemnification clause in your contract. Most lawsuits are brought against publishers because they have deeper pockets than the authors they publish. This, however, doesn't get you off the hook.

Most cases of plagiarism arise from naïveté, rather than from willful intentions. Your publisher may have your book vetted by the company lawyer if he feels there might be a possibility of lawsuits. However, the final responsibility is yours, so be very careful of what you say.

Your Organizational Skills

When your contract is offered and the manuscript delivery date is a year away, you seldom realize just how important it is to get organized immediately. The enormousness of the project usually becomes apparent only as the delivery date of the first half nears and you find you have written only a few chapters. I've mentioned this several times already and will continue to do so in the chapters you have yet to read—meet your deadlines or you will be in serious trouble.

A missed date to an editor is like the dive Klaxon on a submarine—it sets a lot of stuff in motion, and some of it you may not like at all. Therefore, if your editor seems to ask a lot of questions about what else you might be doing while you write your book, take every opportunity to assure him that you will have everything under control. Be open-minded about the suggestions that may be offered to you and honest in your responses to your editor.

Your Understanding of Book Publishing

Your editor will be the person with whom you or your agent negotiates your contract. If this is your first book, you probably know very little about the business, and what you do know may be outdated or may have been told to you by a bitter author who harbors all sorts of baseless grudges against his publisher in particular and all publishers in general. I'm not kidding, and I'm not weighing in on the publisher's side either. I have worked on and continue to work on both sides of the street. I'm a published author, I was an agent and a book packager for 30 years, and I'm a ghostwriter and a collaborator. The misinformation and hostility that I have been exposed to over these years is frightening.

If the first question you ask your potential editor signals any of the paranoid prejudices shown by inexperienced authors who have been coached by cranks, you might just as well kiss your chances goodbye. If the editor really wants your book, he may feel it's worth the effort to teach you enough about the business to ensure a professional relationship, but if it's a toss-up, you just lost.

You will probably be surprised to learn that editors will often suggest that an unrepresented author with a good book idea get an agent. Most editors don't have time to teach Publishing 101 to every new author. And most aren't especially interested in trying to counter the misperceptions some authors arrive with. So they suggest that the author find representation. To this end, they usually provide authors with a list of a number of good agents and insist that the author make his own decision.

It's important to both parties to a negotiation that each has a clear idea of the other's objectives. You, as a first-time author, probably don't have a clue, and you could leave a lot on the table. As much as the editor wants and is required to maximize the advantage of the publisher, he wants the relationship to be fair. No editor is going to tell you that you could have gotten a 15 percent royalty when you accepted the first offer of 10 percent. An agent would know better. And both sides would have been comfortable with the result. Remember that you have both an editorial and a business relationship with your editor and your publisher. Therefore, it's important that you either prove that you know what you are talking about or show that you are willing to learn—but not willing to be fleeced. It's a tough position to be in. Would it surprise you to know that although I have placed more than 600 books and have negotiated just as many contracts, I do not act as my own agent? I am quite pleased to leave this up to Ed Claflin, my agent, and I seldom interfere with his work on my behalf. It's true!

Trust

As much as an editor needs your trust, you need to trust your editor. Don't expect that your editor will pass along secrets that her employer prefers to remain in-house. This aspect of trust is pretty obvious. However, the issue of trust that is most important in the editor-author professional relationship is based on shared goals and the book on which you both are working.

Before a contract is offered, an editor will need to know whether she has your trust. You will probably hear questions about your book such as "How do you feel about …?" "Would you consider …?" and "Have you ever thought of …?" All will be asked casually, but the editor already knows what she has to do with your manuscript and wants to make sure that once a contract is signed the work will go smoothly.

Answer these questions honestly and forthrightly. I know, it's your book and you don't want anyone to monkey with it. However, every book can be improved by sensitive and intelligent editing. And if a book is to carry an important publisher's logo, you should be prepared to listen to and consider very carefully all suggestions an editor makes. In short, if you don't trust your editor, don't sign the contract in the first place. And I can tell you that more than a few books were never acquired by a publisher simply because the editors felt that they could not trust the authors. Remember, your editor wants to see your book succeed as much as you do.

As an author, you also have to have the ability to establish a relationship of trust between yourself and your reader. If potential readers don't trust you, they won't buy your book, and remember, the whole point of publishing a book is selling it.

Your editor will be looking for self-assured writing that is not over the top. If you spend a lot of time covering ground your reader should already know, you will not impress your editor or potential reader. And if you turn up the heat with words like "groundbreaking" and "revolutionary" without backing up your conclusions, you will find it difficult to get your book published.

Your Editor Is Your Advocate

It's the rare editor-writer relationship that has no problems. In fact, it's about as rare as a marriage without arguments. Keep in mind, however, that your editor is your advocate within the publishing company—though, as with any relationship, don't expect that the relationship will thrive if you abuse it.

The element of trust I just touched on is very important, but just as important are the boundaries you and your editor will establish right from the start. The issue really centers on just how much authority your editor has to resolve any disagreements you and he may have. Unless you are an obsessive nitpicker, you and your editor should be able to resolve almost anything that pops up during the relationship, so the need for advocacy to higher authorities within the publishing house seldom arises.

Your editor will try to determine early on in the relationship just how things will shake out. If you are seen as someone who refuses to give up on small issues, your chances of getting an offer will diminish dramatically.

It's not that most editors see themselves in an authoritarian relationship with their authors, but because they usually have at least a half dozen or more books in different stages of development, they want to make sure the edges are defined. On more than a few occasions, I have had to intercede as an agent when some clients got in a snit over points that should have been granted without a fuss. I'm not saying that you have to roll over all the time to keep the peace, but you do have to keep an open mind when an editor might not seem to take his advocacy role as seriously as you might like.

The more senior your editor is within the company, the more clout he has. Unfortunately, some authors take advantage of this when they feel they are getting shabby treatment from a less senior editor. This book is not meant to be a moral guide to the business of book publishing, but I would be remiss if I didn't comment on the practice. I have dropped clients who bullied editors and would continue to do so if I were still an active agent. Other agents I know do the same.

The Least You Need to Know

- Ideas are paramount; you can always get help on the writing side.

- You must prove that you know what you are talking about and that you can back up all your claims with solid research.

- Demonstrate good organizational abilities and you'll make big points with a publisher.

- There must be a high level of trust between you and your editor.

Chapter 17

Negotiating a Fair Contract

In This Chapter

- Why you must read every word of every contract, every time
- How to negotiate better advance and royalty terms
- How to spot the four words that always mean trouble in a book contract
- How to analyze and neutralize the major troublesome clauses found in most book contracts

Whoever gets to draft a contract has an initial advantage over those who must be party to it. This doesn't mean that those who are party to the contract must agree to everything. In fact, most book contracts have a lot of maneuvering room for authors and agents who have concerns about specific issues. You will not always get exactly what you want, but it's not all that difficult to get a lot closer. And you may be surprised at what you can get immediately simply by asking.

Contrary to what you may have heard, most publishers are fair and honest in their dealings with authors. Sure, there are a few whose terms are onerous and some whose demands are absurd. They are the exceptions that are too often thought of as being the way it is with all publishers. I have seen them all. I've negotiated more than 600 contracts with major international publishers as well as with small, regional, and highly specialized publishers.

In all but a very few cases, the publishers were honest and sincere in wanting to do the best they could for the authors they published. However, no publisher is going to give away the store. A publisher may be willing to adjust terms, but none will tell you what their limits are. If you had written the contract, would you offer to tell the publisher that you were willing to take only a 2 percent royalty? I don't think so!

So, then, let's assume that you and the publisher each want to maximize your contractual advantage, that you are both willing to give a little here and there, and that there may be some terms that neither of you will budge on. We now have the start of a negotiation.

Every Publisher's Contract Is Different

Publishers' contracts all address essentially the same concerns and issues, but they all state them differently. The differences are based mainly on the publisher's experience with changing conditions and specific issues that have made the publisher rethink the way it states its terms.

Each publisher has its own house contract, which it presents when it offers to buy your book. Your agent may have done many books with your publisher and he or she may have a "standard" modified contract with that publisher that addresses issues she has already discussed and gotten concessions on. This doesn't necessarily mean that you have to accept that contract if you have issues with any of the terms. However, usually it does mean than many of the smaller issues are already out of the way when your specific contract is offered. Not all publishers do this, so ask your agent if he will be showing you the house original contract or a modified contract.

Publishing Tip _____

Every publisher's contract states the number of free copies it will give the author upon publication of a book. Most contracts call for at least 10 free copies, but you should be able to at least double that with little or no negotiation. Just ask! If, however, you are doing a book that involves expensive graphics and production, it might be more difficult to move the number. But ask anyway.

What is considered a house contract today could become obsolete overnight with the change of a single word. So read every word, even if you have done a dozen books with the house. Years ago, contracts were preprinted and all changes were made in the margins and initialed by everyone. Most agreements today are stored on a computer and printed as needed. This, of course, means that spotting a change of a single word is a lot more difficult than it was before.

Rather than dissect a typical book contract, I will address key issues that I and my clients have encountered most often during negotiations with publishers. In a sense, this can be thought of as your contractual troubleshooter. However, you really should get a much clearer picture of book contracts and your rights and responsibilities under them. Of the many books I have seen and read over the years, the one I'd suggest you read is by Mark Levine, titled *Negotiating a Book Contract: A Guide for Authors, Agents and Lawyers*. It's a paperback published by Client Distribution Services. Check your favorite online bookstore.

Advances and Royalties

The amount of the advance seems to be at the top of most people's lists, so I'll begin with that. An advance is money paid to you that is based on your having presented an acceptable proposal. Further, it's based on your promise to fulfill all of the terms of the contract and to stick to a schedule that you and the publisher agree to. It is money paid in the anticipation of sales.

You will be paid royalties only after sales have resulted in sufficient income to the publisher for it to recover the total amount of the advance. So the higher the advance, the longer it may take to get royalties. Take no advance, and your royalties will begin with the sale of the first copy. (Few people choose this alternative.) However, some publishers are willing to negotiate higher royalty rates if an author forgoes an advance. If you are not planning to live on your advance—few can—ask your agent or editor just how much latitude there may be in this alternative.

Most advances are paid in thirds: the first third is paid on the signing of the agreement, the second third upon completion and acceptance of one-half of the manuscript, and the final third upon the publisher's acceptance of the complete manuscript.

Backspace

Your contract may call for you to supply other material after completion of the manuscript, such as an index or some appendixes that can't be compiled until just before publication. See that your final payment is based on submission of the main text only and is not withheld until the last-minute material is supplied. If this is not possible, the publisher should be willing to make separate payments, one for the complete text and one for submission of acceptable back matter.

The amount of the advance varies considerably. This variation is based mainly on the author's credentials and platform, the number of copies the sales department estimates it can sell, and what income the publisher anticipates from sales of subsidiary rights. If your book will be especially expensive to produce, or if the publisher anticipates an expensive rollout, the advance might be lower than you had hoped.

Now, let's look at some of the issues often seen in the negotiation of an advance.

Timing of Payment of Advances

Watch for a line in your contract stating that the final advance payment is made upon publication—rather than upon acceptance of the final manuscript. This gives the publisher the right to withhold the final advance payment until it publishes your book. You could be waiting for years, unless you insist on payment upon acceptance and state a specific time period during which the publisher must accept or reject your manuscript. If the publisher insists on this, put a cap on the time period. A publisher should not be able to hold your money and your manuscript forever.

Amount of the Advance

No publisher is going to make its best offer immediately. There is always some room to negotiate, but knowing how much room there is and how much to press for is the issue. And it's different with every publisher.

You must know exactly which rights the publisher is asking for before you will be able to determine whether the amount of the advance is acceptable. Most initial offers are for all rights—domestic sales, paperback rights, foreign rights, serialization, and lots more. If you have an agent, she should be able to advise you on which rights are worth keeping and which rights you can afford to let the publisher have. All of these rights—except possibly feature films—are of some value, and you never know when some publisher thousands of miles away will see a way to use your material. If you feel that the advance you are being offered is low, consider withholding the rights that you or your agent might be able to sell. This is one of the toughest areas of negotiation for an inexperienced author without an agent.

If your publisher won't move on the amount of the advance, it's often possible to negotiate bonus payments based on the number of books sold or total income from all sales. Bonuses don't cost the publisher anything until certain goals are reached, and then they usually cost little relative to the income derived from the goal figure set.

Major authors often negotiate bonuses for the number of weeks a book appears on a specific best-seller list, such as that of *The New York Times*.

One option that most publishers are willing to discuss when their offers are considered too low by an author is a pass-through of subsidiary rights income. Ordinarily, all income from the sale of a book, including subsidiary rights income, is aggregated and paid to you semiannually. If the publisher retains a subsidiary right that it is able to sell, the income from that sale is held by the publisher to be paid in a regular royalty period. You could have money sitting in a publisher's account for six months under these terms. If your unhappiness with the amount of the advance is great enough and the publisher wants your book very much, it may be willing to pass-through this income. You don't make any more money, but you get your hands on what is owed you sooner than you might otherwise.

Publishing Tip _____

Most domestic agents are capable of selling all the rights to a published work. However, there are times when a business book might have value outside the United States. Unless your agent is at one of the large, multi-office agencies, your agent will probably work with a network of independent agents in foreign countries to sell these rights offshore. This is common practice, but if you feel there is a potential for foreign sales, ask your agent about how he sells abroad.

Royalty Payment on Net Receipts or List Price

If your contract states that you are to be paid a royalty of 10% of the list price of your book, this means that your royalty will be computed on that number and nothing else. However, some contracts state that you will be paid on the net receipts of the publisher.

Publishers sell to booksellers at discounts of around 45 percent of cover price. If your contract calls for a royalty based on net receipts, this means your royalty is computed on the amount of the list price less whatever trade discount the publisher offers. Ten percent of list price on a $20 book translates to a $2 royalty per book. Ten percent of a net receipts contract, based on a 45 percent bookseller discount, results in a royalty of $1.10, just over half of what you would have received if your royalty was based on the list price.

Most publishers who base royalties on net receipts offer a higher-percentage royalty, but seldom do they offer a figure that fully makes up the difference. The major problem with a net receipts contract, however, is that it is not based on the bedrock of a published list price. Rather, it's based on shifting sands of variable costs and expenses, and it can be especially harmful when booksellers are offered special promotional discounts that exceed the normal trade discount.

Royalties on Subsidiary Rights

If you don't have an agent who will go after the sale of the various subsidiary rights that are available to you, and you don't want to try to sell them yourself, you will probably allow your publisher to be your agent-in-fact for these rights. Some publishers sell these rights to other publishers and organizations quite aggressively, while others do not.

Typically, a contract will provide for a 50/50 split of the income from subsidiary rights sales that the publisher makes. Most publishers are willing to negotiate better terms for these rights. However, the more the balance shifts in your favor, the less interested the publisher usually becomes in aggressively pursuing the sale of these rights for you. There are far too many subsidiary rights opportunities to discuss in one chapter. Again, I refer you to Mark Levine's excellent book for his thorough coverage of this topic.

Reserve Held Against Returns

Books sold to booksellers are sold on a fully returnable basis. Any books a bookseller doesn't sell can be returned for a full refund, subject to some time and shipping considerations. Your royalties are based on the number of books bought and shipped to booksellers. Most publishers include a clause in your contract that states that they may hold a certain amount of your earned royalty as a reserve against future returns.

Backspace

The reserve-against-returns clause is usually stated in terms of "a reasonable" amount. What is reasonable to the publisher may be unreasonable to you. Ask that this be stated in precise terms. It will vary a lot from publisher to publisher, and even from author to author at a single publisher, but your agent should have a handle on the numbers that will work.

There's little or no chance of getting this clause out of most contracts. However, you should be able to negotiate terms that limit the time during which the publisher may hold a portion of your royalties in its reserve account. Try to limit this to one year, but you can feel like you've been successful if you can make this a two-year period.

The Royalty Statement

Many publisher contracts provide for royalty statements to be sent only when more than a certain amount of money is due to you. This means that if money is due and it is below the cap, you won't get a statement and you won't get a check.

These figures are seldom high, and the money held is usually insignificant. However, without a statement you will have no idea of what's happening with your book. The publisher could have shipped a significant number and gotten most back as returns and you would never know. It's nice to know why things like this are happening. If the publisher insists on this clause, try to set the royalty figure as low as possible to ensure you get copies of your statements.

The Copyright

The copyright should be in your name, and most publishers usually agree without fuss to handle the registration. The one major point to watch for is a *work-for-hire contract*. Under the proper circumstances, there is nothing to fear. However, if this is your book, your idea, and all your work, it should be yours and you should own the copyright.

def•i•ni•tion

Work-for-hire contracts are not unlike agreements made with other contractors for certain clearly specified work, except than in book publishing they usually exclude the author from holding the copyright. Work-for-hire agreements are very common in the software development field, and there is a good body of law available, should you ever find yourself in a disagreement with a publisher.

The Option

Most publisher contracts include a clause that obligates you to show your next work to your current publisher before showing it to another publisher. If your publisher really hopes to do more books with you, it might be difficult to get this clause removed.

However, you can usually get the terms softened. The major sticking point usually involves the amount of time before you are allowed to approach another publisher with your next book.

Most contracts prevent you from showing your next work to another publisher until some time after your current book is published. This date is usually negotiable. If your contract doesn't set a time frame for your current publisher to respond to your next proposal, make sure that this is corrected. One or two months to respond should be sufficient.

The real stickler, however, is the line giving your current publisher the option to match any offer made by another publisher. Some less-than-honorable publishers have been known to refrain from making any offers at all until another publisher makes one. This, in a sense, defines the offer level for your current publisher. You won't make any friends at the second publisher if you have to turn down an offer they make on your book. Your agent should be able to get this clause removed from the contract or at least softened considerably.

> **Backspace**
>
> "This or any other ..." These four words can get you in trouble if you do more than one book with a single publisher. They are most often found in the language relating to money due you from the publisher. For example, if your first book has not earned enough money to repay the publisher for the advance, you could find yourself having money deducted from payments due on your second book because of the negative balance on the first. Do a global search for the phrase "or any other" and you will spot where it has been inserted in the contract. Just get "or any other" eliminated and you should be okay. This is referred to as cross-collateralization, or joint accounting. Your agent will know what you mean when you ask him or her about it.

The Definition of a Satisfactory Manuscript

Every publisher's contract contains language that allows it to withdraw from an agreement if the author fails to deliver an acceptable manuscript. When this happens, the publisher is usually granted the right to collect the advance money paid to date.

This is understandable and appropriate. However, suppose you deliver a perfectly acceptable manuscript, but between the date of the contract and the date of submission of the material, the market for your book has dried up. A publisher could invoke this clause and leave you holding the bag. If you just make sure that the clause in your contract defines satisfactory in terms of "form and content," you can usually stop this problem short. And if the publisher has been accepting parts of your manuscript in progress, it will be very difficult for it to reject your final manuscript by saying that it is unacceptable.

You should also include language that states that the publisher must be specific in the comments it gives you and that it must give you the opportunity to rectify whatever it feels makes the material unacceptable.

The No-Compete Clause

Most contracts for business books contain a clause preventing you from writing a book for another publisher that might compete with the current book. Publishers have good reason for seeking this protection, but that protection should be limited as much as possible.

The word "competitive" alone is too broad, and if the publisher insists on including this protection, the word should be clearly defined. Publishers will seldom object to a clear definition of the term, even if it takes a few pages to do it. However, if you run into a hard-nosed negotiator, you can usually get a time cap on the clause. The task, then, is to limit it to as short a period as possible after the publication date of the current book.

In Print or Out of Print?

Your contract will probably have a loosely worded clause that gives the publisher the use of all the rights that have been granted under the agreement for as long as the book is in print. What is seldom defined, however, is what "in print" really means. If, for example, the publisher has done nothing with the book for a few years and does not include it in its current catalog, is it still in print?

There are a number of ways to address this question, but the one I prefer is to specify that if the publisher has not sold at least 50 copies in the last 12 months, the rights automatically revert to the author. This can be tough to get, but you can fall back on a clause that specifies an inventory level for the same period. If the in-stock level drops below the stated figure and remains at that level for 12 months, the book is out of print and all rights should revert to you.

When Your Book Is Published

You may have delivered an acceptable manuscript and even received your final advance, but months go by and you have no news of when your book is going to be published. This happens most often because the market has gone soft for your subject between the time you signed the contract and when you delivered the manuscript. The publisher may just drag its feet unless your agreement specifies a time frame for publication. It's most common for books to be in print no later than a year after a manuscript is accepted.

You should protect yourself by adding language that nails down the publication date. And if that date is missed, you should specify that all rights you granted in your contract revert to you and that you get to keep all money advanced to date. If your contract calls for a payment to be made on the actual publication date, that money should be considered yours as well.

Indemnification

This is an area where those with a litigious turn of mind have a field day. If a suit is brought against your publisher for something you said in your book and it causes the publisher to lose money, you can be bound to reimburse the publisher for its losses. Believe it or not, even if the allegations are proven to be false, you could be held responsible for the money the publisher spent defending itself. You might even have to reimburse others, including booksellers named in the suit.

Many publishers carry blanket insurance that covers themselves and you. However, there is usually a deductible clause that specifies that you, the author, are liable for a certain amount before the policy kicks in. Ask if the publisher has such insurance and what the deductible limits are.

It's seldom possible to get this clause removed from a contract. But with a little effort you can get it softened some. Even though you and your publisher can be sued separately or together and you both can prove your innocence, you may still be on the hook for the costs of the suit. But if you limit your liability to only successful suits, you are on much safer ground.

This is a complex issue, and there are as many ways to soften the blow as there are ways to sue you and your publisher. The best advice I can offer in this limited discussion is to seek the advice of your agent. These suits are not common, but when they are brought they are usually brought by some pretty nasty people. Your agent should be able to provide the language that will offer you protection, but I doubt that he will be able to have the clause removed from the contract. If you are going to worry about something, however, worry about being struck by lightning. Both events are about as likely to happen—unless you have enemies!

It's Not All That Bad

I have never seen a contract that abused all of the contractual elements I have just described. The worst of them have been hard-nosed about two or three of them, but most of these publishers were willing to take softer positions if they weren't willing to drop the clauses altogether. Your job, or your agent's job, if you have one, is to notice the trouble spots before you sign anything.

As I said earlier, the party that writes the contract writes it in its own favor. If you were to write the agreement, you would start with royalty figures far greater than those a publisher states in the contract offered you and be willing to settle for less. The job is to find the point where you and the publisher are comfortable. Although negotiation is based on taking adversarial positions, don't assume the worst about the publisher. I know, I know, there are some pretty bad apples in the barrel, but most publishers are honest and genuinely interested in publishing your book so that you both benefit. If your agent has been in business for a while, he will not only be able to deal with the terms of the agreement, but he should know which publishers to avoid and which to steer you toward.

The Least You Need to Know

♦ Most terms of most book contracts are negotiable.

♦ How far a publisher might be willing to bend usually depends on what you are willing to give in return.

♦ There is a significant difference between royalties based on net receipts and royalties based on the book's cover price.

♦ If you are planning to do more than one book with any given publisher, make sure that you never see these words in any context in your contract: "this or any other …."

Part 5

Writing and Publicizing Your Book

Here's where it gets interesting and where you will meet all the publisher's key players. You won't learn how to write, but you will learn how to put what you already know about writing to good and practical use in your business book. You meet the publisher's sales, marketing, and publicity people and discover exactly what happens as you write, after you write, and as you plan to write your next book.

Publishing is a thoroughly collaborative effort. The publisher needs you and you need the publisher. You learn what your publisher expects of you, in addition to a good manuscript. You learn what you can and should expect from your publisher. And you see why some author complaints about publishers may be justified, as well as why some publisher complaints about authors may be justified, too. In short, you will know more than you thought you had to know about book publishing. I hope that this helps both you and your publisher to write and publish the best book possible.

Chapter 18

Working with Your Editor

In This Chapter

- What happens once you are offered a contract
- How to negotiate your contract with your editor
- How to work with your editor and his or her team
- Your next book

Your first working encounter with your editor may not be quite what you expected. The editor who saw the promise in you and your book, and who went to bat for you when marketing wasn't too impressed and publicity was wavering on your media potential, is now going to negotiate your contract. It's a role most editors dislike. However, it's a role that tradition has thrust on them, and many do it very well.

Just remember, most editors would give you a lot more if they could. Don't hold them personally responsible for the terms of the offer. But do remember that many of the terms in most book contracts are negotiable. It's discovering where there's wiggle room and where there isn't and how much latitude you have that's important.

If you are acting alone, negotiating is your job. If you are represented by an agent, you are spared that encounter. This doesn't mean, however, that you should turn a blind eye to the details. It might be a good idea at this point to read Chapter 13 again before going any further.

If Money Wasn't Involved, Negotiating Would Be Fun

If you are represented, your agent should go over the terms of the contract with you. If you're doing this yourself, you'd better get an education fast. And one of the best ways to do this is to join the Authors Guild. Full membership is available only to those who have already had at least one book published by an established American publisher. However, associate membership is available to those who have a contract with an established publisher for a book yet to be published. Get details at www. authorsguild.org.

When a contract is offered, many of the negotiable terms are stated lower than what the publisher might be willing to accept. Advances are most often negotiable. Royalty rates and whether they are based on the book list price or the net receipts from the sale of the book are tougher to negotiate and sometimes can be deal breakers. Subsidiary rights terms are usually flexible, as are clauses that bind you to submit your next book to the publisher. Unfortunately, most novice authors pay more attention to the clause granting them 10 free copies of their book. They are very pleased with themselves when they get this up to 20.

You will never know what you have left on the table until you do your homework, by using the material available through membership in the Authors Guild.

Actual negotiations are seldom done face to face, either by you or by your agent. If you are represented, your agent will send you a copy of the contract. He may include a brief list of comments on where there might be wiggle room. More often than not, however, the comments will be made over the phone while both of you are looking at the clauses in question.

Remember that an agent is on your team. He works on commission, and the better the terms that can be negotiated, the better the commission money. However, agents also know where the brick walls are and they know the temperaments of the publishers they work with. Some publishers are quite flexible and others are quite willing to shut down negotiations quickly when they feel it might be better to go back to their pile of current submissions (called the slush pile) and look at other proposals.

Publishing Tip _____

Choose an agent carefully and plan to build a long-term relationship with him or her. Agents do much more than just sell your book. If you don't know what subsidiary rights are, your agent will set you straight and could make you more money than you would get from just your advance and domestic royalties. For the whole story, contact AAR, the Association of Authors' Representatives, at www.aaronline.org.

Once you, your agent, and the publisher have agreed to the terms of the contract, work on the book should begin immediately. It may be a month or two before you get the actual contract. In the meantime, you will have agreed to a specific delivery date, and if you are not working on your book, the time you have left to do the job gets shorter and shorter.

Yes, this does mean that you are working without a contract in hand. But you do have a promise of a contract, and in most legal jurisdictions that's almost as good as the paper you will sign when the revised contract finally arrives.

Others You Will Hear From

Even before you get over the rush of thinking of yourself in authorial terms, you will probably hear from others in the publishing company. Your editor may carry the messages, or you may hear directly from the publicity and marketing folks. They will have a lot of questions for you and they will also offer some suggestions. Do everything you can to help them. These are the people whose job it is to make money for the publisher and for you once your book is in print. I discuss your interaction with them in Chapters 20, 21, 22, and 23. For now, I just want to make sure that you take them very, very seriously.

Get to Know Your Editor's Assistant Very Well

An acquisitions editor's main responsibility is acquiring books. If she doesn't get the number of books the company wants during a prescribed period, she is in trouble. This means that the friend you have just made can become a lot more difficult to reach once your book has been acquired. However, the editor's assistant will probably be much more accessible and quick to answer your questions. And it is this editorial assistant with whom you will probably have the majority of contact as you write your book.

Don't make the mistake of not taking an editorial assistant seriously. Editorial assistants are seldom just wet-behind-the-ears beginners. They are usually college-educated people, many with advanced degrees, who probably interned at publishing companies before they got the jobs they now have. Most likely they have taken special courses in book publishing offered outside of their regular course work. More than a few will already have some of their own writing in print. In short, editorial assistants know a lot more about book publishing than you do. They may have to honor the tradition of getting the boss coffee, but few see this as demeaning. The good editors I have known over the years treat their assistants with the same respect they have for their more experienced colleagues.

This may surprise you, but the assistant you will work with just may have been the one who first spotted your proposal and brought it to his boss's attention. Once they prove themselves, editorial assistants are given significant responsibility very quickly. Many serve as first readers of most of the proposals their bosses receive. All serve as the managers of all the details of their bosses' operations. They know where each ongoing project stands, they know when advances are due, and they know when contracts are late. And once they get to know you, they will be both your friends and consultants as you learn the book publishing ropes.

Publishing Tip

Treat the editorial assistant you work with respectfully. He will be your day-to-day connection as you write and your advocate when you have issues in need of resolution.

Here is something else to think about. Just as you may be working to climb the corporate ladder, most editorial assistants are working to climb the publishing ladder. Editorial assistants most likely aspire to become editors, just as editors aspire to move into editorial management. With this in mind, you may end up working with several assistants while your book is going through the publishing process, so be prepared to be helpful.

Remember this, too: the editorial assistant who may have spotted your proposal may become an editor and need a writer like you later on. Publishing is a small world. Be nice to people and give them good material, and you will seldom go without friends in the field.

Be a cranky author and the same grapevine that could pass around your praises will instead pass its pans of you.

Working with Your In-House Contact

You won't lose touch with the editor who signed you up; you will just have a lot less contact with him. Your contact for most of the routine work will be with the assistant. It's this level of contact that will be important for you as you write your book, but you will probably hear from your editor from time to time. These calls may be just atta-boys, or they may involve issues and questions that aren't ordinarily part of the work your editor's assistant might do. As you might expect, you will probably hear from your acquisitions editor more often if your book has been placed with a smaller house. If you are writing for one of the biggies with many imprints, your experience will seem a little more corporate—which it is.

Now, let's look at the path a typical book follows once you have signed the contract. The path will vary somewhat depending on how the house is structured. But whatever the details, the sequence of steps that follows is pretty much the same from house to house.

The Contract's Signed, the Work Begins

You and your agent have negotiated a fair contract and you have signed on the dotted line. Before sending it back to the publisher, be sure to make a copy for yourself. The publisher will send the countersigned agreement back to you, but it is a good idea to have a copy for yourself now to remind you of the conditions and deadlines you have committed to. Also, don't wait until you receive the contract to start writing; get moving now because your deadlines aren't waiting.

There's Nothing Like a Deadline

Your contract outlines the writing deadlines you and your publisher have agreed to. Write these dates down and post them in a prominent place to remind yourself of the work you need to do. Most likely you have a year to write your book, and while that may seem like plenty of time, it will pass quickly if you don't have a plan.

While every publisher is different, chances are that you will be required to deliver half of the manuscript at the midpoint of the contract and the balance of the material at the stated final date.

If this is your first book, you will probably get an occasional how-are-you-doing call from your editor or her editorial assistant. When you get the call, be honest about where you are and be prepared for the advice that will be offered if you are falling behind. It will be a mixture of helpful suggestions and reminders of what will happen if you fail to deliver.

If you find yourself running behind and your halfway point or final completion date is coming up, don't wait for the editor to call to see where the material is. Call immediately and explain just where you are and what you are doing to solve the problem. Being late at the halfway point isn't going to go down well with your editor, but at least you still have enough time to catch up and make the final delivery date.

If you know that you won't make the final delivery date, call immediately. Schedules can be juggled a little if there is enough time. But miss your final date and then tell your editor that you still need a few more months and you just might hear from the publisher's legal department.

Remember, while you are writing, your publisher is scheduling the book's production, planning promotion and publicity programs, and contacting the major chains and online booksellers to alert them of what's in the pipeline. If you miss your deadline, all of this planning must be adjusted.

Keep in mind that you are not the only one writing a book for your publisher. Most likely, your editor is juggling 30 to 40 other books in various stages of development. If you are late with your book, it not only upsets the schedule made for your book, it may throw off the schedules already set for other books.

In some cases, the publisher may outright cancel your contract and require you to repay your advance. If your publisher still wants to work with you, your book probably will be given a lot less attention than originally planned when you signed your agreement.

Pace Yourself to Finish Strong

You have your contract and your deadlines. It's time to make a writing plan.

It is important that you work regularly rather than sporadically. The positive reinforcement of meeting smaller but regular goals is far more productive than the relief of catching up after your editor has discovered that you have been goofing off.

Publishing Tip _____

Stay in touch with your editor and editorial assistant, but don't bury them with stuff. Let them know about the high points, but try to avoid chit-chat and don't expect every note to result in a response. They really are busy people!

While everyone is different, I work by setting daily word counts for each of the books I am working on (as I usually have at least two going on at the same time). Here is the schedule I used for the book you are now reading:

> Total number of words required by contract: 112,000

> Time allowed for delivery: 6 months

> Division of time: 26 weeks or 130 work days

> Number of words per 5-day week: 4,307

> Number of words per day: 861

There were days when I did more and there were days when I did less. But if I didn't reach my weekly goal of 4,307 words, I put in the time over the weekend to catch up. If I did more words than needed for the week, I didn't slack off the following week. This became my cushion for when I did fall behind. All this figuring may seem obsessive to you, but just get a few chapters behind when your editor calls and you will see real frustration.

Initial Editor Reviews

If this is your first book, your editor will probably ask to see the chapters as you complete them. It's better to catch and correct problems early than it is to have to go back over a completed manuscript and make lots of changes. Once your editor is confident that you are on the right track, you will probably be relieved of the responsibility of submitting chapters as you complete them.

Your editor will coach you initially by sending a few pages with detailed edits and suggestions. Most of the comments and suggestions you get at this point will relate to style. If you make the changes he has suggested and stick with the suggestions for the rest of the book, you will be on the right track. This doesn't mean that you must do everything the editor asks. If you have reservations about the suggestions, talk it out.

Just remember that your editor holds the high card. If you turn in a manuscript that the editor views as unacceptable, you will have to rewrite it, correct it, or return the money paid to you so far and have your contract cancelled.

You Have Completed and Submitted the Manuscript

Assuming everything went well as you wrote and submitted material, you probably clicked "send" on your computer or turned your manuscript over to the post office and assumed you would hear back in a few days. Don't hold your breath.

Some editors will acknowledge getting your manuscript and tell you approximately when you will next hear from them. And some won't. And you wait … and you wait …. Randy Ladenheim-Gil, my editor on this book, sends me a simple "Got it" by e-mail and that's all I want. Others use the mail and some will even phone to acknowledge receipt. And then there are those who say nothing, but most editors do respond.

If you run into an editor who doesn't respond, don't assume the worst. Just keep in mind that most editors are woefully overworked. Your editor's editorial assistant may have been promoted or have moved to another house. Or your editor may be at one of the quarterly sales conferences where editors have to present the books they are working on to the sales people. Could be that another author never said that he was going to be six months late with the manuscript of a book that is already in the catalog and being pitched by the sales team. And could be one of the many personal things we all have to attend to that turn up at inopportune times.

Whatever the reason, stay calm. If the publisher has been paying you advances on schedule and you have been told that the material you have been submitting is okay, there's very little to worry about. Whatever is keeping the editor from talking with you is probably not something horrible about your project. It's probably something over which the editor has no control and which must be done ahead of everything else.

You can send an occasional e-mail asking about what's happening. But this is a little like pushing the elevator button repeatedly, hoping that it will make it arrive more quickly. But if, like carrying a lucky charm in your pocket, it makes you feel like you are doing something and it just might work, do it. But stay cool.

Your Edited Manuscript Arrives

If you sent a hard copy to your editor, your manuscript will be edited on the paper you sent. If you submitted your manuscript by e-mail, you will get electronic files in return. Hard copy will have notes and changes written directly on the pages and each page on which notes are made will probably be flagged with yellow Post-it notes.

If you sent your manuscript electronically, your editor will probably have edited your manuscript with the "Track Changes" feature in Microsoft Word turned on. This feature shows in red exactly what the editor has done on your manuscript. It allows you to see what has been changed or deleted, and it allows you to accept or reject the changes.

 Publishing Tip _____

The use of the "Track Changes" feature in Microsoft Word is beyond the scope of this book. Because Word is, by far, the most popular word processing program, you probably have it on your machine. You can turn this feature on by going to the "Tools" menu. Click on "Track Changes" and then "Highlight Changes."

Tracking changes is not difficult to master, but it's best not to learn it while working on your edited manuscript. Pull up something you don't care about messing up and turn on "Track Changes." Play with it. You can either pick up what you need to know on the fly, use the information in the Help menu, or get one of the many books that covers the feature as part of the text.

Now you are looking at a sea of yellow Post-its or a screen full of red changes. Don't panic.

Begin by setting aside a time when you know you won't be interrupted. Start with the first flagged page and just read the comments. Go on to the next flagged section and work your way through the manuscript. This is not the time to start making corrections, even those minor ones that take nothing more than a few keystrokes. The goal is to put the task in front of you into perspective.

If you discover that most of the comments and changes requested are not unreasonable and not demanding, you will be in good shape. If the notes on the flags ask questions like "Please state this more clearly," "What do you mean by this?" and "Why are you repeating this when you said it more clearly in Chapter 3?" you will know that you have some work to do. It's best to know exactly what lies ahead of you when you sit down and begin addressing the editor's questions, comments, and suggested changes.

By the time you get your edited manuscript back, the promotional wheels at the publishing house will be rolling, so this is not the time to take a vacation. There's always a little leeway for the delivery of half of your manuscript, almost none on the date of delivery for your completed manuscript, and none at all on your review and revisions.

You Have Returned Your Revised and Corrected Manuscript

You've worked through your manuscript and made the corrections and revisions needed. It is back in the hands of your editor. This is about the time you will start getting calls from publicity and marketing people at your publisher. They could involve radio talk show spots, interviews for newspaper and magazine articles, and whatever other creative activities the publisher has in mind to move your book.

Your Book Is in Print

Your editor or agent has probably given you an in-stock date for your book, and this is about the time you can expect your author's copies to arrive.

What you do with them is your business, but I'd suggest that you pass out some copies to your local media—newspaper, TV, and radio shows. It may not result in a lot of sales locally, but it's nice to let those who thought you were kidding when you told them that you were writing a book know that it is now in print. Everyone needs and deserves a little gloat-time. Enjoy it!

Time to Think About Your Next Book

Judging from the response your publisher gets from wholesalers, distributors, chains, online booksellers, and independent booksellers, this is usually the time when your editor or agent might ask whether you have another book in mind.

If the response has been good, publishers like to follow up quickly with another book. The ultimate decision to do this will probably not be made until your publisher knows how the sell-through goes: that is, how well the book does with the market for whom it was written. But if your publisher has gotten enough interest for your book early on, they will want to move quickly to get your next book in the works.

Sadly, and with what I think is marketing nearsightedness, you are usually only considered as good as your last book, unless you are already a "name" author. But you should still be aware that this can be something to look forward to.

Some Words of Thanks

By the time your manuscript has been turned into a book, your editor has signed a lot of other books and your in-house development team has moved on to the next projects on their lists. You probably won't hear much from them, but if you have had a good experience, tell them so. They are no different from the rest of us: they like to know that their work has been appreciated. Even a simple e-mail message will be appreciated, but a handwritten note will really make any editor's day. And don't forget your agent!

The Least You Need to Know

- ◆ Your editor will negotiate your contract and be your main contact during your writing.

- ◆ Most of your routine contact will probably be with an editorial assistant.

- ◆ Never, never fail to return your edited manuscript on time.

- ◆ Take some time off and do a little brag-and-boast when your books arrive.

Chapter **19**

Voice, Point of View, and Style

In This Chapter

- ◆ How to write in a style that will appeal to business readers
- ◆ Why serious writing often needs a light touch
- ◆ Pacing, spacing, and placing words, sentences, and paragraphs for perfect pitch

Have you ever wondered why so many business books are published each year and why most of them pass without notice? Many editors will tell you they failed because the authors never had clear images of their readers' needs. They will also tell you that the writers' goals were probably not those of the readers they were trying to reach. Many of these books might have been well written, but that's like speaking eloquent English to someone who only understands Old Norse.

Before you begin writing, be sure you are absolutely clear about what you want your writing to achieve. Then ask yourself who you want to reach and influence with your words. Until you have a clear picture of your goals and the wants, needs, and characteristics of your readers, there's little point in writing anything.

Until you know your reader and are fully aware of why you want to reach that reader, discussing style is pointless. If I were to write this book in a humorous style, you wouldn't take me very seriously. If I were to assume that all my readers understood why active voice is a stronger style than passive voice, I would lose or at least annoy many of them. So define your typical reader, know what he or she wants to get from the pages of the book you plan to write, and make sure that all this is in sync with your goals for writing the book and the style you plan to use.

Why Do You Want to Write a Book?

Don't get lofty and give me a Miss America answer. Peace, justice, and profits for all just won't cut it. I'm not being cynical when I suggest that you probably want to write a book to further your career. There's nothing wrong with that. But you must bring more to the page than that if you want to interest a good commercial publisher.

Okay, so writing a book to move your career is not a bad idea after all. Writing a book to further your career without offering value to your readers probably won't get you published unless you do it yourself. While there is nothing wrong with self-publishing, a major publisher's colophon on a book is the seal of approval that no one gets when they self-publish.

Do this now: in 50 words or less describe your typical reader and state your reasons for writing your book. It might help to consider the following: Are you trying to explain something, to describe it, to analyze it, to argue a point, or to provide advice and help that the reader needs?

Now, in a 72-point font, print out what you wrote. Tack it up where you will see it every time you work on your book. This is your writing mission statement.

Puncturing a Balloon

Contrary to what liberal arts grads like to say about their M.B.A. colleagues, business-people do read a lot. It's likely, however, that neither group would recognize the other's favorite authors. The major difference is that business book readers read mainly for content. They will wade through some of the most atrocious writing to get at the nugget the guru du jour has buried somewhere in his recent best-selling book. Their liberal arts friends, meanwhile, read for style and will quickly abandon a book they are reading if the author is a clunky writer. In fact, many will reread a book just to enjoy good writing.

Because much of business and the writing about it are based on real-world experience, many writers contradict one another regularly. This is not a gauntlet-throwing exercise. It's just that each author has a different take on a particular subject, and each will describe that take in his or her own way. It's here that the better business writer has the advantage. Write better than the others in your field, and when the other marketing mavens contradict one another, your eloquence will make the difference. If you doubt this, spend a day in a courtroom and listen to the attorneys' pleas. You're sure to hear at least one case decided on flimsy evidence just because the attorney was a better speaker. It's no different when you write a business book.

Publishing Tip

TQM. MBO. AIMS. Quick, tell me the names of the people credited with these inventions. These people had good ideas and they made them memorable by creating acronyms that resonate and are easily remembered. Each introduced his ideas in books and articles in major periodicals. There's something about rolling "TQM" off your tongue in a staff meeting that makes you feel good. Give your idea a three-letter name and you might be the next Tom Peters.

In general, businesspeople read books because they have to. Those who find pleasure in reading do so just for that pleasure. If you have the next TQM and you write about it badly, you may get some people to read your book. If you write about it well, a lot more will read your book.

Now let's see how you can use words to communicate clearly and efficiently with your business book–reading audience.

But Enough About Me

If you have read anything at all about writing style, you are probably more confused about it than you were before you read a word. Style counts, but only as it reveals your thoughts clearly and as it leads your readers effortlessly from page to page. Don't confuse this with the Dick-and-Jane school of writing. It's not the number of words you use but how well you use them.

Think of the business books you have read that helped you in some way, that were actually a pleasure to read, and that didn't give you an overblown image of the writer. You will probably notice that the authors inserted themselves only when it was necessary to make a point more clearly than it could have been made otherwise.

In short, keep yourself in the background. Business book readers are conscious of style only in that they know it's easier to read one writer than it might be to read another. Deliver the goods in as few words as possible, and deliver them without hogging the page yourself, and you will have done what many business writers never learn to do.

It's Not Plagiarism to Copy a Style

Plagiarism is stealing a writer's words and ideas. Adapting a writer's style is not plagiarism. In fact, it's one of the best ways to learn to write well. Read the business book authors whose style you admire. In fact, read any nonfiction author on any subject with an eye on style, and you will do more to improve your writing than by doing just about anything else. Read any of David McCullough's books and you will see a master of nonfiction at work. Read Richard Rhodes's *The Making of the Atomic Bomb*, and you will meet another great nonfiction writer. Read Alan Axelrod's *Patton on Leadership*, and you will read a historian who writes business books far better than most.

I don't mean to imply that you should simply imitate another writer's style. You should, however, try to get a sense of how it would feel to write like a writer whose style you admire. When you do, you will probably notice that your own writing comes a little easier and that you are more productive than you have been before. Just don't force it. Many editors will tell you the best style is really no style at all. Style, in their view, is affectation, and unless you are writing fiction, affectation can detract from the quality of your prose.

In My Opinion

Unless your book depends on specific opinions that you hold, avoid the use of this equivocal statement. "In my opinion" at the beginning of a sentence softens the blow, makes your point wishy-washy, and detracts from any positive image the reader may have of you. Say what you want to say, but don't do it in a qualified way.

If you must make uncertain statements, say things like, "according to so-and-so, this adds up to …." Weasel words? Of course, but they take the heat off you when you must make a comment on something that, in your opinion, is less than certain.

It's the Details That Count

After you master style, you need to pay attention to some of the details. By this, I mean everything from the grammar, to the voice, to the number of words you use or don't use, to the acronyms you think your audience will understand, and even some of those things that English majors understand, but maybe not business writers. This section covers a mixed bag of the many details you'll want to consider to make your manuscript a quality manuscript that even your editor will be proud to read.

I Never Met an Adverb That Couldn't Be Cut

The editor who said this was one of the best. She had edited a client's manuscript and used a bright purple pencil (this was pre-marker days) on adverb problems only. Everything else was marked in red. She had a thing about adverbs and wanted authors to know it. "Don't be overly concerned about …" would get a purple pencil.

Then there's the ultimate red flag—turning words that shouldn't be adverbs into adverbs. Over has become "overly," as in, "don't be overly concerned." Apart from the linguistic mishmash this creates, it can have an effect opposite that which most novice writers intend. How much is overly? Does this mean that there is a scale of how much concern is necessary in the situation being described? Wouldn't it have been better to just say, "Don't be concerned"?

As language continues to change, this adverb thing just might become accepted usage. Language does change and customs that were once rejected are now accepted. If you insist on using "overly," just be overly cautious about using it too often.

But This Is Serious

I can't remember how many times an author has used this line as a defense against an editor's comment that his or her language is above the level of the intended reader. And this comment goes for those who are writing for highly educated readers as well as for those who are writing for a general audience.

Long, complex, and heavily punctuated sentences are not only signs of an inexperienced writer, they send readers back to comic books quickly. Don't write them. Big words don't send good signals either. If you are writing about chemistry for chemists, there is no escaping the use of the terms they understand. But if you are writing for chemists who want to start a small business, there's no excuse for obfuscation. Look that word up in your computer dictionary! It's not even in the synonym finder of mine.

But I Have to Explain It All

Yes, you do when writing about a business subject that may be unfamiliar to most of your readers. But once you have done it clearly, move on. If you feel that making your point from several perspectives might make it clearer, you are in for trouble. Explain a salary compensation system from a human resources manager's perspective and then do the same from an employee's perspective, and you will dig a verbal hole that won't be easy to climb out of. (Yes, I did end that sentence with a preposition, and there's nothing wrong with that.)

If you are writing a business biography, a lot of explanation gets boring quickly. Good biographies make use of dialogue. Choose the words of your subjects that make your points, and let them lead the reader to the conclusions you might be tempted to spell out in a more conventional narrative style. Readers like to think they have come to their own conclusions.

Blah, Blah, Blah

We all tend to overwrite. I do it. You probably do it, too. There are times when the words just won't stop coming. I know when I am filling files with worthless words, but I also know that there are times when there are no words to put on paper. For me, it's a lot easier to cut away the words that add nothing than it is to put words on paper when I just can't think of the right ones.

The real issue here is the timing of your self-editing. I tend to do it as I write. One of my colleagues claims he doesn't stop writing until he has made his daily nut, which is 3,000 words. Then he edits his stuff all at once. Another claims to edit when the words stop coming as easily as they did earlier in the day. There is no time that's best for all.

My reason for editing as I write is that when I used to do it at the end of a day's writing I'd sometimes discover flaws in the writing—or even the thinking—early in the day's work that made the rest of the work almost useless. I hated that!

I seldom stop to edit short paragraphs as I go and will occasionally hold off until I have completed a thought, which could include several paragraphs. However I do it, it's done in manageable chunks, and when I'm finished I am comfortable about moving ahead. I think of it like building good foundations first. You may work differently, and I urge you to use whatever system works best for you.

The main goal of ongoing editing is to maintain the pace and to ensure that you stay on track. Overwriting and drifting into pointlessness often means that most of a day's work ends up removed. Writing is like hiking a trail with many forks to consider. Choose any wrong fork at any point and you are in trouble. Editing in short gulps helps you get back on the trail before you waste too much time.

It's a lot easier to edit your stuff today than it was before the word processor replaced the IBM Selectric typewriter. Cut and paste is done instantly with keystrokes, without scissors and glue. And just in case you change your mind after doing an edit, you can always pull up your original text—if you save it.

I urge you to learn how to use the "track changes" feature that is part of most word processing programs. You can master the elements you need in less than an hour and you can save many hours of frustration.

> **Publishing Tip**
>
> If you are uncomfortable editing your material, find a freelance editor to help you. Don't ask Cousin Maggie, whose A in English was granted 30 years ago. A local librarian might be able to suggest someone.

Tracking changes records your changes in a different color and give you every opportunity to manipulate your text. Rather than have to sort through stacks of different versions of some text, you see it in easily understood markings right on your screen. When you are happy with what you have, just hit the "accept or reject changes" button and your final manuscript is on the screen. All the iterations of your revisions can be saved so that future editing can be done just as easily.

But Everyone Knows What NRA Means

Everyone is familiar with your acronyms, right? Wrong! If your reader is a bit past retirement age, that acronym will conjure up the federal National Recovery Act. Someone younger will see the National Rifle Association. Federal bureaus and most business associations are often referred to by their acronyms, but not all your readers will know what you mean when you use one without clarifying it. The safest thing to do is to include the full name of the organization the first time you mention it and then just use the letters. If a few chapters pass before you mention the group again, reintroduce it by its full name.

Keep Your Reader Interested

If you have read any of the writers I mentioned earlier, you probably noticed that it was more than subject matter that held your attention. These writers are a pleasure to read. Others you have read may have been rough going, even though the material was of interest to you. What made the difference? Pacing is one factor. A mixture of short and longer sentences is always more interesting than a steady stream of all long or all short sentences.

A blend of shorter and longer paragraphs is just as important.

There are as many formulas for creating "perfect" structure as there are people who think they have found the secret. Many are helpful, but the best helper you have is your ear. You don't have to speak your writing out loud to use your ear; your inner ear will do just as well.

Read your writing as though you are actually speaking—you can even move your lips if you want. The idea is to slow you down from your customary reading speed to a point where content is less important and where rhythms begin to show themselves. Writers who vary their pace skillfully will grab you, whatever they are saying. Writers who have no idea of pacing will put you to sleep.

This may seem unusual, but if you have a collection of favorite music—rock, marching bands, opera, whatever—put your all-time favorite piece on the player. Listen only for the rhythm instruments. This won't be easy at first, because the music is familiar and you will be listening mainly for melody. If you have a Puccini overture on, listen for the bass drum. He loved that instrument and it's easy to pick up the rhythm. Listen for the guitar bass lines by any of the better rock musicians. If jazz is your favorite, listen for the bass in a small combo. You will quickly discover that this is what holds everything else together.

The same is true when you listen for the rhythm of your writing. Without rhythm, the best soloist simply sounds ordinary. Without verbal rhythm, good words can't make the impressions they should.

You Don't Have to Be One of the Boys

Every field has its special words and its own vernacular. You can't write about marketing without referring to a distributor and without wondering whether an inexperienced reader might wonder why you are talking about an automobile engine part. If you must use a word that has different meanings in different contexts, explain it.

Now that you are a nascent author, you might be tempted to dazzle your reader with your knowledge and use words that set you apart from everyone else. Don't do it. If the use of jargon can't be avoided, either explain it or use it in a context a reader will recognize.

Apart from the special words of your field, you should avoid use of any of the language that could be classified as slang. It's okay to be one of the boys, or girls, in casual conversation or even in writing when you want to make a special point. But to write that a deal is going down after all the honchos get a chance to throw an eye on it will cause you to lose serious readers and make others wonder what you are really up to.

Just in Case You Have Forgotten

Sometimes it takes more than a few words to build a case for a point you are making. An occasional reminder of where you are headed will help readers follow you. You can do this with an intentional remark or by inserting text with key words that will keep your reader focused. "As I mentioned earlier, you should be looking for profits before the end of the year" is the kind of remark that can do the trick without slowing the reader. You may have to offer more of a reminder depending on how much time has passed since you introduced the topic, but this should give you an idea of what I am talking about. This will help you stick to the point, too.

Use Active Voice

For those who like rules, the subject performs the action expressed by the verb when active voice is used. It's just the opposite with passive voice. But enough about grammar. All you need to know is that active voice is direct and more vigorous than passive voice. If you ever have the feeling that what you are reading is important enough to continue with, yet it's a real slog, it's probably because the writer seldom uses active voice.

Which of these do you prefer?

1. The report is being read by the entire staff.

2. The entire staff is reading the report.

The second is active voice, the first is passive. Doesn't the second seem more lively than the first?

1. The share price offer was rejected by half of the brokers.

2. Half of the brokers rejected the share price offer.

Again, number two is the better of the two.

You don't need to know the rules; all you need is an inner ear that hears the difference. It's a feel thing, and with a little practice you can pick it up and use it in your writing.

One warning, however. Once you see how easy it is, you will probably try to force all your writing into an active voice mode. Be warned that this gets breathless and can be just as deadening as sentence after sentence of passive voice. As with sentence and paragraph length, variety is the key.

Words That Belong Together Should Be Kept Together

Thoughts that relate to one another should be expressed together, especially in longer sentences. For example,

1. She saw a major contradiction in the contract that appeared in clause 12.

2. She saw a major contradiction in clause 12 of the contract.

Sentence 2 keeps the two central ideas of the sentence together.

Choosing Your Words Carefully

There are times when it is just too uncomfortable to make bold statements, and there are times when only the bold will do. When only the bold will do, you may need to say negative things in a positive way. Confused? Read these two sentences:

1. We didn't really believe that the finance officer was making the right decisions.

2. We distrusted the finance officer's decisions.

Neither sentence puts the finance officer in a good light, but the second lays it on the line. The second is a stronger statement. You might find the first sentence used in a mea culpa letter to the company's shareholders and the second in a jury's comments on why they decided to send the finance officer to jail.

Relax

If writing isn't what you do regularly, you probably grope for individual words rather than laying down sentences. Get your ideas on paper quickly; you can always cut, change, and add to what you have written. Begin by groping and you will continue to grope. Begin by getting on with it, and you may have to cut and paste later, but you will be better off than if you hack it one word at a time.

As I mentioned earlier, your ear is one of your best writing tools. Read aloud, or read as though you were reading aloud, and listen to the rhythm of the words, the sentences, and the paragraphs. Long sentences mixed with short, complex words mixed with simple ones, and a drumbeat that keeps your reader interested is all it takes. You don't have to learn a single rule of grammar. You don't even have to be able to spell well. All you need is a sense of what good writing sounds like, and you have had the course. Read the good business writers and practice writing like the writers whose words you enjoy reading, and you will be okay.

The Least You Need to Know

- Emulating a style is not plagiarism; it's one of the best ways to improve your writing.

- Active voice is stronger than passive voice, but don't overuse it.

- Edit mercilessly: don't be afraid to throw out writing that doesn't work.

- Finish what you begin, and never leave a reader hanging.

Chapter 20

Working with Your Publisher's Sales and Marketing People

In This Chapter

- ◆ Why you will hear from your publisher's sales and marketing people long before you finish writing your book

- ◆ Why you should negotiate a pre-print buy-in if you are planning to buy a significant number of your books

- ◆ How to work closely with your publisher's subsidiary rights people

- ◆ How to make the most of your subsidiary rights in the emerging electronic marketplace

Just when you get used to working with your editor, the next player in your literary life will probably make an appearance. Depending on the size of your publisher and the emphasis it puts on sales and marketing, that person could be anyone from an assistant to a vice president. Whatever the person's title, this is the beginning of the selling of your book—even though you are still writing it. More than likely, this encounter will take place sometime after you have submitted half your manuscript and have responded successfully to your editor's requests and suggestions.

The first call is usually just a let's-get-acquainted call and a heads-up on things to come. The person calling will tell you what may be in the works for your book and what will be expected of you. In case you forgot, your contract probably calls for you to do radio and television when asked and to arrange your life so you can do book signings and personal appearances, sometimes with very little advance notice.

The early conversations will center mainly on information the marketing people can use to pitch you and your book to the industry, not to the readers you are writing for. Your publisher may have its own sales force, or it may work with independent reps, wholesalers, and distributors to get your book to the trade—the booksellers who hand sell your book to readers. Some use a combination of all of these services, and many have salespeople whose only job is to sell to the online booksellers like Amazon and chains like Barnes & Noble.

The initial sales effort is critical. If a book doesn't "advance" well, your publisher could see this as a bad sign and might cut its promotional budget even before your book gets to the stores. *Advance* in this case refers to early sales to the book trade. Just another example of how publishing terms can mean different things in different contexts.

Keep in mind that whatever promotion and publicity is done for your book will be concentrated in the first few months after publication. After that, the focus shifts to the books that will follow yours a few months later. So pay close attention, be flexible, be creative, be cooperative, and do whatever you can to help get your book successfully launched. Complaining that it's not your job is not appreciated by the publisher, who is just as interested in making money as you are. Whether poor sales can really be blamed on your reticence is seldom provable, but you will get more than your share of the blame. And you do want your book to earn royalties, don't you?

Apart from publicity, this is what you can expect as the sales machine cranks up.

Putting the Package Together

The first call you get from a marketing person is critical. The person you talk with is not only looking for facts, but also is trying to size you up as a promotable author. He probably has your bio and whatever material you submitted with your proposal, so the questions asked will go beyond those details.

Once again, you're being tested. You passed your first test when the publisher agreed that you had good ideas and could write well enough about them. You also passed the initial "platform" test at that time. That is, you have the credentials the publisher needs to help move the book you will write. Your platform is the sum of the characteristics you posses that can be tapped to sell your book. This can include not only your professional qualifications, but your personal skills and abilities as well.

The marketing person talking with you is making notes as you talk. Words like *enthusiastic*, *bright*, and *energetic* make points on a marketer's scorecard. *Quiet*, *non-responsive*, and *inarticulate* are the kiss of death. Marketing has only a limited portion of the sales cycle budget to spend on your book. Fail this test and your portion may get even smaller.

The best way to ace this test is to know yourself, know your subject, know your readers, and speak authoritatively. Don't dominate the conversation, but don't allow for much dead air between topics. Keep the ball rolling in a positive way.

You will also be asked for the names of people the publisher can contact for endorsements. Try to have these lined up long before you get the call from marketing. The people you suggest should be known to your readers or have credentials that will make a big impression on potential buyers. If you have a connection with an especially important person, see if you can line up this person to write the foreword to your book.

Publishing Tip

If you belong to any associations or groups that publish magazines or newsletters, contact the editors. Many editors have connections with people who would be known and would be pluses as foreword writers. While you might not be able to get the attention of a big-name person, the editor probably can. Better yet, if you can get the head of the association to make a call on your behalf, you are pretty much assured of access to someone whose name next to yours can help sell books.

Any media connections you have should be mentioned. Radio and television people, journalists, and writers are key prospects. Other book authors should be considered as well. The more prominent the persons the better, but include everyone.

Pre-Publication Buy-In

This topic may have been discussed during your contract negotiations. If it hasn't, this is when you will be asked about buying more books for your own use than the 10 free copies most author contracts call for. Publishers place their print orders with their printers well ahead of the printing date. The larger the run, the lower the unit cost to the publisher. If you plan to buy a significant number of copies, you may be able to buy in on the publisher's initial run.

Most publishers offer authors a price based on a discount off the planned cover price. This can save you some money, but it's seldom that much of a bargain. Remember, the discount to booksellers hovers around 50 percent of the cover price. A bookseller pays the publisher $10 for a book with a $20 cover price. If you are offered a 20 percent discount off the cover price, which is a common offer, you would pay $16 a book. Sounds good, but wait.

If you want a significant number of books, try for a price based on the publisher's production costs plus a markup. It's beyond the scope of this book to tell you all the items a publisher can come up with to include in a per-unit production cost. However, I can tell you that the figure will always be a better base to work with than a discount based on the cover price.

Just to illustrate, assume that the book priced at $20 retail has a production cost of $8 and you agree to a 50 percent markup of cost. Your cost per book would be only $12. That's $4 less than the price offered based on a discount from the cover price.

These numbers can vary widely, but you can bet that even with the kitchen sink loaded into the cost, your cost would be lower if you could swing a deal based on a markup of production cost.

It's important to remember that you will have to make a legal commitment to buy the books at whatever price you agree to. And you will be expected to pay for your copies as soon as they are shipped.

It's just as important to plan in advance for the storage of your books. A few pallets of books will fill an ordinary one-car garage. And if you have any temperature or humidity problems with your storage area, be sure to insist that the pallet be shrink-wrapped and sealed in plastic. That costs more, but it's worth it.

The publisher will probably ask you to agree not to sell the books you buy in any way that would compete with the way your book is sold through regular channels. These are books that you would have to use as giveaways at conferences or as handouts when pitching business. This gets sticky, but your agent should be able to clarify your rights and responsibilities when you buy in bulk.

Secondary Rights Sales

If you didn't pay close attention to the clause in your contract that deals with secondary rights, you probably gave away a lot of money. If you work with an agent, she knows where the bodies are buried in these clauses and you should be in good shape. Again, there are several words used to mean the same thing. When you see *secondary*, *subsidiary*, and *ancillary*, they all mean pretty much the same thing—any rights other than those which the publisher considers as primary for its own use.

Copyright law provides for the use of these rights by the copyright holder:

- The right to reproduce the copyrighted material
- The right to prepare derivative material from the copyrighted work
- The right to distribute copies of the copyrighted material
- The right to perform a copyrighted work publicly—which I doubt you had in mind when you decided to write a business book
- The right to display the copyrighted work publicly

You'd be surprised at how many ways these rights can be split and interpreted when money is involved. In some cases, subsidiary rights can far outearn royalties on trade sales. If you have granted all subsidiary rights to your publisher, you have in effect appointed the publisher as your agent to either use or sell the rights and to pay you a portion of the proceeds it earns from these sales.

Some publishers are especially good at mining the sub rights of the books they publish, while others are not. Whether they are good or bad seldom relates to their size. In general, however, the larger the publisher, the more interested and the more capable it is of making profitable use of these rights. And, I should add, the more aggressive the publisher is in trying to retain these rights.

Whether you own the rights or share all or some with the publisher, their sale will produce money for you. And it's at this point that you, or your publisher, should begin to take a serious interest in just what is planned for their use.

Publishing Tip _____

Most agents will pursue the more lucrative sub rights deals that might be available for your book. Some of the larger agencies have separate departments for this work.

However, most of the efforts of these people are devoted to pursuing movie deals. There's little chance that your business book will attract a Spielberg offer, so you may have to go after the lesser rights deals yourself. Just remember, your agent works on commission, and a $100 commission for the work involved in selling serial rights for your book on managing new employees is not going to get an awful lot of attention.

What follows is a description of the major subsidiary rights that can be exploited by you or your publisher. If your publisher retained some of the rights, do whatever you can to help sell those rights. It's a mistake to sit back and assume that because the publisher has been granted certain rights, it will exploit them. And if you are going to handle them yourself, now is the time to get the ball rolling.

Paperback Rights

In general, popular business books are published as originals in either hardcover or as trade paperbacks. However, it's not unusual for a book that has sold well in hardcover to warrant a follow-up trade paperback edition. A trade paperback is the same page dimensions as a hardcover book. The even smaller paperbacks are called mass market paperbacks.

Publishing Tip _____

Generally speaking, the only thing that differentiates a trade paperback from a hardcover book is the soft cover. Paper quality is usually the same for both. There is no difference in page size. Trade paperbacks are published mainly to be marketed in bookstores whereas mass market paperbacks, the smaller of the two types of paperback, are produced mainly for sale in outlets other than bookstores. Trade paperbacks are priced lower than hardcover books, and the choice whether to publish first in hardcover or trade paper is usually based on sales estimates for each. Trade paperbacks are priced lower, so the assumption is that more trade paperbacks might be sold than if the book were published originally in hardcover.

The publisher that published the book as a hardcover edition may elect to do the trade paperback itself, or it may decide to sell the right to issue a trade paper edition to another publisher. A follow-up trade paperback edition is seldom considered until the hardcover publisher sees the market for its edition drying up. Or it may produce the paperback if it sees a niche market where trade paperback sales won't endanger the sale of its current hardcover edition.

Whether you or the publisher controls the paperback rights, it makes sense to do everything you can to help make a sub rights sale of the edition. You will make money either way.

If you control the paperback rights, all the proceeds from a sale you make will be yours. If the original publisher has retained the rights, the split of money will be based on the terms to which you agreed in your contract. It's not inconceivable for paper-back earnings to exceed the earnings of the original hardcover edition. This is why it's good to have a savvy agent on your side. The commission your agent earns will be worth it, especially when you consider what you would have to do to find the best publisher yourself and make the best deal.

Even though you may control all the paperback rights, you may still have to adhere to certain restrictions imposed by the publisher of the original hardcover edition. After all, you could conceivably become a competitor to your original edition. Again, your contract will spell this out clearly.

Although it's unusual, there are some business books that do find their way onto the mass market paperback racks. This is where you see the romance, western, sci-fi, and action-adventure titles. The attraction for the publisher is the racks in airports, hotels, and other places where businesspeople gather. I doubt that your handbook of advanced accounting practice will ever become a mass market paperback. However, if you are writing a book about how to start a home-based business or how to be a suc-cessful consultant in your field, there's a good chance that some publisher might be interested in mass market rights.

Book Club Rights

Book clubs are less of a power than they were a few years ago. The book clubs that will be interested in your book will probably be operated by organizations that do specialty publishing in your field. Or they may be part of one of the periodicals that serves a field, or business in general.

Book club sales are most often made well in advance of the publication date, to allow the club to buy in on the original print run of your book. So it's important to start talking with book clubs very early. These rights are most often sold by showing the club buyer a copy of your proposal plus as much of the manuscript as might be available.

Try to negotiate nonexclusive deals with book clubs. If you were to make an exclusive deal with the accounting book club and later discover that a general book club thought it could sell your book to its members, your exclusive agreement would prevent you from doing this.

Translation and Foreign Rights

Some business books travel well, but most don't do all that well in foreign markets. However, you just never know whether yours is one of the lucky titles until you try to sell it abroad. I have had a few that made lots of money in translations and others that I would have thought were winners that weren't.

Selling foreign and translation rights is, as you might expect, a lot more complex than selling the same rights domestically. Here, I would really urge you to locate an agent with a network of offshore agents in the areas where your book should do well. If you are using a domestic agent, chances are she already has a relationship with such agents and makes good use of them for clients.

There are a number of annual international trade fairs at which publishers and agents buy and sell foreign rights. Check them out in *Publishers Marketplace*. Your local library probably has a copy of this directory. It may not be in the general stacks or even the reference stacks, however. It's a librarian's tool and is probably kept in the librarian's office. Most librarians are happy to let you use it.

Translations can be expensive, but books that are sold where English is the main language, or at least a well-understood second language, are where you might consider getting your feet wet. The British Commonwealth alone is a huge market.

If you are handling your foreign rights yourself, be especially careful that you don't sell or give away rights that your original publisher already owns. This is an area where many inexperienced people can get into serious trouble. Be especially watchful of the territories that you grant your offshore licensees. Everyone sees their territory differently, and if you are not careful you just might grant some overlapping territory. You don't want to create an international incident, do you?

Also, watch the term you grant. It's better to grant the shortest period possible along with the right to renew under terms that you specify. Also, you must be mindful of local taxes that have to be collected and paid to the country in which your book is published. And try to arrange for payment in U.S. dollars, not the currency of the country in which your book is being published. If finance is your field, you may be able to do better in terms of exchange rates. Otherwise, stick to dollars.

Some offshore publishers pay royalties annually, or on cycles that differ from that of your American publisher. If you have left foreign rights in the hands of your publisher, you should have negotiated a pass-though clause. With this clause, any money your publisher receives from an offshore publisher is remitted immediately to you. Without this provision, a publisher will simply deposit foreign rights receipts in its own account, and only remit your share with its next half-year royalty statement.

Electronic Rights

The translation of words into bits and bytes has become a major industry. It has also become a source of some pretty expensive lawsuits brought by writers whose words have been appropriated without attribution and without payment. However, for those who buy material and respect copyright laws and those who write the words, a new and profitable market exists.

Selling the rights to your copyrighted material on the Internet is pretty much the same as selling other subsidiary rights. The major issue usually is just how the licensee will use your material and whether that use will interfere with the rights you or the publisher own.

Internet publishing is a relatively new thing. You will run into people who make honest mistakes in their deals as well as those who make dishonest ones. It is so easy to slice and dice material electronically that those with a different slant on life than you and I have steal with impunity. Some get caught and some hire very talented people to rewrite your material for less money than they might pay to license it legally. I know, you're shocked, shocked! But it does happen and there's very little you can do to either prevent it or to collect damages when you think you have been ripped off.

In the meantime, the Internet really does provide excellent possibilities for subsidiary rights sales of your material. It's not uncommon to see electronic business publishers publish excerpts from books and even license entire books for serial electronic publication.

The technology keeps changing, so you will probably see a line in your contract relating to electronic publishing which, after its attempt to define the medium adds something like "or any media created hereafter." Words to this effect are sure to appear in the subsidiary rights clause of your publisher's contract and should be seen in any licensing agreements you make with an e-media owner.

Remember, you can only license rights to material you own. If you have licensed material from someone else and use it with permission in your material, you will need the copyright owner's permission to license your material to someone else.

Dramatic Rights

It's highly unlikely that your book on financial management for biomedical laboratories will be optioned for a Hollywood movie. However, it is possible that someone might want to use some of the material in a training film or a video. I have never encountered this situation, but it does exist and you or your agent should think about it.

Serial Rights

Magazines, newsletters, newspapers, and other periodicals frequently buy the right to serialize material in books. The rights and terms of use of your material will be a major portion of your book contract. I discussed this in some detail in Chapter 17, but it's worth repeating that if you don't pay attention to the details, you could give away the potential for a fair amount of money.

There is hardly a business book that doesn't address an audience that is covered by at least one periodical. And many of the more general business books have a much wider potential. Write a book on how to be a consultant and I can't imagine any of the major or minor periodicals not being interested in at least some of the material.

Even if you made the mistake of granting all serial rights to your publisher and failed to negotiate the terms under which these rights were acquired, you should do everything you can to place your material in as many periodicals as possible. Whether you make the deal or the publisher makes it, it will be money in your pocket.

Backspace

Just a reminder: if your publisher controls your subsidiary rights, negotiate a pass-through clause in your contract. With it, any money the publisher collects for the use of your material from others will be paid to you when the publisher gets its money. You don't want to wait until the end of the six-month royalty period to get what is owed to you.

It's best to start making contact with the periodicals you feel would be best for your material long before your book's publication date. Periodical editors plan their issues well in advance. If anyone is planning a section on the use of regression analysis in market research six months out, you could have a shot at getting some material on the subject in the issue. Be sure to tell the publication editor that your material is copyrighted and that any fee negotiations would have to be done with the book publisher. Also, ask your editor about how much material you can show. If yours is a groundbreaking book, the publisher may want to keep his cards close to the chest.

When Your Publisher May Want to Use Your Material in Other Formats

Smart book publishers are always looking for ways to make more money from the books they publish. They will occasionally assemble chapters from different books they have published on the same subject into something resembling a handbook. It's not uncommon to see sets of paperbacks created from books that they had originally published in hardcover. And some publishers are even more imaginative.

Regardless of how it's done, you should be compensated for the use of your material. Some contracts call for authors to be paid a flat fee for any use of material by the house in any other form than that specified in the contract. Some have even begun to do limited work-for-hire deals in which the author is given an advance and paid royalties only on traditional trade sales. However, these publishers are quite ingenious about assembling material in different forms, and these forms may not mean money for the authors under some limited work-for-hire agreements.

This may sound like a rip-off, but it isn't always. If you are paid well enough up front as an advance, and you are happy with the royalty terms, you may not be giving up much on the work-for-hire side of the deal. As long as you are not bound by a next-work option and are not bound by a rigid non-compete clause, these deals can be okay. Again, an agent in the loop can interpret the language and might even be able to negotiate softer terms on the work-for-hire part of the deal.

The Least You Need to Know

- ◆ Anything you can do to work with your publisher in selling your book will usually translate into bigger royalties.

- ◆ If you are planning to buy copies of your book for your own use, make the deal before the publisher goes to press. You will get your copies for a lot less than you would if you decided to buy after they are printed.

- ◆ Coordinate your efforts with your publisher's sales team and don't hesitate to offer suggestions to them.

- ◆ Subsidiary rights income can often amount to more than royalties earned from general trade sales.

Chapter 21

Working with Your Publisher's Publicity People

In This Chapter

- Why publicity is a major factor in the success of your book
- Creating your own news and buzz for your book
- Getting and profiting from endorsements of key people in your field
- Using personal, social, and business networks to boost your book sales

Dollar for dollar, the money spent on publicity and promotion yields a better return than the money spent on advertising business books. This doesn't necessarily mean that your publisher is going to throw lots of publicity and promotion money at your book. If you are writing a book about sales, marketing, or advertising, you probably know this already. But if you are writing on any other business subject, this may be news to you.

A few years ago, business books could be sold very effectively by direct mail advertising. Publishers with books aimed at large enough segments of the general business population could sell single titles through the mail with fairly elaborate promotional packages. However, as postage and shipping costs rose, book sales didn't rise enough to make direct mail worth the expense and effort. A sales conversion of 1 percent to 2 percent was considered a real success then. When the number dropped below 1 percent and postage and shipping costs continued to rise, the selling of single titles through the mail pretty much ended.

For a while, publishers were able to create mailing packages for several related books and still make their margins. That is still done successfully by some houses. Then the "deck mailings" were tried. These mailings contained postpaid reply cards for many books. This still works for some.

Now, the big book retail chains and the Internet booksellers pretty much account for the bulk of sales of business books. There is still some pretty aggressive direct mail selling being done by specialty publishers and independent bookselling organizations. The engines that are driving these sales, however, are mainly publicity and promotion. And, incidentally, this is one of the reasons why you were interrogated so intensely about your "platform" before you were offered a contract. Your publisher wanted to know how well positioned you were to promote your book and how promotable you would be if a publicity program were to be launched.

Publicity and the Business Book Sales Cycle

In the last chapter, I mentioned that you would hear from marketing, sales, and publicity even before you had delivered your manuscript. Their early contact was aimed mainly at getting your book launched to booksellers, whether they are selling via the Internet, by direct mail, or through the traditional brick-and-mortar stores.

The strength of the early responses from these organizations gives publishers the data they need to allocate the publicity and promotion money aimed at potential readers for your book once it is in place with retailers. Strong early orders usually mean than you will see strong publicity and promotion efforts after the launch. Needless to say, the opposite is also true.

Publishing Tip

Don't be afraid to contact your publisher's publicity people if you are well past the halfway mark in your writing and have yet to hear from them. Your editor can put you in touch.

I apologize for revisiting this subject here, but it's important to remember that your book has only a short time to prove itself. As soon as your book is in print, you should do everything you can to help move your book yourself and to work closely with your publisher's publicity and promotion people.

Publishing Tip _____

Always tell the publicity person who has been assigned to you what you are planning and doing. If you don't, you may not only waste time because of duplicated
effort, but you can also gum up the works if you start duplicating each other's efforts.

Book Reviews

A good way to create early buzz for your book is through book reviews. You don't
have to wait until the book is printed and bound for this to happen.

Once your manuscript has been edited and accepted, it will be converted from your
hard copy pages or electronic copy to the page images that will be your book. These
early proofs are called galleys, and it's these sheets that your publisher's publicist will
send to the appropriate reviewers.

Publicists will usually ask you for a fixed number of names to send galleys to. Pick the
recipients carefully.

If you belong to any groups or associations related to your book subject, and they
publish magazines or newsletters for members, include them. Your publicist probably
already knows the editors and publishers
of the general business publications, such
as *BusinessWeek* and *Entrepreneur*, so try to
focus on the specialty people who will have
a well-focused interest in your book. And
avoid sending a galley to your hometown
newspaper with a circulation of just 500
subscribers.

Publishing Tip _____

Galleys are what your original manuscript is converted
to before being printed. They
are called *galleys* because of the
galley trays in which metal type
was stored. While metal type is
no longer used, the name has
stuck.

If you have a business degree and the school that granted it is in touch with its grads,
be sure that a set of galleys is forwarded to the right person at the school. You may
not only get a pop in the alumni magazine, but the prof who heads the department in
which you specialized might even place an order for ancillary text use.

If your book has "legs" and can be used overseas as well as domestically, send
galleys to the appropriate international editors. Chances are that your publicist will
be concentrating on the domestic market, so this can be an opportunity for you to

help where there is little possibility of any duplicated effort. This used to be a very expensive proposition before the Internet made it possible to e-mail all the text in galley form—not only without cost, but without having to pack and ship many pounds of paper.

Publishing Tip _____

If you can manage to get a good early review, make copies of it and include it with the galleys that you or your publisher continues to send to potential reviewers.

Write Articles and Op-Ed Pieces

Articles in the publications that serve your field and in the business sections of the general press will do a lot to move your books. It's best to coordinate this with your publicist. He probably knows the key players, or at least knows how to get in touch with them.

You can help your publicist by preparing a list of articles you are capable of writing that would be appropriate at the time that your book hits the stores. The publicist will probably ask you to do short précis of a few of the articles, mainly to give editors an idea of what you plan to write about and how you plan to handle the material.

As helpful as articles under your byline can be, articles by people your potential readers would recognize immediately can be even more effective. The articles don't have to be specifically about your book. The author should just write on a subject that allows her to quote from your book liberally.

Publishers with well-known authors can sometimes be prevailed upon to approach their authors with a request for an article. Seldom does money change hands, but this is a quid pro quo situation, and you might be expected to return the favor sometime.

Publishing Tip _____

Check the masthead pages of the periodicals you might like to write for. The larger magazines list their department editors by name, and some even give telephone or e-mail contact information. They need you as much as you need them.

If your agent represents many business book authors, he can probably tap into his network. Be sure to ask early on about help in making a contact. Timing is critical. Some agents even trade these favors with other agents whose clients might be appropriate for the task.

If you are going to pitch articles to magazine editors yourself, get your query letters out early and be sure to mention the anticipated publication date of your book. Don't send the entire manuscript; only send the portions that relate specifically to the subject you would like to write about. Include a copy of your bio and highlight the points that would be of special interest to the editor.

Do not expect to be paid for writing an article that is tied to the publication of your book. Some publications will pay you their standard fee whether or not you request it. However, don't ask for money!

Volunteer for Speaking Gigs

Your publicist will be mainly responsible for setting up radio and television appearances, and it will be pretty much your responsibility to set up any other personal appearances. Seminars, training sessions, corporate and stockholder meetings—these and any other gatherings for any reason that bring potential customers together should be considered.

Most of the gigs you will set up will probably be pretty close to home, so the expenses involved will probably be yours. However, if you are able to set up any speaking engagements that will attract a big crowd or that involve national publicity, your publisher might be willing to pick up the tab, or at least pick up some of the costs.

Whether you plan to give away books or sell them when you speak, the cost will be yours. However, you should be able to negotiate a discount at least equivalent to the publisher's conventional bookseller figure.

Speaking engagements can be opportunities to get media coverage. Be sure to notify the appropriate publications, editors, and journalists about your plans well in advance of the date. Also send them all a reminder a few days before.

Create Your Own News

Most business books published by general publishers add knowledge to the field for their intended readers. Outside the field, however, that news is seldom earth-shattering. This means that a press release about your new book will probably get published only if it happens to be a slow news day or if you are already a name author.

A press release announcing the book is just not going to get an awful lot of attention. But there are ways to get that attention and to get it when you need it—when your book is first available for sale.

The best way to get that attention is to tie your book to some current news. The announcement of a book just published that relates to ongoing and exciting news will stand a far better chance than will a release simply announcing the book. If, for example, you have written a book about an aspect of banking that touches on the scandals being exposed daily as I write this book, a tie-in line or two will help a lot.

Here's a conventional press release headline for such a book:

> NEW BOOK COVERS ALL ASPECTS OF BANKING WITH FRESH INSIGHT

A headline like the next one could put the release on the top of the "run" pile:

> NEW BOOK REVEALS WHY BANKING SYSTEM IS FLAWED AND WHAT CAN BE DONE TO PREVENT FUTURE LOSSES

The text should, of course, touch on the aspect of your book that addresses this news event in sufficient detail to satisfy the curiosity the headline created.

If your book is not too narrowly focused, you can tailor your press releases to the magazines and readers you want to reach. One of the biggest mistakes most authors and quite a few publishers make is to try to create one press release that will work for all the book's audiences. Yes, it takes work and is more costly to do separately focused releases, but it is well worth it. Chances are that your publisher will go the one-size-fits-all route, so think about adding to the effort with releases of your own or releases that you have an outside publicist create for you. Again, coordinate your efforts with your publisher's publicity person.

Remember, the news you tie in with must be current. Your press releases should have a slightly breathless quality to them. You want to create the impression that your new book has arrived just in time and that you are the expert readers should turn to for answers.

Pitch Yourself as a Source of Material

Some of the best book publicity I have seen only mentions the book tangentially. And the publicity was not sent out as a traditional press release; it was sent to magazine editors with the idea of getting the author on the editor's go-to list.

Every magazine editor keeps a list of individuals he or she can count on for information on stories being written. Once you are on that list and have proven your ability to the editor, you will be called when your specialty is the subject of a planned article. A long quote in an article in an important journal with a line like this is priceless: "According to Jane Smith, author of the recently published book *How to Invest in Gold*, the market for bullion will soon …." A pop like that will do much more for sales of your book than you might imagine.

Getting on an editor's go-to list is not as easy as it might seem. An editor or staff writer has to know enough about you to consider you to be a reputable and practical source of information. He has to be able to trust you and your judgment. And the best way to build this trust is to send a copy of your book, a resumé, and a letter saying that you would be willing to help with a story whenever needed. You should also mention that you have other contacts who might be helpful with the story and be prepared to make the introductions.

The best way to get this ball rolling is to identify the editors who write regularly on subjects that you can help with. Your first letter might just be a note commenting on a recent article one of the editors wrote. Don't be obsequious, write as one professional to another. Needless to say, the letter should include all your contact information and a simple offer to help if the editor is planning a follow-up on the current story.

You probably won't make the A-list immediately, so if you don't hear right away, don't push it. Wait until you see another piece by the same editor and send another note with material that he or she might have found helpful in the initial writing of the story. In time, you will make the list and you and your book or books will get those little notices inside big news stories that really help sell books.

Backspace

Avoid an ego trip. Stick to the facts that would get an editor interested in you as a potential source. Forget about the glitter. Instead, stick to details that would impress an editor on a tight deadline who needs a source for an immediate quote.

This approach works just as well for radio and television journalists as it does with print people. The fact that you have a book in print with a reputable publisher gets you in the door. That you are willing and able to contribute to a story or feature gets you the exposure you want.

Remember, being quoted regularly in any medium means that you can use that status when you talk to your publisher about your next book.

Make the Most of Your Contacts

In addition to asking you to provide a foreword by a well-known person, your publisher will probably ask you to provide names of people who would be willing to write short endorsements. These are the lines you often see on the back flap or back cover of a book that say wonderful things about the author and the book. Their most important use is at the point of sale: in a bookstore where a potential reader is deciding whether to buy your book or another author's. Two or three short endorsements by people your readers might recognize can do wonders for your book at that particular moment. However, there are also other ways you can turn your endorsements into selling tools for your book.

If you have several good endorsements, create a separate sheet to send with your press releases and your queries to magazine editors. Keep it simple: just a bold head like "What others are saying about this book" at the top of the page is all that's needed.

Most authors in most fields don't look at other authors as competitors. If a reader reads one author's book on your subject, she will probably read some of the other authors' books as well. It's this kind of friendly competition that makes the work not only more enjoyable, but also a lot more profitable.

Check the books you already have on the subject you are writing about and you will probably see many of the same names showing up as writers of endorsements and even lengthy forewords. Of course, we all think our own books are better than all the others, but most of us realize that it's better to cooperate than compete when it comes to book marketing.

One of the best ways to line up the right people for your foreword and endorsements is to contact them early in the writing of your book. Have a specific question in mind and tell the author that you would like to quote him or her in your book. Only the most egocentric or naive of authors will fail to respond with the material you want and permission to use his or her quote in your book. The bigger the name, the better, of course. And you will be surprised at how many really famous people will be willing to respond to you.

Publishing Tip

When seeking endorsements, make it clear in your request that, as a published author, you would be more than pleased to return the favor.

Once a person has agreed to be quoted in the pages of your book, he most likely will be willing to write an endorsement. You will, of course, have to see that your publisher sends him galley proofs to read. This often leads to a quid pro quo in which the authors who blurbed your book will ask you to blurb their books. You are now part of the in-group!

Those who endorsed your book are often willing to help you beyond the few words you might ask for. It's not uncommon for authors to ask others to take part in promotional programs to which they have been invited. If you are used to tooth-and-nail competition elsewhere, you will be very surprised at how little of this exists among authors of business books.

Networking Gets You Places You Never Thought Of

Networking is not a new concept, but it's a concept that must be managed carefully—or you may find your network managing you. You have written a business book, which means that you are an expert in your business field and you are a writer. It's tempting to network in the writing area, but this could be a mistake, unless you want to make writing your main field.

Active participation in any network takes time and patience. If your book is an extension of the work you do in business, stick to networking in your business field. Networks are made up of people with common interests who want to meet others in their field. To be considered part of the net, you must be willing to give as well as to get. For this reason, look for network links with people who are operating at least at your level, but hopefully well above your level. When you are the big guy in your network, you have no one to turn to. This may feed your ego, but it does little to promote you and your book. Good networks operate like well-coordinated sports teams. They have a common goal and they realize that there are times when even the bench-warmer can make a contribution.

The new Internet social networks, such as Facebook, Twitter, and LinkedIn, are tempting to use for networking. However, you should be prepared to deal with a lot of contact that will not only be unproductive, but that can bog you down if you try to deal with everything. The narrower the focus of your networking, the better your responses are likely to be.

Tie In with Someone Already in the Spotlight

If you have any connections with people already in the publicity spotlight, see if they will help you with contacts or tie you in with their existing publicity activities. Established authors are often willing to go to bat for new authors. Your agent may already represent other business book authors and might be willing to put you in touch with her other clients.

Your agent is as interested in seeing your book succeed as you are. Her commission is tied to book sales, and anything she can do to help you sell books will help boost her agency's income. Don't hesitate to ask your agent about making connections.

Tie In with Your Employer's Publicity

If you work for a company that already does publicity for its products or services, see if you can tie in with its efforts. Pitching an employee who has become a published author is as good for your employer as it is for you and your book.

Many of the clients I represented when I was a literary agent worked for major corporations and universities. The bigger the employer, the smarter it is about the value of this kind of publicity. The earlier in your writing cycle that you make this contact, the better. Your employer's public relations department or its outside agency will have contacts that will be impossible for you, as an individual, to tap.

Beyond the publicity angle, your employer may even be able to help you during the development of your book. Several of my clients were given short leaves of absence to research or complete the writing of books. Needless to say, your employer must see some value for itself in your book to do something like this.

Don't Waste Too Much Time Locally

Becoming an author in your own backyard is a real feel-good experience. You should enjoy every moment of it. However, unless your backyard includes some turf that will account for a lot of book sales, you can get bogged down in a lot of relatively unproductive effort.

Being the guest author at the local library book club or a speaker at the local chamber of commerce lunch will not do an awful lot to put royalty money in your pocket. Try to focus your publicity efforts on the big picture. Here is where your publisher's publicity department can help a lot. The department has a pretty good idea of how many of your books will be sold in the first year, and it will be focusing its efforts on the people and places where those sales should be made.

As I have already mentioned, publicity for your book will begin long before your manuscript is complete. It's tempting to avoid anything that will take you away from the job of finishing your writing, but you should do everything you can to help the publicity people do their jobs. And the more enthusiasm you show, the more enthusiastic they will be about working with you. Depending on the size of the publishing company, your publicity person could have a few titles or an entire catalog of books coming out in each publication period. The earlier you cement your relationship, the better for you and for your publisher.

Always Have Your Own Sound Bites Ready

You never know when a publicity opportunity will show itself. Imagine you are attending a national sales conference and you hear the speaker say, "I've just been told that we have an author in our midst. How about telling us about your new book, Tony?" The spotlight is on you, and you have to describe what's in your 100,000-word book in just a minute or two.

Or you are on the train going home at the end of the day, when someone who knows you casually asks about your new book. Your stop is coming up and you don't have the time to give the spiel, but you happen to have a publisher's press kit in your briefcase.

Never be caught short when it comes to blowing the horn about your book. Have your pitch on the tip of your tongue, and have the press releases at the ready. Never flounder. Missed moments are missed sales.

You might even consider creating a "sampler" CD that features key points in the book as well as chapter summaries and some sample text. And, of course, it should include specific ordering information. If you are capable of creating such a disc, your only cost will be duplication, which should be only a few pennies per disc. A professionally prepared disc could be more expensive, but it might be worth it, especially if you are "asked to say a few words" at a meeting and just happen to have a bunch of discs to hand out to those who are interested.

> **Publishing Tip**
>
> If you already have your foreword and blurbs in hand, either memorize them so you can repeat them easily or give a printout to anyone who might be interested.

The Least You Need to Know

- Exposure is the key element in book sales, and good publicity is the way to get it.
- Become the go-to source by sharing your ideas and information freely.
- Endorsements from key players can be gotten, but you have to be ready to return the favors.
- Never miss an opportunity to pitch your book.

Chapter **22**

Working with Independent Publishers, Distributors, Media Trainers, and Publicists

In This Chapter

- ◆ Where to turn when a commercial publisher says no
- ◆ How publicity consultants can turn your story into a newsworthy event
- ◆ How a media trainer can cure your jitters and turn you into a sought-after media guest

Most of this book has been focused on publishing your book with conventional book publishers. You probably recognize their names. They pay an advance for manuscripts and take care of editing, designing, printing, and distributing the final product. They also are quite choosy about the manuscripts they accept.

Maybe your proposal is one of those that was kindly rejected, but you believe that what you have to say is important and valuable to a particular group of readers. Maybe your potential audience is very small, but what you have to say will take more space than a magazine article or a white paper. All is not lost. There are other ways to get your book into print, some a bit more practical than others.

Independent publishers, self-publishing, print-on-demand systems, or subsidized publishing may be options for you. This chapter examines the different alternatives available.

Who Goes the Independent Publishing Route?

Most of those who go the independent route have first tried to interest conventional publishers in doing their books. After all, a conventional publisher will not only pay you an advance against future sales, but it will also undertake all the editorial, distribution, marketing, sales, and promotional tasks the book needs to get to readers. But when a small potential market closes that door, it doesn't mean that all the benefits of having a book in print are closed.

Suppose you wanted to write a book about how to do test marketing for manufacturers whose products are sold only to clinical diagnostic laboratories, a very small market for a book publisher. You write well and you know that there is a need for one book that pulls together all the techniques that work and tells why the others aren't to be trusted. There is a clear need for the material, yet every agent you talked with said no, and the few publishers you contacted were kind enough to send a preprinted thanks-but-no-thanks form letter.

Publishing Tip

You have probably read many books that were first self-published. A few of the more notable include *In Search of Excellence, What Color Is Your Parachute?,* and *The Elements of Style.* You are in good company if you go the independent route.

What you want to say requires more space than a magazine article or even an extended report or white paper. The practical route is to do it yourself. But which of the alternatives is the better way to go? Let's look at the issues from the perspective of independent and subsidized publishing.

Costs

If you had been able to attract a conventional publisher, you would have had no out-of-pocket costs. In fact, the publisher would probably have given you an advance of money against sales of the book once it was published. Any of the other options, however, will cost you money.

You might end up paying less to do your book with a vanity publisher or just by working directly with a printer. However, if you see your book as reflective of yourself and your ideas, you may be disappointed by the results.

Most of the independent publishers operate pretty much the same way as conventional publishers and not only provide hands-on editorial assistance, but also some first-rate talent when it comes to design and book production. Many also provide considerable help on the distribution side of the equation.

Costs should always be considered, but when it comes to working with independents, printers, and vanity presses, the quality of the finished product is critical. Be sure to ask to see copies of books each has done and ask for cost data. Independents will probably turn out to be more costly, but from the books I've seen done by some, it's the safer bet over a printer and a vanity-type press.

Who Owns the Rights to Your Material

When you work with a conventional publisher, even when you hold the copyright to your material, you assign certain and sometimes all rights to your publisher. Go with any of the other systems and the rights are all yours. This may seem like a great thing, but it also means that it is up to you to make appropriate and profitable use of these rights. Unless you know what you are doing, you could miss out on a lot of money and a lot of exposure for your book.

What About Timing?

A conventional publisher can put a book out in a matter of weeks if there is a market for it. But under most circumstances, you won't see bound copies in less than six months after submitting your manuscript, and it's more likely that it will take a year.

Sponsored Books with Conventional Publishers

As I mentioned before, a conventional publisher's colophon is in many ways a stamp of approval. There are times when these publishers get proposals for books they really like, but they know they can't sell them well because of their small market.

Some publishers will offer to do what is called a sponsored book, which goes through the complete editorial and design process and carries the publisher's colophon. However, the author agrees to share the costs by agreeing in advance to buy a certain minimum number of copies. Needless to say, the cost per copy can be higher than it might be to do the book with a printer, a vanity press, or an independent. However, you are getting all the attention you would get otherwise from the publisher and you are getting that valued colophon on the spine of your book. Also, these books are usually carried in the publisher's catalog, even though there is little hope of selling a significant quantity of them.

> **Backspace**
>
> Rejection is part of publishing life. John Creasey's first story was rejected 774 times before it was finally published. He then went on to write 564 books, using 14 different pen names.

Don't mistake this for any kind of vanity publishing. Sponsored books must meet all the editorial standards of the other books the publisher does. It's just that they seldom meet the publisher's economic goals without the sponsorship.

Many of the corporate histories you may have read have been done as sponsored books. There are writers whose specialty is writing corporate histories. These writers usually work closely with the sponsoring company's public relations department or its outside public relations or advertising agency.

Becoming Your Own Publisher

This is, by far, the most difficult and potentially the most costly route to go. . You will have to work with editors, designers, marketing and sales consultants, printers, book distributors, and wholesalers on your own. It's not as simple as just handing your manuscript to a printer and waiting for your books to be delivered. Not being published is better than having a badly done book with your name on it.

But if you are set on going this route, here are a few tips to help you make the best of it.

Find a Good Editor First

Everyone received occasional praise from one of the English teachers he or she had in high school or college. And because nobody has the guts to tell someone that his or her current writing is terrible, the image lives on. Primed with early praise and over-blown authorial dreams, too many people publish their own books without help and live to regret it. It's not only costly, but it can also be very embarrassing.

So before you do anything else, find a good editor, book doctor, or collaborator.

What It Costs to Be Your Own Publisher

If you are working with a printer, either you or the printer will have to do the prepress work. This includes design, keyboarding, and all steps necessary to bring your material to the point where it can be put on a press. Outside designers are costly. A printer may include design as part of the package, but if you don't like the work, you are either stuck with the deal or have to hire a designer yourself.

The larger the press run, the smaller the unit cost should be. These days, however, it's possible for many printers to do relatively small runs for a lot less than it cost only a few years ago. Regardless of the quantity, however, you are going to invest some significant money in prepress, printing, and post-press binding services.

Subsidy publishers will handle the prepress, printing, and binding operations. Costs will vary, and because there isn't a lot of competition in this field, it will be difficult for you to know whether you are getting a bargain or not. By the time most authors decide to go this route, they simply want to get on with it, and they seldom get competitive estimates. Take the time. There are some excellent subsidy publishers to choose from.

> **Backspace**
>
> Your cost to print may be the smallest cost of your self-publishing plans. Marketing, publicity, warehousing, distribution, sales, and other costs will probably amount to a lot more than your total printing bill.

Where Do You Want Your Books Delivered?

Few who go the self-publishing route think about what they will do with all the books once they are published. Unless you have already made arrangements with a book distributor or wholesaler, you will have to store your books yourself.

Let me give you some numbers to conjure with. Two thousand 6×9×1.5-inch books take up 162,000 cubic inches. Add the space taken up by the pallets, and you better have more room available than just the spare bedroom. And that space better be at ground level or at least on an extremely well-supported floor—or you may have to add the cost of some major structural damage to your cost of doing business.

Who Will Sell Your Books?

The stories you hear of authors who pack their cars with their books and hit the road to make fortunes are usually true, but for everyone who makes it to the big time, thousands don't. You have become an author and a publisher, and now you must take on the sales job.

Fortunately, there are quite a few smaller distributors and wholesalers who work with independents and self-publishers. The larger distributors seldom are interested in taking on a one-book publisher; it's just too costly for them.

Most of the smaller distributors can walk you through pricing and other issues related to dealing with book retailers. Remember, however, that the book retailers have pretty much the same concerns about dealing with a one-book publisher as a distributor does.

All of this adds up to your sales and distribution costs being higher than they would be per unit if you had more titles to offer.

As you can see, the most difficult part of this self-publishing drama is that of selling the books you wrote and published. But there is a way it can be done effectively, and that is by working through another publisher who already had a good sales and distribution network in place. Many small publishers who are selling titles related to your book would probably be interested in making a distribution deal with you. The deals can vary considerably. Most publishers who do this usually require you to store and ship the books that their sales force sells. So you may still be stuck with the storage problem.

Many authors sell their books directly on the Internet, and others make deals with both the large and small Internet booksellers. This can be an excellent way to move your books, but, again, you should be prepared to pack and ship the orders the Internet sellers get for you.

Consultants and Associations That Can Help

The alternatives to publishing with a conventional publisher are many, as are the pit-falls and advantages. If this is a route you are seriously considering, I would suggest that you talk with a consultant about your ideas and get a good plan of action before you go any further. There are many good people in this field, and most walked the walk before they started consulting.

Type "small publishing consultant" in your search engine and you will find more than a few pages of consultant listings. Look at all of them and call those who seem to be closely aligned with you and the type of publishing you are considering. Two consultants whose names have been mentioned by several of my colleagues are Cross River Publishing Consultants (www.pubconsultants.com) and Self Publishing Resources (www.selfpublishingresources.com).

There are a number of associations for those who self-publish, but the one most often mentioned by my colleagues is Self Publisher's Association of North America (www.spannet.org).

As with many things, it probably isn't wise to rush into self-publishing. A consultant or one of the associations of self-publishers can get you started on the right road at a leisurely pace. But if you are writing on a topic that will soon be out of date and need to move quickly, a consultant should be able to give you a self-publishing crash course.

Take a Course

Many major colleges and universities offer courses on a wide variety of publishing topics. Some of the courses are part of the course work in undergraduate and graduate programs and others are specialized noncredit courses offered by departments of continuing education.

Quite a few of the programs are offered as evening courses or as concentrated mini-programs, usually during summer break. Many of these programs are designed for college graduates with degrees in English to pick up a fast working knowledge of book publishing before heading out to look for jobs.

New York University (NYU), for example, has an extensive and highly rated program within its School for Continuing and Professional Studies. Most of the courses are given in the evening and are taught by professionals from many of the major international publishing companies headquartered nearby.

Of the more than 40 courses listed in the Spring 2009 NYU catalog, many would be perfect for the person who is thinking about self-publishing. Here are just a few of the courses that could help any self-publisher:

From reader to writer: An introduction to book publishing

Everything you need to know about digital publishing

How to get your book published

Book publicity and promotion

Book marketing in print and online

The business of book publishing

There are many others, but these few give you an idea of what is available at NYU. A quick check of other major universities showed that most of them have similar offerings. Pull up the continuing education bulletins of the schools near you and see what they offer.

Most of these courses are taught by working professionals, so you not only get real-world material, but you also just might meet a publishing pro who can set you up with good local publishing contacts.

Working with a Freelance Publicist

Whether you are planning to self-publish or have found a commercial publisher who wants to do your book, you will probably find yourself using some of the services offered by publicity freelancers or larger public relations organizations.

If you are being published by a commercial publisher, you will probably get the publisher's standard treatment, unless you happen to be a big name or are writing a book that everyone agrees will hit the best-seller charts immediately. Then you move from the publicity B-list to the A-list.

Most major publishers' standard publicity treatment for new authors ranges from good to great. Few really do a bad job, mainly because their money is on the line and they want to recoup it as soon as possible. If you find yourself getting the bad treatment, you may want to work with someone who can do more for you.

If you decide to do this, be sure to let your publisher know what you are doing. Nobody will be annoyed with you. In fact, your publisher will be happy, because your effort will help sell more of your book and you will be paying for it. In fact, some publishers are happy to give you the names of publicists with whom they have worked in the past and can vouch for. The publisher just needs to know what you're doing to avoid duplicating any work that your publicist is planning to do.

Work on publicity for your book usually gets started well before the publication date. It goes into high gear when books should be reaching the bookstores. Timing of events is critical, because there is such a narrow window to launch a book. It's every author's bad publisher story—you got a guest spot on Oprah, interviews on NPR and some of the key radio business shows, and the local papers reviewed your book with high marks. But your books aren't in stores. Talk about lost opportunities! All those people primed by your performances to buy and read your business book, and there are none to be had.

Most independent publicists and publicity agencies can help by providing separate elements of publicity, or they can do the whole package. What you need really depends on what your publisher has planned and what you might require beyond the publisher's package.

A typical business book publicity program can include elements focused on print, public appearances, the Internet, and broadcast media. However, because you are a new

Backspace

Remember, most advertising is not all that effective in selling business books. Don't be tempted to spend your own money on ads if your publisher refuses to advertise your book. If you are going to invest some of your own money, spend it on publicity and promotion.

author, your in-house publicist will probably focus on the one or two areas believed to offer the biggest and fastest bang for the publicity dollars allocated to your book. If you choose to include an outside publicist in your plans, she will probably review the publisher's plan and suggest where additional attention should be focused.

Print Media Publicity

The very least most publishers do is create and distribute press releases to the print media they feel would be most interested in your book. Some may do a lot more, but you may have to turn to an outside person or group to take on print media publicity beyond the basic release.

One of the best ways to promote a book is by writing and placing articles about the subject of your book. Publishers' publicity people seldom do this for authors other than their A-list.

An outside publicist can usually handle everything from selecting the appropriate media and journalists to the actual writing of the material. The material created is more like a white paper than a press release. It's often written as an article that the publication can either publish as is or use as the basis for an article that a staff writer develops.

Good publicists know the publications and the staff editors and writers well enough to pitch the stories personally. They are also prepared to offer whatever assistance the media writer might need to flesh out the story, get exclusive author quotes, and provide other contacts to add to the story.

The ideas for these placements may come from you, but more than likely they will emerge from conversations you have with your publicist. Don't hesitate to send ideas to your publicist whenever you have them. Don't be too upset, however, when your ideas are either rejected or ignored. A good publicist knows what has been published on your subject recently and what has not been in print for a while and might get a periodical editor's attention.

It's not uncommon for a publicist to pitch an article based on a minor point of your book, rather than on the key issue. He knows what might get the attention of each publication and writer. Although the pitch might not focus on the key issue of your book, rest assured that the publicist will see that the key issue is part of the story that is sent and that, hopefully, will be published. It's a matter of getting attention first, then massaging the material appropriately.

Apart from actually placing material in appropriate publications, a good outside publicist will also pitch you as someone his media contacts can go to for information. If your book deals with subjects currently being covered by the media, you may soon hear from a writer in search of information and quotes from an authoritative source. Be as helpful as you can, and you will be called again the next time the writer addresses the same subject.

Broadcast Media Publicity

If your business book has a wide enough general audience, your publisher's publicity people will probably try to book you on radio and television shows that have a business focus. Get on the right shows and you can move a lot of books. If your publisher's publicity program seems a little thin, and the publisher is unwilling to do anything more, then consider working with an outside publicist with the right connections. Again, nobody will be offended.

Working with an outside publicist on a broadcast media publicity program is pretty much the same as working on a print media campaign. Your publicist will make the appropriate contacts, send back-up information, and pitch you as a good candidate for shows.

The major difference, however, is that you become an active participant, whether the show is taped for later airing or if you appear live. A television gig means that you must go to a studio for a live show or to a production studio where a show is taped. However, there is no escaping doing an on-camera performance.

Many radio shows are done live to take advantage of the immediate call-in potential for listeners. However, most radio shows don't require you to go to a studio. Most are done over the telephone. You may have heard dogs barking or children screaming in the background of another author's radio interview. I'm willing to bet that those authors never had any media training, or they would have made sure they were in a locked and nearly soundproof room at home for the interview.

Publishing Tip

As practical as cordless home telephones and mobile cell phones are for routine calls, they can present problems for on-air radio interviews. If the battery goes dead during the interview, you are off the air and probably won't be asked back. These phones are miniature two-way radios and on certain frequencies are subject to interference from other phones. Use a hardwired landline handset just to be safe.

One of the major benefits of doing television with an important host is the potential for taping your segment and using it as a calling card or for other promotion. Be sure you know exactly what you can and cannot use and how the show grants you the right to use the material. In general, as long as you don't sell it or use it in a way that implies media endorsement, you should be okay. But be sure—not sorry!

Doing broadcast media is a lot more tricky than working with print media. You could travel across the country to do a television show only to find that at the last minute you have been bumped. The scheduling, coordination, and management of television appearances often requires constant contact right up until airtime. Unless you are ready to handle these details, an outside consultant is usually the best way to go. On the other hand, if you have been bumped from a radio show, it was probably a phone-in gig, so no time has been lost.

Other Public Appearances

Some of the best publicity you can get will be at business conferences that attract big audiences. National and international trade shows, seminars, and professional meetings provide you—and your publisher—with a tightly defined audience for your book.

Some book publishers do a pretty good job of booking authors for these venues. But some don't, and a good outside service can do the trick. Speakers' bureaus, sometimes called meeting planners, can be a big help here. One good way to get leads on a good one is to ask authors who have spoken at programs you have attended for the names of the people or organizations that booked them for their current gig. A quick Internet search will prove that speakers are in demand. Do the usual refined search to come as close to your subject and target audience as possible, and you will be surprised at how many bureaus there are, who they represent, and what they say they can do for you.

Media Training

Most first-time authors are usually quite inexperienced presenters or guests. You may think of yourself as a good speaker, but let your publisher's publicity person be the judge. A lot of work goes into setting up media contacts and arranging for interviews and other appearances, so make sure that you know what you are doing. A spot on a major television business show will sell a lot of books if you are an impressive guest.

Most publishers' publicity people can give you the basics and the encouragement to do your best. But because they are usually working with more than a few authors at any one time, they seldom can take you by the hand and turn you into a super guest. If you are a first-time big-name author, some publishers will pick up the tab for coaching. But for all the others, the tab will be yours.

If you are concerned about the cost—it's seldom inexpensive—consider that the training will also help you in any of your other public appearances. Just doing your job running your company's sales meeting can be improved with good media training. If you work for a company that would also benefit from your media exposure, see if the company will pick up the tab.

Most media consultants have long menus of training programs. Some provide comprehensive and media-targeted programs. Others address individual elements in a cafeteria choice situation. If you have been told by your publisher's publicity person where you might need help, go for the individual sessions that will do the job. If you are really not media-savvy, it's probably best to go for the whole show.

In general, most media appearances involve you as either the presenter or as the person being interviewed. There's a lot of crossover in both situations, but being interviewed is definitely not the same as giving a speech. A good media trainer can show you when to lead and when to be led, when to respond and when to defer, when to move on and when to go deeper in the current topic. If you ever want to return to a show that had you as a guest, you'd better know how to respond to the host appropriately in every situation that is likely to occur.

Media Training for Presentations

Whether giving an invited lecture to a large group or addressing a small group of your peers, you are seen differently from the way you are seen when you are not in front of a group. It's a control issue, and unless you know how much to exert, you can either come off as a hero or a flop.

A good media consultant will explain the difference between engaging an audience and grabbing an audience. You should learn how to translate the language of your field into a language that will resonate with most of the people in your audience. You should also get coaching in the nonverbal factors, the body language aspects of giving a speech. And, as elemental as it may seem, you should learn how to work with props such as slides, sound, and individual items that relate to the topics you are discussing.

Media Training for Guest Appearances

Even experienced public speakers have moments of sheer panic. This may not be a comfort to you, but many of the people you have admired for their cool on the podium are complete wrecks in the wings as they await their introductions. Once on stage, they are in total control.

Training just to handle the panic can be well worth it. But just as important, you should probably get some training in how to stay focused, handle controversial questions, and deal with the totally unexpected events that can destroy an otherwise perfect media appearance.

The Least You Need to Know

◆ There are many more ways to become a published author than just going the traditional routes.

- Self-publishing has a long and honored history of success.

- Media consultants can turn even the most stage-frightened people into dynamic presenters.

- You don't have to be a big name to get on broadcast media if you connect with the right independent publicity organization.

Chapter 23

Usual and Unusual Ways to Promote Your Book

In This Chapter

- ◆ It pays to do more than your publisher plans to do
- ◆ Promoting yourself is one of the best ways to promote your book, but avoid an ego trip
- ◆ Tap the promotional strength of those you interview in your book
- ◆ Marketing your book when you self-publish

The publicity you and your publisher will do for your book when it's first published is designed to do one thing only—to sell books and to get them moving as quickly as possible. It's critical to establish a buzz for the book in order to get the bookstore and online sales moving as quickly as possible.

If a publisher's first efforts at promoting your book are successful, there is every chance that the publisher will continue to spend money promoting your book.

However, book publishers don't throw good money after bad, so if the book doesn't catch on quickly, very little will probably be done to make it work.

There are just too many other books in a publisher's pipeline that might catch on quickly and be worthy of the investment and time.

But you already know this if you have read the earlier chapters of this book. What you don't know is that there are other ways to promote your book than the standard model most publishers use. Your publisher may take advantage of some of them, but more than likely it will be up to you to help get the job done. Here are a few ideas you can play with.

Publicizing Yourself

Unless your personal credits far outweigh those of the other authors on your publisher's current list, chances are your publisher won't do much more to publicize you than it does for the other authors on the list. However, the more you bring to the table personally, the better your chances of making a case for a publisher to put in some extra effort.

More than a few authors I have represented over the years have made good use of some form of self-promotion. Those who worked for companies that could see a benefit in spending their publicity dollars to promote an employee with a new book encouraged their companies to do so. For my self-employed clients, self-promotion usually meant kicking in their own money.

In either case, I can say that many carefully planned and professionally managed personal publicity campaigns were successful in boosting sales. One client, a university adjunct professor, claimed that his book and his personal publicity campaign moved him from the adjunct ranks to the ladder of the tenure-track faculty. Another, the marketing manager of a manufacturer, got a raise and a bonus and, last I heard, was being considered for a significant promotion.

Obviously, publicity focused on you must still be based in some way on your book. And the best way to make this work is by the old tried-and-true route of sending press releases and querying magazine editors and broadcast bookers. If you are especially knowledgeable on a subject currently in the news, an offer to editors and bookers of broadcast guests will probably get immediate attention.

Using Current Events as a Publicity Hook

It's usually better to focus on topics of immediate interest. As I write this chapter, banking and investment scandals are breaking everywhere. If I were still an agent, I would urge my financial writer clients to focus on issues that would provide background for the breaking news. Just about anyone with a current book published by a well-known publisher who could be quoted or interviewed would be likely to get a call. If the media host does a live phone interview with you, you are sure to be introduced as "Mary Smith, the author of the recently published book *Money, and How to Get It.*" Enough of these spots on the appropriate shows will move a lot of books.

Apart from making hay based on current issues, it's still a good bet for any business book author to work hard at becoming a go-to resource for any medium seen, read, or listened to by potential book buyers. When the publisher's initial publicity push comes to an end, if your book isn't moving well by itself, you will have to do things on your own to continue or enhance the momentum. Once your book is no longer the "new" book, the focus has to shift to you.

Make Use of Your Professional Memberships

If you are a member of a professional association, you may be able to get some help from it. Professional associations are always trying to recruit new members, and by connecting with you, "the author of the recently published book on ...," they get new member attention and you get sales. The best way to kick this wheel is to volunteer to speak at meetings you think will be covered by the press or to write for the association publications. This can only be effective with organizations whose members would have a real interest in you and your book. Speaking at the annual meeting of the National Association of Model Train Enthusiasts won't get you a lot of notice with potential readers of your book on business to business communication.

You should probably avoid trying to get attention for your book by appealing to a writer audience unless your subject is writing. It's nice to be known among and associated with writers, but from a purely business point of view, it's probably a waste of time.

If your academic background relates to the subject of your book, your college connections may be a good bet. Pay your alumni dues and tell the editor of the alumni magazine about yourself and your book. More than a few of the writers I represented when I was an agent went this route, and many who were independent consultants claim to have landed nice assignments from the connection.

Networks Can Be Very Productive

Don't hesitate to turn to friends and professional colleagues for help, too. Everyone in business has connections that can be tapped without offending. This kind of networking can be one of the most effective ways to expand your reach. No one knows everyone who can help promote a book, but everyone knows others who know others who can help with the job. It's one of those situations where everyone wins. When your friend mentions to the editor of the journal in her field that she has a friend who wrote such-and-such book, attaboys land on all concerned. Don't be shy about asking.

Syndicated radio and television business shows offer excellent opportunities to gain personal stature. Once you get on their call lists, there's a good chance you will be called whenever your subject is a topic of a show. Radio is often easier to do because most of the shows are done by telephone. You stand a better chance of getting on the television business shows if you live near enough to the studios that you can be on stage easily and inexpensively, especially when a breaking news story has to be covered.

Most call-in radio business shows use screeners, people who check you out before putting you through to the on-air host. Be sure to mention that you are the author of a book that relates to the current topic and the chances are good that you will be called on as a guest for future shows. One of my clients discovered this quite by accident and used the technique to get herself on the go-to lists of several good shows.

Publicize the People You Write About

The chances are good that somewhere in your book you quote a few well-known people. More than likely, these are people of some stature in the field of the subject of your book. If you have done interviews, even short ones on the phone, for your book, you have established connections that can be tapped later.

Publishing Tip

Buzz is one of the current catchwords in book publishing. It's best defined as a mixture of everything that is happening to your book and what everyone is saying about it. It's your book's momentum, movement, and status relative to other books on the same subject. One of the best ways to get the buzz going and keep it going is to see that those you quote in your book talk up your book. Obviously, the more people you quote, the more buzz there can be.

It would be presumptuous, of course, to ask the person to pitch your book, but he will probably do it without being asked. When someone can tell his friends, associates, prospects, or employers that he will be quoted in a forthcoming book, that book gets a plug. The real strength of the connections, however, comes from your being able to mention—in the right places, of course—that so-and-so is quoted in your book. It's prestige by association.

A query to a magazine editor that includes the name of someone who would be recognized by the magazine's readers will get some pretty serious attention. Needless to say, if you have interviewed and quoted a few people, the possibilities expand nicely.

Several of my clients do this regularly and report that not only do they get paid for the articles, but the magazine editors are also far more likely to review their books when they are published.

Also, it's not uncommon for people who have been interviewed for a book to invite the author to speak at appropriate programs. The twists and turns of this kind of networking can produce an almost endless list of possibilities. But it all begins with interviewing the right people and maintaining some kind of connection after the interview.

Publicize Your Competitor

In a sense, no book on any subject really competes with another on the same subject. However, too many authors get defensive and even possessive of what they see as their turf once they are published. Anticipate this problem by quoting your "competitors" positively. It can be very disarming for a person who thinks the turf belongs to her when another author calls and wants to say nice things about her. Once you convince a person that you are the genuine article and that you have no hidden agenda, you have made a friend of someone who might have rained on your parade once your book was in print.

As I mentioned earlier, most authors will write blurbs for authors whose books might compete for the same book buyer dollars once they realize that it's just good business to do it. In case you haven't noticed, more than a few of the cookbook authors sing one another's praises publicly. They may wish that the others die of food poisoning before their next books hit stores, but for public consumption they are all buddy-buddy. I'm sure the same holds true in any field where author star-power is deeply craved.

Publicize Up-and-Comers

There are always people who are working their way through the chairs of your field. They are easy to spot, are usually very anxious to help, and are often the source of good connections. Do an article for a magazine based on your book, and a few quotes from the bright new stars will make your own star shine even brighter.

Unaccustomed as I Am to Public Speaking

Your book, whether it's fresh off the press or has been in print for years, is always a good card to play when seeking speaking gigs. Public speaking is as good a way to launch a new book as it is to keep an old book alive on the sales charts. And one of the best ways to make business connections is to get the attention of an undergrad, graduate, or continuing education school of business near enough to you for you to talk at it regularly—or even become an adjunct professor.

Guest lecture spots at university continuing education programs present a really good opportunity to meet and influence potential book buyers, and even potential users of your services if you are an independent consultant. I have met several people who not only have gotten regular consulting gigs by being a guest lecturer, but who have also been responsible for the school using their books as part of their programs.

Publishing Tip

Teach a course yourself in a major university's continuing education program and you can be identified as part of the university faculty. You won't be tenure-track or have all the benefits of full-time faculty. But you can say that you teach such-and-such a course at Bigname University. Being identified with a good school is great publicity.

Continuing education programs in all fields have become a major revenue source for colleges and universities all over the country. Not only do individuals see them as ways to improve their skills, but companies often see them as excellent ways to upgrade current employees. Many major international corporations send their promising young executives to these programs and pick up all the costs—including the books. If your book can be used as a text and you get a gig at a local university, you will move quite a few books and even be paid to teach the course. And, who knows, you could meet your next client or even your next employer at one of your lectures.

Send Copies of Your Book to the Right People

First of all, everyone who is quoted in your book should receive a free copy inscribed with thanks from you. Apart from just being the right thing to do, your kindness can pay off in surprising ways.

An author once told me that he had quoted someone in his book and sent a copy to the person upon publication. The quoted person had about a dozen books on the credenza behind his desk, and this book was added to the collection. Not long after, the quoted individual was the subject of a story in a major financial publication that was dotted with talking head shots of the individual. In almost every picture the author's book spine was not only visible, but plainly readable. The author claims that his publisher saw a significant bump in orders following the publication of the story, even though the author and his book were never mentioned in the article.

It's entirely possible. After all, remember that all that stuff you see in television settings is the result of paid-for product placement. If you think the star of a television show is swilling Old Overshoe Turnip Soda because he likes it, you need to go back to school for a refresher course in marketing.

Send free copies to your mentor, your business colleagues, your clients, your potential clients, and whomever might be able to make a decision that involves the purchase of more than one book. A free copy of a book on sales techniques sent to the sales director of a company with a big sales force could move him or her to make a bulk buy for the entire sales force. It does happen!

Make Calls with the Publisher's Salespeople

It's not uncommon for major book distributors to invite a famous author to speak at the sales conference where the author's book is being presented. Okay, so you're not a major author yet, and you probably couldn't wrangle an invitation to address such a conference. But if you live in an area with a heavy concentration of book wholesalers and chain retail customers, think about offering to make calls with the salesperson. Be aware that when a publisher's salesperson calls on wholesalers and retailers, she has a long list of titles to push. If you do get the opportunity to make some calls, don't step on the salesperson's pitch for the rest of the line. If you do, you may have to walk home.

Fill in the Holes in Your Publisher's Marketing Plan

Most publishers have good marketing plans, but they are based on covering the best sources of sales as fast as possible and with as much firepower as the budget will allow. There are plenty of other opportunities to sell your book, but from the publisher's perspective they are not all that cost-effective.

You can't blame the publisher for this, really. You may feel unappreciated when you see that the lead book in the current catalog gets a full-color spread while your book shares a two-color page with three other books, 20 pages later. Chances are the lead author paid his or her dues on the back pages a few years ago. But there are ways to kick the wheel that publishers often pass on.

Your publisher may see your book's biggest potential with Internet sellers like Amazon. Most major business book publishers have at least one person whose full-time job is selling only to the buyers at places like Amazon. If you are willing to invest time and possibly some money, you may be able to pick up the lesser markets yourself. If you plan to do this, coordinate your efforts with your publisher. Don't try to sell into markets that the publisher covers, and don't sell into markets that might diminish sales the publisher makes itself.

> **Backspace** _____
>
> Don't ever pick at the weak spots you see in your publisher's marketing program. Nobody's perfect, even you and me. However, don't hesitate to offer help when you really can be helpful. Any offers you make should be built on specific suggestions and proof that you will not only be able to do what you say you can do, but also that your efforts will not interfere with what the publisher is planning to do or already doing.

For example, if your publisher sees most of its sales for your book coming from online and only plans a small budget for library sales, there may be an opportunity for you to cover the library market yourself. If you are willing to spend the money and promote in a way that would be as professional as your publisher might, there are publishers who are willing to discuss all sorts of deals.

Almost anything is possible. All it takes is some discussion. Your agent should know something about what the publishers she works with are willing to do and not willing to do. The major go/no-go decision always boils down to your not interfering with the sales plan the publisher has for all its other business titles and your representing yourself and your book in a way that would not embarrass the publisher. Keep in mind that any effort you make that would undercut the sales the publisher's retail customers have will kill any deal immediately.

Special Editions of Your Book

It's often possible to find an organization—perhaps your employer—that might be interested in having a special edition of your book printed for use as holiday gifts or as a promotional tool. A deal like this usually requires a commitment to a fairly large number of books. That number differs from publisher to publisher and also varies in cost depending on the production parameters. It's always best to make the deal before the initial press run so that savings can be made on paper quantity costs and press time expenses.

Special editions often involve different cover designs, or at least modifications of the cover used for the general edition. The actual text is seldom modified, but there is usually considerable latitude in the front and back matter. This is where the sponsor of the special edition gets to place its message or messages.

If the book has a removable paper dust jacket and the sponsor is willing to have his or her message on the jacket alone, without making any internal changes, the cost can be a lot less than that involved in adding front and back matter between the covers. I imagine that any publisher would be willing to rejacket copies from its current stock of a title for fewer copies than it would require for a remake of the interior.

Special edition copies are made on a not-for-sale basis and have no prices printed anywhere on them. The copyright page usually includes a line stating that the book is a special edition.

It's also possible to have individual chapters bound with special covers if enough copies are ordered. I've never seen this done, but I think it would be a good idea to make smaller booklets of a book and to mail them periodically to customers and good prospects. Twelve chapters means a prospect sees your material 12 times, not just once as a complete book. It's also a way to be able to get in to see prospects—you've "just dropped by to deliver the current installment." A book in itself is a superb "calling card," but why not slice it and multiply your personal exposure?

Take On Distribution in Markets Not Covered by Your Publisher

In addition to all the regular distribution channels for business books, there are channels that some publishers feel are not productive enough to bother with. If you have access to any special markets, ask your publisher whether you could take on the distribution to these markets yourself. Most publishers are willing to go with deals like this just as long as your sales to these markets don't interfere with the publisher's traditional sales channels.

You might be willing to take on distribution to certain smaller markets yourself, or it's possible that one of the many specialized book distributors can do it for you. You may even find a small publisher who has strong connections in a small, specialized market that might be willing to acquire limited rights to your book from your original publisher. It's worth checking this out.

Using Your Book as a Premium

If your book has the potential to be a premium for the purchase of something else, talk to your publisher about what kind of deals might be made. Premium use usually involves only a bulk sale at an agreed-upon discount. Some publishers will add a line to the sales agreement stating that the books are not to be offered for sale in any of the sales channels they traditionally use.

Try using your book as an enticement for early sign-up for a seminar or program you teach. Most people who are on the lecture circuit sell their books at the seminar site at full cover price. If you use your book as a premium for early sign-up, tell the early signers that they can pick up their books at the seminar and send them a chit that must be presented to get the free copy. Obviously, you want to avoid giving away books to people who have no intention of showing up.

Publishing Tip

Many of the ways of moving books I have just discussed involve sales that are not royalty inclusive. For example, you may not get royalties on deeply discounted bulk sales of books that are to be used as premiums. Every case is different, and it's important to discuss this with your publisher. Chances are that your contract already covers most areas in which royalties are not paid. Royalties are mainly based on the publisher's sale to wholesalers and retailers. Library sales are usually commissionable, but at different rates than retail sales. The royalty clause of your contract will have all the details. Just remember that if you are doing more than one book with different publishers, each publisher's approach to royalties will be a little different.

Piggyback Sales, Too

Are there any products or services being sold with which the marketer could piggyback your book? Some distance-learning organizations, for example, offer books for sale on the subjects they teach by mail or over the Internet. These books may not be the actual texts they use in their programs, but they offer them as ancillary reading.

The best way to understand this market is to check out the distance-learning programs themselves. The literature they send may contain a catalog of discounted items that enrollees can buy. If there are any books in the package, check out the names of the publishers. If your publisher has books in any of these piggyback programs, ask about how the deal was done.

If your publisher doesn't actively call on these accounts, consider doing it yourself. The deals can vary widely depending on when, how, and how many books might be involved. From what I have heard, though, most of them are single-title drop ship deals with either the publisher or a distributor that specializes in this kind of marketing.

As a businessperson, you are probably on many different mailing lists. Check out each of the mailings you get and see which companies offer books for sale in addition to the merchandise or services that are their main offerings.

Discs and Tapes

You probably granted your publisher the rights to audio production of your book in your contract. However, if your publisher isn't planning to exercise the rights and produce audio materials, you might be able to get them back or at least make a deal to use them yourself.

It's much less expensive to duplicate and mail a CD than it is to print a book and ship it. If you have a good enough voice or can afford to have a professional do the reading, all you need is the master to make copies when you get orders. CDs of business books are not all that popular, but as premiums and promotional giveaways they make excellent items. Nobody refuses a free CD.

The Least You Need to Know

- ◆ Your publisher will probably do a good job, but you can do a lot more to make your book a real success.

- ◆ Tooting your own horn is a good way to get attention for your book.

- ◆ Tapping the promotional strength of those you quote and those you know is one of the best ways to get attention for your book.

- ◆ You may be able to take on some of the sales activities that your publisher is not that interested in.

Part 6

Using Your Published Book to Enhance Your Career

A book in print is a sign of accomplishment. A book in print with a respected publisher is a tacit endorsement not only of your writing ability but also of your ideas. More than a few business careers can be traced to an author who has been published well and whose ideas have been accepted by the people the author saw as potential readers.

In this final part, you learn how to make the most of your book. You will probably be surprised at some of the avenues that will open to you once you become a published author. Ideas are the real currency of business, and authors of business books not only enjoy the added income of publisher royalties, but they also benefit from the opportunities that become available with publication. Careers are launched and enhanced by publication. These final two chapters tie the ribbons to your efforts as an author in some very interesting ways.

24

Enhancing Your Career and Growing Your Business

In This Chapter

◆ Writing a book can lead to radio and TV appearances and magazine and newspaper reviews

◆ Your name as an author becomes a lasting personal brand

◆ A book in print brings quality inquiries for your business that the Internet cannot provide

◆ Being an author puts you on the career fast track

You're at a business meeting and being introduced as Jane Smith, the author. Sure beats being introduced as just Jane Smith, doesn't it? Your credibility goes up more than a few notches immediately. People who have read your book will talk with you about it. Those who haven't read the book will be curious enough to ask about it. In short, you have gone from just another person at the meeting to someone a lot more interesting. I don't know whether anyone has researched this, but many of my clients claim that the books they wrote lead to promotions, greater responsibility, and higher incomes from the companies that employed them.

A book in print is a passport. It can get you past the well-guarded gates of the prospects you have been trying very hard to reach. It can give you credentials almost immediately that would take you forever to build any other way. In short, once you are in print you have joined the major league of your field, and doors open a lot more easily. This chapter shows you how to make the most of your book.

Nothing Beats a Book for Building an Image

A few years ago, it was a lot easier to explain why writing a business book was good for your business or your career. A book in print with your name on the title page was seen as a passport to profits. And in most cases this was true. Today, however, a short blurb on the Internet is seen by many as the way to go. So why are you planning to knock yourself out by writing a book when you could whip out a few paragraphs and plop them on the Internet immediately? Here are just a few of the more important reasons.

◆ The actual benefit from most material published on the Internet is fleeting.

When was the last time you threw out a book? How many times have you gone back to an article that interested you on the Internet? A book has substance, literally and figuratively.

◆ Most people have finally realized that one of the greatest benefits of the Internet is also one of its greatest weaknesses.

Anyone can say anything on the Internet, whether or not they know what they are talking about. A book in print, however, says that a publisher has reviewed and edited your material and is confident enough in you and what you have written to invest a sizable amount of money, time, and effort to print and publish your book. An article on the Internet may register a large number of hits, but only a book in print establishes real and lasting credibility. A copy of every book published is part of the collection in the Library of Congress.

◆ A published book opens more doors than even the best material on an Internet website could.

Books are reviewed by media. Book authors appear on radio and television, and make guest appearances at meetings and conferences. If the Internet is the ultimate answer, why do some of the biggest bloggers also write books? They do it because of the cross-marketing possibilities and because they, too, feel that books convey stronger credentials.

♦ As a book author, you stand alone and you stand out.

An Internet article will be surrounded by all sorts of distractions, ranging from pop-ups to the blurbs of others who are looking for the same attention as you. And you never know who you might have to share a page with on the Internet.

♦ Anyone who spends the money to buy your book is far more interested in what you have to say than a casual browser on the Internet.

> **Quote/Unquote**
>
> In 1959, the famous American artist Andy Warhol said, "In the future, everyone will be famous for 15 minutes." When was the last time you actually spent 15 minutes reading one piece on the Internet? I'd say that Warhol was off by at least 10 minutes.

Book readers tend to be more serious about what they read than those who browse the web. And the time they spend reading your book far exceeds the time they spend reading even directly relevant material on the Internet.

♦ Anyone who takes the time to read your book will have a much better image of you and what you want to convey than is possible to transmit on the pages of a magazine or on the Internet.

The choice, however, should not be a book or the Internet; it should be a book and then making the most of it on the Internet. I talk more about this later, but for now let's look at all the major benefits of having a book in print.

A Book Makes a Strong Statement About You

One of my author clients once told me that he is seldom introduced as "Bob the sales manager," but instead as "Bob the sales manager who wrote that great book on direct marketing." To use a popular term, he has been branded.

The famous author and management consultant Tom Peters is usually credited with having introduced the term and the notion of branding, and it makes a lot of sense when you think of his career. Tom Peters himself is thoroughly branded by the many books he has written. He has differentiated himself from his competitors by writing about subjects on which he is an expert and on which many others need help and guidance. Anyone who has taken the time and made the effort to build a strong personal brand will tell you that the perceived value that comes with authorship is worth its weight in gold.

Most experts in the personal branding field agree that one of the key issues of personal branding is letting people know where you stand on a particular subject or how you can be of benefit to them. You may be able to get a glancing whack at this with a magazine article or an Internet blurb, but there are no substitutes for the strength of conviction that can be built with a book. You have plenty of space to build a case.

> **Publishing Tip**
>
> A personal brand is a combination of reality and image. A book is reality, it has heft, and it says that you and the publisher have real credentials. A book creates an image of you as an author, an expert, and someone whose words should be read and heeded.

Writing a book gives you the opportunity to clearly differentiate yourself from all the others. It's hard to stand out in a competitive crowd with the few thousand words that make up most magazine articles or Internet blurbs. A book gives you the opportunity to present your case and to build it in steady, logical steps. This is the kind of writing that is remembered and often most persuasive.

A Book Builds Business

Business books are written to stimulate business: your business and the business of the people who read your book. Suppose for a moment that you are thinking about changing advertising agencies for your company. You have narrowed the search to two agencies and invite both to make final presentations. The first agency makes a knock-your-socks-off presentation and you are ready to sign it up. But courtesy demands that you at least listen to the pitch of the second agency. Its pitch is great, too. Then, the account guy opens his briefcase and hands you a copy of a book he has written on your kind of advertising. "If I haven't answered all the questions you have," he says, "you might find the answers in my book." Who are you going to choose?

> **Quote/Unquote**
>
> "To read a book for the first time is to make a friend of an acquaintance; to read it for the second time is to meet an old friend."
>
> —Chinese saying

Here are some of the ways books are regularly used to build, keep, and enhance business.

Prospect Identification

To get new business, you have to identify the most likely prospects for your product or service. You can choose to cast a broad net with the Internet or a magazine article, or you can choose a tightly focused approach by writing a book. There are plenty of products and services that would benefit far more from an Internet quickie, but if you are looking to establish higher-quality customers and build longer-lasting relationships, most will agree that writing a book is the best way to go.

A client I worked with a while back wrote a book on selling through independent manufacturers' representatives. The only reference he made to himself was in his introduction. He was at the time the CEO of a major association of independent sales reps. After his book had been in print for a year, he told me that the number of membership applications for the association had tripled over the previous year, and most applicants referred to the book as their source of interest. He also said that the number of leads converted to paid memberships was far greater than any of the paid advertising or direct mail the association had ever produced.

I don't want to give you the impression that you should not take advantage of every promotional tool that might benefit your company. A good marketing plan covers all bases but stresses the techniques that work best for the product or service with which you are involved. And though you will spend time writing a book, you may even be paid an advance by the publisher for doing it. Now, there's a bargain that is hard to turn down!

Prospect Qualification

This may sound elitist, but I'm okay with it. The leads generated from people who read your book will be of much higher quality than the leads you generate just about any other way. While giving an invited address at a major university or professional society will turn up better leads than your book, how often can you take time away from your work to go on the lecture circuit? And a book in print is out there working for you all the time.

Depending on who is telling the story, the percentage of leads that become customers from paid advertising and carefully placed articles is small. In fact, more than 70 percent of most leads are never even qualified. I've also seen reports that claim that 45 percent of the leads you do follow up on will ultimately go with a competitor. So much for getting big numbers by way of magazines or the Internet!

A phone call, letter, or e-mail from someone who has read your book and wants more information is pure gold. Such a lead is as close to being qualified, vetted, probed, and screened as any inquiry will ever get. In fact, it's better to think of such leads immediately as prospects, not unqualified leads. Anyone who bought and read your book *is* a prospect.

Turning Prospects into Customers

One of the most productive ways to turn prospects into customers is to give away a free sample. People who read your book will want to get in touch for something more. They usually have specific questions, and in most cases, all you have to do is give them enough to convince them that paying for your service or product is the best way to go.

Offering a free 15-minute telephone consultation is often the most productive way consultants have to convert their prospects to customers. Think about it: a phone consultation is pretty much a pitch for your services and it is done without ever having to leave your office. You can do one in your pajamas or at poolside if you happen to have a pool.

If your company produces a product that can be sampled, offer it and see what happens. Remember, you have a pre-qualified prospect list made up of people who spent real money for your book. So sampling can work with the right product.

Turning Customers into Better Customers

Most good marketing people agree that their work doesn't end with a sale. Keeping customers satisfied and turning good customers into great customers is just as important as signing them up in the first place. And as you might have already guessed, a book works well here, too.

Asking a newly acquired client or customer to supply the names of a few of the key people in his organization so you can send them complimentary copies of your book is a great way to solidify your relationship. I bet you can't think of anyone who has a typical office and who doesn't have a few books on display. One cynical publisher I knew years ago used to refer to this as being part of the "furniture." Your book and your name as author on the spine are on display in key spots and are a constant reminder to the customer that he made the right choice. Oh, by the way, be sure to get the correct spelling of each individual's name and autograph each copy.

Because most publishers can be convinced to give you the bookseller's discount if you buy enough copies, giving books away can be a lot less expensive than buying a customer a good lunch. And far more filling, too!

Think about offering to give free copies to all new employees of your clients or customers with whom you will have some interaction.

Securing Your Lock on Business

A lot of business today is done on a contract basis, which calls for regular reviews and comparisons with your competitors. This means that no matter how well you have been performing, you still have to submit to a review and resell your services. A book is about the fastest way to differentiate yourself from your competitors. Remember, many business books are revised every few years, so there's always an opportunity for you to send the new and revised edition of your book to those who make the decisions. Incidentally, it doesn't hurt to send revised editions to everyone, regardless of whether or not you are facing rebidding.

Put Your Show on the Road

As a new author, you will probably be surprised at how little your publisher spends to advertise your book. And if advertising is your business, you will probably be severely incensed by the number. The truth is, however, that dollar for dollar, publicity does more to move business books than advertising, with the exception of dollars spent on direct sales promotion.

If you have a book that appeals to a well-defined market and the people who make up that market congregate for seminars, conventions, or other meetings, your publisher will probably work hard to get you speaking engagements at appropriate venues. Depending on the publisher and the size of the anticipated audience, many publishers will attempt to sell books where you speak. In smaller situations, some authors will take over that chore themselves. I discuss this in greater detail in Chapter 20, but the point for this chapter is that your publisher-sponsored speaking gigs are super opportunities to sell your services or products as well as copies of your book.

The publisher's publicist will probably try to get you spots on business-oriented radio and TV shows and also some appearances on interactive business websites. Just keep in mind that exposure is the key issue. The more you are seen and heard, the better your book sales will be and the better your chances of expanding your business or enhancing your career.

Get a Better Job

Not everyone who writes a business book has a business or a service to promote. Many are employed by others, and more than a few have landed new jobs or been promoted as a result of having a book in print.

A resumé that highlights a book you wrote tells a potential employer that you have something none of the other candidates have. A resumé that is accompanied by your published book has real impact. However, this can be an expensive way to look for a job.

Unless you are sending only a few resumés with books or can really get a deal on the copies you need, consider doing what one of my clients did. She has a book in print with a major publisher, but the list price of the book is more than $50. Even at the bookseller discount, her cost per copy was in the high twenties.

Anticipating a job change, she placed a pre-pub order with her publisher for 100 copies of the dust jacket, the wraparound cover that is used on most books. Then she had one chapter, the one critical for the job type she was seeking, printed and bound by a local printer. The combination of the publisher's dust jacket and the sample chapter got her interviews with everyone she wanted to work for and several good offers to choose from.

You may not even be looking for a job, but when a good one comes along, who wouldn't consider it seriously? Actually, this happens all the time to many authors. One author I know has moved twice as a result of such offers. He was quite happy where he was both times, and he was recruited by headhunters in both cases. Each recruiter had seen his books and each saw potential for a search in progress. In fact, if you just want to salt the mine with a recruiter—but are not actively looking for a change—send a copy of your book.

Advance with Your Current Employer

It's not uncommon for people employed by larger companies to be given either leave or a work schedule that allows for writing while also benefiting the employer. It's probably more common in the sciences, where breakthroughs are the currency of growth and published books are a hallmark of a company's effort. But don't rule out the possibility of getting some sort of reduced schedule to write your book if your employer in any industry sees a benefit in it for the company.

I've seen companies provide the help an author might need in the production of an appropriate book. Some actually provide ghostwriters for people whose skills lie in fields other than word arrangement. Some offer assistance from staff in their corporate communications departments and others, I've been told, pay special bonuses to employees writing books for them to hire the help they need themselves. In short, forget the novel for a while.

Writing Company Histories

People have egos, and companies have collective egos. Sometimes this adds up to an interesting story for a book. You've probably seen company histories that range from beautifully written and illustrated books to little pamphlets. Size doesn't matter; both are company histories and both are usually written in the service of growing a business even larger.

There are a few writers who do nothing but corporate histories and who are known in the industry both for their skills and the fees they command when a book is commissioned. If you can see the value of a company history for your current employer, pitch the idea yourself. As a current employee, you probably have access to the information you would need to at least get the ball rolling. And if writing is not part of your current work assignment, you really should seek extra compensation for the effort, unless you are excused from your current responsibilities to undertake the project.

Writing Executive Memoirs

Few CEOs can resist the idea of a book being written about them. The person who heads up the company you work for is probably not an exception. Here, however, unless you have a great story to tell, your book will probably have to be privately published. There are many excellent organizations that specialize in this field and can provide everything from the writing and editing to the art, design, and printing.

Writing someone's memoir is probably one of the more difficult business writing assignments you will encounter. There are egos involved and there are events you want to include that your subject would rather forget. It's a minefield, but it's navigable.

Writing for Professional Associations

If you work in a field that is supported by a large trade or professional association, there could be an opportunity to do the definitive book on the association, or even on the entire field. One of the activities that heads the list of interests of most associations is telling the story of the field and the people who work in it. And one of the ways many who manage these associations achieve that mission is by having a book written and published.

Writers who have done books for associations tell of massive amounts of data being made available to them, but also of incessant requests to include every minute detail. And they tell of having to work with and satisfy the demands of far too many people.

One writer who has done several books for professional associations claims that he won't take on a project unless he has only one person to report to. He wants access to everyone who can help, but he will only work with one point person.

Forget Your Day Job ... for the Moment

There are other ways to put your writing skills to work. If you have a hobby or a special interest, you are probably familiar with the names of the people who have written on your subject. Most of these people don't make a living writing about collecting art, ham radio, or needlework. But they are paid for their efforts and some actually get paid quite well. And some do become rich and famous. Just recently the author of a huge number of books on antique collecting died, and his obituary in *The New York Times* was illuminating and quite inspirational. This gentleman turned a hobby into an industry that he ran from a garage into a worldwide enterprise.

The Least You Need to Know

- ◆ If you want to be seen—and remembered—write a book.

- ◆ Book authorship creates personal brand credibility that is impossible to create any other way.

- ◆ A book in print not only produces leads for new business, but it's also the perfect tool for turning leads into sales, clients, and customers.

- ◆ Whether you are employed by someone else or work for yourself, a book in print is the perfect growth tool.

Chapter 25

Building a Career Based on Your Book

In This Chapter

- ◆ Write a book and create your own personal brand
- ◆ Using your book to win promotions and raises
- ◆ How a book can help you launch a business
- ◆ Then, of course, you can even be a full-time writer

I've seen buzzwords and catchphrases come and go. I've written books for clients on some rather flimsy stuff, and I've worked on others based on ideas that never faded. As I write this book, the notion of personal branding is riding high. It would be presumptuous to say that branding is just another gimmick until we see how well it plays a few years from now. I will say, however, that the underlying notions are sound. As with all that came before and all that will follow, branding is derivative. It's not based on new research. However, it is based on using tested and proven concepts in ways that are fresh and productive.

Combine tomatoes, olive oil, oregano, basil, and salt and pepper, and you can make a basic pasta sauce. Combine the same ingredients in different proportions, and you will have a nice tomato basil soup. Combine the concepts of personal branding as it's defined today and you have a concept that works whether you are employed, self-employed, or just getting your start in the business world.

One of the major elements of personal branding is promoting yourself in carefully defined ways. Read anything on the subject, and you will surely see the suggestion to write articles and books that will enhance your personal brand. Writing a book to toot your own horn makes sense, but it's most effective when you do it in a much broader context, such as creating your own personal brand. And that's what this chapter is all about—how your book can be a part of your personal branding and lifetime career plans.

What Is a Personal Brand?

You are more than the simple sum of your experiences and personal characteristics. In math, 5 and 5 always add up to 10. In life, however, you are more than just a simple sum of your parts. As in my tomato soup metaphor, you are what you are because of the way you assemble the ingredients of your life. Don't think of your brand as a "new" you; think of it as the "real" you. It should be created from everything you have achieved and blended with what you want to achieve. Branding is not a makeover. Your brand is a tightly focused image of your life's realities that you want to project to others.

> **Quote/Unquote**
>
> You have to decide what image you want for your brand. Products, like people, have personalities, and they make or break them in the marketplace.
>
> —David Ogilvy

You can and should have more than one brand: a business brand and at least one or more personal brands. For now, we'll stick with the business brand you want to create and how writing a book can help you.

Your Brand and Your Book

Before you even think about your book, you have to decide which elements of your business life can be combined to create your brand. Keep in mind that the work you do or the job you have is simply not enough by itself to be your brand. It's part of it, as are all the other experiences that make up the image you want your brand to project.

You may have devised a superior system for qualifying sales leads that you want to write about, but your book has to be more than just a handbook on the subject if you want to create a brand. Your brand builds confidence in you and what you are writing about. Your brand says that you have done what you write about successfully. Your brand sets you apart from others who may be doing similar things. It should give you a competitive advantage over others doing the same work. Your brand inspires trust. And it must do this without a hint of bragging and boasting. This is where things start to get sticky for many people, even those who are good enough writers to write their own books and to get the attention of major publishers.

Many of the people you see quoted in the media today got their start with books that captured popular imagination. Tom Peters and Bob Waterman wrote *In Search of Excellence* way back in 1982. That book launched careers for both. The first and other books they wrote are still in print and the image they created continued to get them major consulting, lecturing and media assignments. Ralph Nader, whether you agree with him or not, launched a career that got him to the fringes of a presidential nomination with a book about how the auto business failed to consider safety, *Unsafe at Any Speed.*

What you say about your subject and how you say it tells more about you and your brand than bragging and boasting. A brand is an image, and that image becomes reality when your reader invests his or her trust in you and what you say on the page. Think back to the days when branding was related mainly to products, not people. Texaco

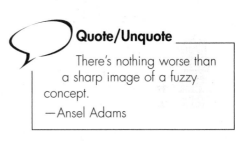

Quote/Unquote

There's nothing worse than a sharp image of a fuzzy concept.

—Ansel Adams

gasoline used a star in its logo. And under the star this line made the point: "You can trust your car to the man who wears the star." For the most part, gasoline is gasoline wherever you buy it. But the image of the brand coupled with the word *trust* was a very persuasive message. This is what you are aiming for in your personal branding.

Using Your Brand and Your Book to Get Ahead in Your Job

In the previous two chapters, I discussed how to move books, how to boost sales, and how to get the kind of exposure needed to earn royalties. Now let's look at some of the ways you can turn your book and your brand into a career tool.

Writing a book can help you move up the corporate ladder, and it can also help you create your own corporate ladder. Let's look at each use individually.

How a Book Can Help You Earn More Money

In my experience as an agent, about half my authors wrote business books to improve their employment stature and about half of them wrote them to start or build their own businesses. A book in hand that relates to the work you do when asking for a raise or a promotion is pretty close to an automatic okay. But it takes more than just depositing your book in the company library and hoping that the right people will see it. It takes a little creative imagination, some work on your part, and a projection of your personal brand in the right places to make things happen.

Probably the easiest thing to get with a new book in print is a raise. Most companies have pay ranges for all jobs, and unless you have topped out in your grade and are not ready for a promotion, a book will likely produce some extra money in your paycheck quickly.

If more money is your goal, be specific about it. Plan your approach accordingly and don't leave anything to chance. In other words, don't beat around the bush. One of my clients told me an amusing story about how he parlayed his book into a substantial raise. He planned his pitch to coincide with his annual review. He knew that typical raises were not all that great, and he wanted more than the usual. On the day of his review, he brought a copy of his new book, but he kept it hidden in his briefcase.

The discussion was the usual cookie-cutter compensation review. His manager told him the number that had been planned and was preparing to close the session. My client then brought up that the company had been getting very little mention in the press lately and wondered what they were paying their PR agency for such poor results. The manager didn't know, but guessed it was a lot of money. My client then casually mentioned that even a few mentions in a good book would be worth the agency's fee, and his manager agreed.

With that, my client pulled the book out of his briefcase and handed it to his manager. Sticking from the pages were more than a dozen yellow Post-it notes. My client said that each tab represented a mention of the company and suggested, wryly, that maybe there could be a bit more of a raise.

His boss was impressed and said he'd get back to my client. When he did, the raise was significant. And about a year later, my client's boss was promoted and my client was promoted to his boss's job. Last I heard, he is working on a much more ambitious book. It will be interesting to see what he has in mind this time.

It's not uncommon for business book writers who work at higher-level corporate jobs to include the more discreet headhunters on the distribution list for their new books. Their notes usually say nothing more than "I thought you might like to have this." A noncommittal note like that to a headhunter is usually enough to set some wheels in motion. After all, a headhunter is only as good as the people he or she recommends. And a published author as a client makes the headhunter look pretty good.

A Boost Up the Corporate Ladder

One of the more interesting sections of any major business publication is the obituary column. These columns provide tightly focused glimpses of the lives of important people in the business world. Apart from the usual mentions of school connections, family, and positions held, books written usually head the list. I'm not suggesting that you write a book to enhance your obituary, but I am saying that authorship is always seen as something important. It is an inferential jump, but it's hard to avoid the conclusion that the deceased got where he or she did in part because of his or her credentials as the author of one or more business books.

One of my clients told me that in addition to a sought-after promotion, her employer bought a significant quantity of her book to present to clients and to use in the company's new business development activities. The bulk sale was royalty inclusive, so my client got a promotion and a nice royalty check from her publisher as well.

Another told me that he had been on the short list for promotion and the book got him off the list and into the job he had hoped to get a week after its publication.

> **Publishing Tip**
>
> Get enough copies of your book to circulate to key people in the company that employs you. Don't forget to write a short personal note to each person on your list. And be careful not to give Alice's book to Joe!

A Book Can Put You in Business

Books in print have launched more than a few businesses for their authors. Some authors have done it accidentally, others intentionally. It's probably possible to launch a manufacturing business with the help of a book, but you are most likely to get some kind of consulting business off the ground with a book. If you are already in some business other than consulting, however, a book in print will always be more than helpful.

Books that launch businesses usually feature the author's different slant on a problem that potential customers wrestle with regularly. The most obvious of these are the books on management systems. No company, regardless of how well managed it is, can't be improved by using a newer system. The improvements can be huge if the company is badly managed to begin with, or the improvements can be small if the company is already reasonably well managed. The point is, however, that all companies can be managed better, and this means that there is a perennial source of readers for books like this.

Get a book published that gets good press notices, and you will probably have to either quit your job and start your own consultancy or hire people to help you if you are already in business for yourself.

Remember, a management consulting business has a brand and that brand is carefully intertwined with the brand of the key player or players. And one of the best ways to expose that brand is by writing and publishing a book.

Do You Have a Second Act?

Book publishing is based on building brands. Overall, the publisher's brand is the image it has with the primary readers of the books it publishes. You probably wouldn't buy a novel published by a house known for its textbooks on accounting. But if you taught accounting and were reviewing textbooks for your students, you would certainly consider the brand the publisher has created for itself. And you would just as likely consider the brands the publisher's authors have for themselves.

If your book is successful, your publisher may suggest possible titles for you to write, rather than just hope that you have another book in you. The publisher has, in part, created your personal brand, and now it wants to capitalize on it further.

Being asked by your publisher for your next book is an invitation to keep the personal brand alive—yours and that of your publisher. You may feel that you just don't have another book in you, but listen to what is said and consider it carefully. If your publisher really wants another book from you and you aren't that excited about the idea, your publisher will probably suggest that you do the book with the help of someone else. Some will even suggest possible collaborators or ghostwriters for you to work with. Either way, the expense will be yours, but in many cases the advance you will be paid will cover most of—or maybe even more than—the cost of working with a writing professional.

> **Quote/Unquote**
>
> An image is not simply a trademark, a design, a slogan, or an easily remembered picture. It's a studiously crafted personality profile of an individual, institution, corporation, product, or service.
>
> —Daniel J. Boorstin

If you are considering the possibility of writing a second book, but are concerned about the cost of a ghostwriter or a collaborator, compare that cost with the cost of launching any kind of public relations program that would get you the same attention as a book. There's seldom a contest when the numbers are viewed in this context. At best, a book will cost you nothing, and at worst it will cost you a lot less than comparable PR fees to get the same exposure. And a book's impact lasts a lot longer than most PR campaigns.

But what do you do as a second act? Chances are that you said just about everything you had to say in your first book and aren't ready to do something different. Second books are usually more practical extensions of first books. The central concept of your first book is introduced briefly and with any refinements that you've added since you wrote your first book. Then, if possible, dwell on more practical applications of your ideas. Try to include more material from people who have had hands-on experience with your ideas.

You can only refine good material for so long before you have to do something new and different. If you have been successful with your first few books, it's usually a good idea to move on to something new and different. If you have established a base of dedicated readers and you don't jump too far afield, they will follow you. It's probably not a good idea to step too far out of your reader's frame of reference. First, your publisher may balk, and second, you take the chance of diluting the brand image you have carefully built and nurtured so far.

Is Writing Better Than Your Job?

What if you discover that writing is more fun than your day job? Now you are talking about a big jump. It could mean abandoning a successful career to switch to writing. But it's like any other career change you might consider: it has risks and it has rewards.

It's comforting to think about people like John Grisham, who has degrees in accounting and law and who is now one of the most celebrated American novelists. Isaac Asimov, probably the most prolific writer of the last century, spent his early life teaching biochemistry. And Kurt Vonnegut once worked for the public relations department at General Electric. It is a long list, and more than a few writers have toiled in business before crossing the border.

The life of a novelist, playwright, or nonfiction author can seem awfully attractive when your boss has a hissy fit or when you lose your largest client. But even if you have the talent, you have more competition that you can possibly imagine. I am not trying to discourage you; I just want you to know that no matter how good a writer you are, there many others as good as or better than you who have tried and tried hard but never made it.

So pardon the cliché, but it's not smart to quit your day job unless you don't have to worry about money or have a contract for your first novel in your pocket. Most writers do start out doing other things. My degrees are in psychology. Many of the authors I represented had business degrees. Several were physicians, and quite a few others had advanced degrees in fields that weren't even distantly related to writing. But they did it, and most of them were quite successful at it.

So if write you must, do it! Read everything the writers you admire have written. It's the best way to learn to write, other than to be lucky enough to have an editor discover you and help turn your life around. It does happen!

The Least You Need to Know

- All it takes is one book to launch a career, get a raise, receive a major job promotion, or start your own business.

- A book can become the image of your personal brand.

- Your second book will be a lot easier to write than your first.

- Who knows, you may even quit that senior vice presidency, return the key to the executive washroom, and join the ranks of the terminally insecure—writers!

Index

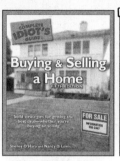
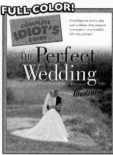
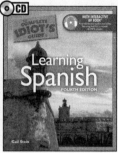

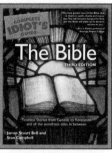
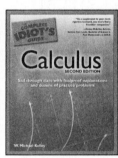

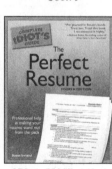